# LEARNING TIME with LANGUAGE EXPERIENCES
## for young children

LOUISE BINDER SCOTT

Virginia Sydnor Pavelko
Olive M. Amundson
Robert L. Douglass
Christina R. McDonald

**Webster Division, McGraw-Hill Book Company**
St. Louis, New York, San Francisco, Dallas, Toronto, London, Sydney

Senior Author

Louise Binder Scott (Ed.M., Boston University) is Associate Professor of Elementary Speech, California State College at Los Angeles, and has Clinical Competence in Speech Pathology with American Speech and Hearing Association. She is author of many publications in language arts. Her most recent contributions are: *Tell-Again Story Cards,* Levels I and II; *Workers in Our Neighborhood; Learning About Our Language Filmstrips;* and *Time for Phonics* series. As senior author, other publications include: *Rhymes for Fingers and Flannelboards, Singing Fun, More Singing Fun,* and *Talking Time* (Second Edition).

Contributing Authors

Virginia Sydnor Pavelko (M.A. Spanish, Stanford University), teacher of art appreciation and United States history, San Marino Schools, California, and former primary teacher, has contributed to *Talking Time, Singing Fun,* and *More Singing Fun,* and has coauthored *Book R, Time for Phonics.*

Olive M. Amundson (B.A., California State College at Los Angeles), Reading Specialist in the El Rancho Unified School District, Pico Rivera, California, and former teacher of Project Head Start, has contributed to *Rhymes for Fingers and Flannelboards.*

Robert L. Douglass (Ph.D., University of Southern California), Professor of Speech and Chairman of Speech and Drama, California State College at Los Angeles, has written articles for many professional journals and has conducted studies on language development of young children.

Christina R. McDonald (B.S. Ed., University of Kansas), is Curriculum Specialist and Director of Preschool Programs, El Rancho Unified School District, Pico Rivera, California; lecturer; former teacher; and contributor to professional journals.

Copyright © 1968 by McGraw-Hill, Inc. All Rights Reserved. Printed in the United States of America. No part of this publication may be reproduced, stored in a retrieval system, or transmitted, in any form or by any means, electronic, mechanical, photocopying, recording, or otherwise, without prior written permission of McGraw-Hill, Inc.

ISBN 07-055800-0

12 13 14 15 HDHD 79

# Foreword

Language and learning are interwoven, for much of formal and informal education consists of translating learning experiences into words and using those words to understand more fully the meaningfulness of the experiences themselves. An individual who is limited or deficient in language is similarly limited or deficient in his ability to learn.

It is easy to take talking for granted. Beginning with the first cry at birth, the development of speech in a child appears to the casual observer as a spontaneous outpouring of sound which flows normally from crying into babbling, from babbling into jargoning (this has many of the characteristics of rhythmic and inflectional normal speech) and, finally, from jargoning into the verbal symbols of words. Like the physical movements of walking, the mouth motions of talking seem to be a natural and an appropriate activity for a human being.

Teachers, parents, and others may too readily assume that the learning of language consists solely of adding words to a child's vocabulary, or that once a child has learned how to pronounce a word, he then understands it. Nothing could be farther from the truth. True oral expression is an *original* and *creative* process based upon learning, not an automatic act of echoing back that which has been presented by others.

What, then, is in a spoken word? *Our senses are in a word*, for we have heard the sounds and have felt the sizes, shapes, and textures of the world around us, and from these raw materials are the words of language spun. *The mind is in a word*. From others are received the language labels which we attach to sights, sounds, and feelings. We have used these verbal symbols to represent our understanding of the world in which we live. *Our mouths, too, are in a word*, for through the articulated sounds of expressive speech we have linked our thoughts with the thoughts of others and have shared in a sense of belongingness as a member of the human race. The spoken word, then, is but the final act in a whole sequence of events: absorbing experiences, synthesized information, comprehended meanings, and translated ideas.

It is the basic philosophy of this book that *all* children should be immersed in a learning environment which stresses the *whole process of language learning*. For those young children who have been handicapped because of emotional, social, or educational deprivation, an educational program which provides a rich and meaningful exposure to skills of language and oral self-expression may make the crucial difference between later success or failure in school and in life.

The authors believe that the teacher must understand that language, like learning, is a basic part of living, and that words are interwoven constantly through day-by-day experiences. The teacher will find this book to be a guide of practical materials, appropriately arranged in units which will make it easier to plan the day's activities. She will find, as she explores the contents, that a wide variety of language-oriented, learning experiences have been originated and collected. These language techniques are designed to meet the aesthetic, social, emotional, and physical needs of young children.

*Learning Time with Language Experiences for Young Children* consistently follows the philosophy that any learning program for early childhood must be of the spirit and be concerned with the feelings and understandings of the young child. Both teachers and children can grow in knowledge and understanding by following the pathways to better communication suggested herein.

—ROBERT L. DOUGLASS, PH.D.

# Contents

INTRODUCTION

CHAPTER 1: **THE CHILD AND LANGUAGE**    **1**
- Helping the Child to Develop a Satisfying Self-Image    6
- Children Are Poets    15
- The Child Uses Language    25
- The Child Shares Language    40
- Language as a Social Skill    45
- Improving Articulation of Speech Sounds    59

CHAPTER 2: **SENSORY AVENUES TO LEARNING**    **65**
- Listening as an Aid to Language Development    70
- Observation as an Aid to Language    77
- The Sense of Touch    101
- Smells and Tastes    119

CHAPTER 3: **THE WONDERFUL WORLD OF PLAY AND MAKE-BELIEVE**    **123**
- Toys Are Magic    126
- Dramatic Play    130
- Expressing Without Words    133
- The Traditional Nursery Rhyme    139
- Action Rhymes    147
- The Story    157
- Bringing Young Children and Good Picture-Storybooks Together    164
- Using Pictures    168
- Playing a Story    173
- Quiet Times    176

| | | |
|---|---|---|
| CHAPTER 4: | WHERE WE LIVE, WORK, AND PLAY | 184 |
| CHAPTER 5: | SPECIAL DAYS | 209 |
| CHAPTER 6: | ALL THE YEAR ROUND | 251 |
| CHAPTER 7: | CREATURES TO LOVE | 268 |
| CHAPTER 8: | GOOD TIMES AT THE CIRCUS AND ZOO | 284 |
| | EPILOGUE | 300 |
| | INDEX FOR UNIT INTEGRATION | 303 |

# Introduction

How teachers can best provide for the young child's learning presents an overwhelming challenge in today's education. This book will help those concerned to meet this challenge because it treats of the skills of language which are basic to all learning.

Chapter 1 begins with an explanation of language and its stages of development. Emphasis is placed on the relationship of the communication skills with all concept formation within an intricate design for learning. The teacher is given a wealth of aids for helping the child with defective speech and also the child with a non-English speaking background.

At whatever age the child enters school, his beginning experiences help him to develop a favorable concept of himself and strengthen and preserve his sense of personal worth and self-confidence. In Chapter 1, Louise Binder Scott describes the kinds of interaction the child experiences with people and the impact of this interaction upon the image the child has of himself. Before he can communicate freely, he must identify with adults and with children of his age. Thus, the teacher sets about helping the child to discover himself and his potential and to believe in himself as a successful person.

Since poetry is the natural language of young children, sound, syllable, word repetition, and vocal play are described as necessary parts of the child's speech development. This natural, rhythmic speech can be kept alive through encouragement of self-talk and exposure to poetry, pantomime, and music. These activities help the child to give free rein to his creative impulses.

Because children from limited backgrounds sometimes have few patterns for simple greetings and courtesies, there is a section in Chapter 1 entitled "Language As a Social Skill." Original stories invite critical discussion on values.

The child develops more oral competency in coping with the English language through participation in games which deal with sentence structures, grammar, antonyms, synonyms, and contractions. Chapter 1 presents such games plus stimulating ideas for practice in making comparisons, expressing feelings, describing and rendering value judgments. Rhymes and devices for the improvement of speech sounds are contained in the final section.

Chapter 2, "Sensory Avenues To Learning," provides a discussion on the multisensory approaches to learning. Included are many suggestions on how to awaken the interest of the young child and help him to use his sensory powers creatively and constructively. Specifically related units are: "Listening as an Aid to Language Development," "Observation as an Aid to Language," "The Sense of Touch," and "Smells and Tastes."

Chapter 3, "The Wonderful World of Play and Make-Believe," is replete with creative ideas for dramatic play, finger plays, action rhymes, storytelling, picture-storybooks, creative dramatics, pantomime, nursery rhymes, and relaxation activities. All of these can become flexible parts of the daily program.

It is the teacher who, through her attitudes and actions, sets the stage for creative learning through discovery. She helps to establish a physical and emotional environment which will encourage young children to inquire, reach out, and explore. This is the creative approach which is *individualized, personalized,* and *flexible.* This is the creative approach which *Learning Time* emphasizes.

So that creative and investigative approaches may be used freely by the child, the following learning areas are suggested:

A playhouse center equipped to promote social learning;
A listening and audio-visual center where records and filmstrips are available;
A talking center where the children may gather with the teacher for share-and-tell or story time;
A library center well stocked with a supply of high quality picture-storybooks so that children may be motivated to browse and "read" pictures;
A science center that provides things to think about, touch, feel, smell, taste, and discuss;
Work centers with groupings of chairs and tables with flat surfaces.

Other centers may include those for indoor and outdoor games, block building, painting, nature, puzzles, numbers, and alphabets.

Chapter 4, "Where We Live, Work, and Play," describes the child's community life as it is now extended to a larger group where he can begin to relate to new adults and to children of his age. Again, language skills are emphasized as the child engages in dramatic play. Many ideas for involvement of mothers in the program are presented in this chapter.

The child's eager anticipation of "Special Days" is recognized in Chapter 5. Ideas for observances focus on holiday meanings and touch the various cultures. Many chalk talks, stories, finger plays, and rhymes help the child to continue his use of language skills.

Chapter 6, "All the Year Round," emphasizes seasons, and provides a background of materials about nature.

A child's relationships with animals can be of life-long value to him. Most of the benefits in this association come from interaction between the child and the pet. Chapter 7 suggests these experiences with "Creatures To Love," which are first in surveys of children's natural science interests.

Chapter 8 describes the circus and zoo with that magic charm of the clown and the merry-go-round which can provide experiences a child long remembers and cherishes.

The materials in *Learning Time* are grouped into chapters and units, which have been identified as major interest areas. This format may appear structured; yet what is structured to one person may actually be unstructured to another. To some teachers, structuring may be ritualistic and forced learning, while to others, structuring may mean planned teaching. The teacher should feel free to use any part of this handbook at any time during the day. Each area is introduced with a descriptive presentation of background information and suggested use of materials.

Because integrated learning is difficult to explain, it often is hard for observers to identify what children are actually achieving. It is important, therefore, to help others to understand that *process* more than *product* is a major goal of early childhood learning. The content of the program suggested in this book is adapted to the child's individualized needs and interests, and to his abilities to use and adapt to the program.

As stated previously, *Learning Time* is a language-oriented book designed to give the teacher a wealth of materials that will help her to meet the challenge of the many levels of child development and maturity for which she must plan. Language emphasis is based upon these four fundamental premises:

The recognition of the relationship between oral language and self-concept;

A recognition that language is a tool for thinking and is essential to social, intellectual, and emotional growth;

A faith in the power of good children's literature that will enrich and inspire children to love language;

An acceptance of the findings of linguistic research which has demonstrated that competence in language—listening, speaking, reading, and writing—is rooted in the language development of the early years.

Emphasized within the chapters in *Learning Time* are ways in which language is acquired by the child through:

Sense perception, which includes aural discrimination and identification of sounds, visual perception, tactile experiences, balance, chemical senses of taste and smell, and speech;

Interaction with people; thinking; reasoning;

Spacial relationships;

Comprehension;

Verbal and body expression;

Retention.

The alert teacher should explore the rich language potential within this book and use the ideas and techniques as enrichment experiences, applying them to fit the needs of individual children.

As stated in the foreword, a program for young children must be of the spirit and concerned with feelings and understandings. Built into the sensitive educator's responsibility is a commitment to provide each child with well-researched materials that promote physical well-being and intellectual growth. One who accepts the challenge of educating young children constantly seeks time-tested materials and surveys professional literature and procedures which will help him to better insure that each child will realize maximum values from his daily experiences.

—THE COAUTHORS

CHAPTER 1

# The Child and Language

Learning to talk is a long and complicated process. That a very young child can acquire and speak the English language with its eight parts of speech, its homonyms, and involved sentence structures is remarkable. That he can use rhythm, rising and falling inflections, and a variety of loud and soft utterances peculiar to the English language within a relatively short span of time is amazing. That he can develop sentence sense, use many adult sentence patterns, and speak with clarity by the time he enters school is almost miraculous. Yet the young child does develop motor skills in such ways as to produce a multitude of speech sounds blended into word symbols which have meaning for him and are used in connected speech. This act requires a high degree of coordination.

A difficult language *is* learned by the child because he has innate potential for learning and growth, and an ability to imitate. He learns speech through imitation of the mother, father, and others in the immediate environment, and he learns it without apparent instruction. He moves ahead in progressive steps from stages of vocal play to articulate speech.

However, deeper motivation to learn speech transcends the process of imitation and acts of parent approval. The child has a physical and an emotional need to maintain secure contact with the parents in order to move into verbal abilities and to exert control over his environment. Unless there is warm identification with the parents, there is no assurance that the child can survive socially in a chaotic world. Severe insecurities, fears, and hostilities may develop if the child is not understood, is not given motivation to talk, or is isolated. The child must be motivated *to learn about and to master the world through his need to have mastery over it*. Language provides the key to this mastery.

As the child learns to label his experiences, he comes to understand what he can do with language and is provided with new ways of expressing himself. Thus, he can control his world, and attain power through the use of words. As he acquires vocabulary, he is provided with a variety of ways of expressing himself. A small child has no other channel for draining off energy, which is either normal and healthy or filled with anxiety, except through motor acts of which speech is one.

The child's ability to communicate begins to develop when he makes the sounds of crying. Though many authorities feel that crying is not to be interpreted as true speech, there are indeed differences in the child's cries which, within a few months, can be understood by the mother to mean hunger, thirst, pain, or general discomfort. "At first, these are the only sounds he (the child) makes when he is uncomfortable. Otherwise, he is quiet." [1]

When crying, the child uses lips, tongue, palate, nasal passages, and vocal mechanism. These same structures are used for talking.

About eight weeks after birth, the child begins to babble, and this babbling activity continues for many months. He contentedly plays with sounds and derives pleasure from doing so. By now, he is producing a variety of vowels, consonants, diphthongs, and syllables. Eventually, he hears these repetitions. Delighted with his discovery, he imitates his own output over and over. The child would not learn to talk at all without this ability. Imitation of his own babbling becomes an activity which gives him a sense of achievement and pleasurable aural sensations as he uses varieties of rhythms, pitches, and loudnesses.

"The private babbling and social vocal play continue strongly during this period from eight months to a year. We now find the baby using inflections which sound like questions, commands, surprises . . . Grunts and wails, babbling, socialized vocalization, and inflection practice . . . continue throughout the period of speech development." [2]

The enjoyment of listening to his own voice inflections and sounds forms a basis for the next stage: imitation of adult speech. As the child imitates adult *work* in dramatic play, which helps him to face adulthood, he also imitates adult *speech,* which helps him to become a socially acceptable individual.

---

[1] M. M. Lewis, *How Children Learn to Speak,* George G. Harrap and Co. Ltd., London, 1957, p. 15.

[2] Charles Van Riper, *Speech Correction: Principles and Methods* (Fourth Ed.), Prentice-Hall, 1963, p. 81.

While in the process of learning to talk, the child does not acquire one word at a time before progressing to another. He explores sensory avenues—many of them—and tries them all. The word he says may fit innumerable situations. *Coat* may mean "go in the car" or "play in the yard." *Ball,* because it is round, may mean orange, apple, or balloon. At first, the child articulates poorly. Gradually, as his nervous system matures and his memory span develops allowing him to imitate words more accurately, a refinement process takes place. Many children indulge in jargon (or unintelligible, continuous speech) which begins around the age of ten months and often continues for seven or eight months.

Between fifteen and eighteen months, while energy is concentrated upon walking, progress in talking may be slow. However, at this time the child may listen more intently to what others say.

By eighteen months, many meaningful words appear along with continued jargon. At the age of two, there is increased vocabulary, perhaps as many as three hundred words, mainly nouns and action words. Other parts of speech (such as adjectives and adverbs) appear later, as well as pronouns like *me* and *my,* since the child is now becoming aware of himself as a person. The words which he learns are in reference to what he hears, sees, and experiences. He now realizes that everything has a name and he derives talking pleasure from verbal exchanges by asking, "What's this?" This verbal exchange is extremely important since it is through communication with others that the child becomes a sensitive, investigative, and thinking individual.

From three to five, the child moves forward linguistically, provided that his language development has been given impetus. There must be *incentive* for him to speak and there must be *need* for oral communication.

All races have the same physical equipment needed for talking. Any normal child can learn a language, particularly if it is the first one he learns. Then why are there deviations in a child's ability to communicate when he enters preschool or kindergarten?

Although language patterns are largely set by the time a child enters school, we find an appreciable number of children who mispronounce speech sounds in the English language, or perhaps cannot talk intelligibly. This inability to produce all sounds of the language, in many instances, is a part of normal speech development. Yet the teacher can provide aural stimulation and speech-sound fun through games, poems, and stories which help the child move forward in his speech development more rapidly.

It must be remembered that parents are the first teachers and models. Comforting verbal responses during the time when a child is acquiring speech will accelerate its development. Parents are the gardeners, but they do not make the seed grow. They provide the fertile soil so that the child's mind will be surrounded by what it needs as it matures and develops.

Parents should provide aural and verbal exchange and speak carefully, slowly, and plainly. They should imitate the child's speech "tries" in pleasant tones of voice, and thus give him added stimulation and appreciation for his efforts. They should provide happy play experiences. Words can be made treasures for the child if the parent reads to him frequently, allowing him to follow pictures in a book. Parents should answer his questions, and remember that the child wants to be answered in terms of action and sense perception, and not in terms of reason. *He thinks with his senses and muscles,* not through reasoning of cause and effect.

If the child is friendly and outgoing, probably he has had friendly and honest responses at home and good motivation to speak. Oddly enough, however, some children can grow and develop normally in home situations in ways which seem almost incredible, while children from homes where more material advantages and experiences have been offered may use baby talk and even be delayed in speech development. The richness of experience and good interpersonal relationships do not necessarily relate to income bracket.

"The feeling relationships between parent and child appear to be a tremendous factor in the child's learning of language. The child who avoids talking because he fears the lack of acceptance, the child whose feelings are not understood, the standards of eating, toilet training, and behavior which are imposed too soon, and emotional tensions existing in the home, can create surface symptoms produced by a child who attempts to cope with an unsatisfying and hostile world."[3] A friendly, hostile, aggressive, or timid child *has learned his behavior.*

*We can help and understand the child with defective speech:*

> By giving him support, accepting him for himself, trying to identify with him, being warm and friendly toward him, and by alleviating his fears, distrust, and anxiety;

---

[3] Robert Douglass, "Basic Feelings and Speech Defects," *Exceptional Children,* March, 1959, p. 319.

By providing a happy speech environment so that he will acquire speech in pleasant ways;

By helping him develop a good self image so that he can adjust better to himself and others;

By encouraging him to make sentences and stimulating him to ask questions so that his curiosity for learning will be heightened;

By refraining from criticizing his speech and instead, using interesting games and activities where practice can result in new and more acceptable patterns;

By remembering that true growth is slow, and being sensitive enough to realize when a child is ready for the next step of learning;

By recognizing when professional help is necessary, and by becoming aware of the facilities in school and community which can give the child essential help needed.

*We can understand and help the child with a non-English speaking background.* It must be remembered that a child coming to the center with no English speaking vocabulary must depend upon his native tongue to some extent in communicating with those who can understand it. The child born of foreign-speaking parents is at a disadvantage when the English language is suddenly thrust upon him. We cannot expect him to drop his native tongue entirely. English will develop in time if proper incentives are used.

Some bi-lingual children will have had the background and experiences which will make transition to English easier. Others will have had narrower and meager experiences and will need special encouragement and motivation for learning a new language. Some children will not be able to communicate well in either language.

The teacher will need to speak slowly and distinctly. She will need to provide excursions and experiences for these children so that concepts of learning can take place. The child must have these concepts and meanings before he can express himself in words. The general procedures under "We can understand and help the child with defective speech" may apply also to the child with non-English speaking background.

As stated previously, the child acquires speech through communication with others. Association and personal relationships enable him to become aware of people and share with them, to listen more effectively, to have something to say, to influence others, and to gain confidence in his ability to use his language.

However, language is more than an avenue of communication. It leads to the revelation of feelings and emotions. Accompanied by body movements, it helps the young child to identify himself, escape for awhile from feeling "little" to being "big." Also, it helps to release and redirect emotions that otherwise could be repressed. Language provides the child with a valuable cathartic function, giving release from emotional tensions and aiding in personal and social adjustment.

—L.B.S. and R.L.D.

## HELPING THE CHILD TO DEVELOP A SATISFYING SELF-IMAGE

Each child has the need to relate to others in satisfying ways, to be loved, recognized, and admired for his individual accomplishments. He needs to explore his surroundings, to manipulate his world, and to express himself verbally and bodily. In order to test his perceptions, and to grow socially, emotionally, and intellectually, the child needs to communicate and identify with the people in his immediate environment. He needs, also, to learn about himself as an individual, separate and distinct from his family. If some or all of these needs are not met, social and emotional ills can develop.

In the early childhood education center, the child who exhibits a negative "me" concept is struggling for self-identity. This "me" concept probably is the least definable and most vaguely understood of all patterns in the child's make-up. It is difficult to know exactly how a young child thinks and feels, but research shows that the child's self-concept has been shaped by adult relationships during the early years. A word, a look, a movement, a smile, or a touch contributes to this shaping. It is this social interaction upon which full development of potential for learning depends.

A child from affluent surroundings may come to the center with a self-image as negative and with needs as urgent as the child from the most impoverished slums. No amount of material wealth can balance feelings of not being loved, needed, wanted, and approved.

In an atmosphere of restriction, apprehension, and rejection, the child is often unable to clarify *who* he is. With no chance to develop healthy attitudes, preferences, or sense values of fairness, responsibility, self-discipline, or graciousness toward others, his social consciousness can be weakened. His senses may be dulled through lack of use, and he cannot derive pleasure from learning.

Part of discovering oneself is being able to express wishes, thoughts, and feelings verbally. Language is important to the fulfillment of all the child's needs. If he cannot talk spontaneously and limitlessly, he may discover that talking is threatening, frustrating, and unpleasant. Who could find ease in communicating when there is no verbal or auditory exchange, when one is criticized and admonished, is ignored, rejected, or penalized in unfair ways? When communication cannot flow freely, fear and anxiety develop. A child cannot think freely when others do his thinking for him and do not consider his responses worthwhile.

A child can scarcely believe in himself if the adults upon whom he must depend tell him that he is no good and undermine his self-esteem. He cannot learn to trust when he is treated ambivalently and does not know what to expect. When discipline is "do as I say," or accompanied by consistent physical punishment, we can expect severe retardation in emotional development.

Although the child with a negative self-image may be deprived of love, status, and feelings of importance and accomplishment, he is emotionally different from another child having experienced the same deprivations. One child may be painfully introverted and quiet, afraid to try new things because he has no faith in his own powers. Another may be aggressive and outgoing with performances lacking in purpose, direction, and meaning. Still another child may be sensitive and fearful. Many rejected children exhibit restlessness, nervousness, resentment, and hostility. Thus, each child must be handled differently because of his individual make-up; his actions and responses may need preferential treatment if a positive concept is to be built.

Above all, the child must *be* loved and *feel* loved. Being loved in a demonstrated and affectionate way gives him that first sense of safety and value of himself as a creature of significance. "If prior to language development, a child experiences feelings of being loved, the groundwork for self-respect is established. The child then can branch out to loving others. If one has never felt loved, he can never fully respect and love himself. If the parents love each other, they indirectly tell the child it is safe to love oneself and others." [4] Being loved in the home gives the child security to try his own wings at something else, to experiment freely, fearing no adverse consequences for his actions. Love is that manifested and serene feeling which tells the child he is truly loved, even

---

[4] Glenn R. Hawkes and Damaris Pease, *Behavior and Development from 5 to 12*, Harper and Row, New York, 1962.

when he has fallen short of adult expectation. "Love is a special way of feeling," [5] as one author aptly expresses it.

The teacher in the education center is a potent force in helping the child to gain confidence in himself and others. She must establish a one-to-one relationship through which the child can learn to love and trust an adult—perhaps for the first time. She must build an atmosphere of regard and encouragement in which he can feel secure and grow in independence. Empathy is a powerful factor in creating positive attitudes and security when a child is crippled emotionally.

The teacher encourages the child's attempts, through stimulating and satisfying learning experiences, until he is sure of himself and does not need encouragement and approbation each time he performs a task. She creates a climate of interest so that he will ask questions. Knowing that he cannot learn much if he is hungry, unhappy, or angry, she comforts and feeds him both food and affection. She makes it possible for him to learn with his senses, his mind, and his muscles, realizing that tremendous innate drive for satisfying his curiosity through play and experimentation. She helps him to project his feelings with his eyes, ears, fingers, and voice, and she becomes excited with him over his new-found experiences. She makes possible many aesthetic experiences and creative achievements for him which nurture emotional satisfaction and personality development. Occasionally, she gives him very *special* attention so that his worth is enhanced. Knowing that anthropomorphism is a stage in which he now lives and enjoys, she provides opportunities for him to give animation to the inanimate, thus opening the door of communication.

In this atmosphere of acceptance and understanding, the child's concept of self grows and changes. In time, the shy child acts out "The Little Red Hen," and the real "me" begins to emerge. The too verbal child is able to listen to others. The unsure child proudly shows his painting and talks about it.

Jean Piaget, the Swiss developmental psychologist, tells us that intellectual and emotional growth are inextricably interwoven. The child adjusts or "accommodates" himself to his surroundings. He then tries to understand and to make that knowledge a part of himself.

The concept of early childhood education implies concentration upon emotional, intellectual, social, creative, and aesthetic development, as well as emphasis upon physical health so that the child will develop

---

[5] Joan Walsh Anglund, *Love Is a Special Way of Feeling*, Harcourt, New York, 1960.

a healthy personality and a favorable self-image. The teacher needs to explore the rich language potential of the child's everyday world so as to instill pride in his culture and community. Helping him to build self-identity will give direction and impetus to more broadening experiences.

It is not enough for the teacher to be aware of the child's needs. She must also help the parents to understand his needs and her philosophy and methods so that school and home may cooperate more effectively in supporting the child. Whenever this relationship becomes a reality, the child shows almost miraculous growth in attitudes, and in ability to work and play constructively with others. Even when parents are hostile or apathetic and do not reinforce the learning carried on in the education center, they should, nevertheless, be consulted and be given sympathetic explanations of the program goals. Gradually, these negative parental attitudes may be supplanted with more positive ones which will contribute to more favorable development of the child's self-image.

The stories, poems, devices and activities included in this unit are originated to give the teacher some applied language and other techniques which will help the child to become aware of himself as a *person* and to gain self-confidence.

—L.B.S. and R.L.D.

## NOBODY JUST LIKE ME
### (A Discussion)

There is nobody just like you in the whole world, and there is nobody just like me.

Everyone has two hands, two ears, two eyes, two cheeks, two lips, two legs, two shoulders, two knees, and two feet. (*Children show or point to their body parts named.*) But hands, ears, eyes, cheeks, lips, legs, shoulders, knees, and feet are never exactly like someone else's.

Everyone has one head, one nose, one chin, one forehead, one neck, and one whole body. But your head, nose, chin, forehead, neck, and body are never exactly like someone else's.

No two people like quite the same things, either.

Some people like vanilla ice cream and some like strawberry. What kind do you like? (*Responses.*)

Some people like the smell of tar on streets and others like the scent of freshly cut grass. What do you like to smell? (*Responses.*)

Some people like to feel cool water running through their fingers; some like the silky fur of a kitten. What do you like to feel? (*Responses.*)

Some people like to watch a silver plane as it skims across the blue sky, while others would much rather watch purple violets in a flower pot on the window sill. What do you like to watch? (*Responses.*)

Some people like to hear rain on the roof at night, and others like to hear drums in a parade. What do you like to hear? (*Responses.*)

It is true that no two people are alike.

I look in the mirror, and I know that I am not like anyone else. I am *me*. I don't look like you and you do not look like me.

Even if you have a twin brother or sister, *you* know which is which.

Isn't it a good thing that people are not all alike? What might happen if they were? (*Responses.*)

Would you like to be like everyone else? (*Responses.*)

Life wouldn't be much fun, would it?

I'm glad I am *me*. How about you? (*Responses.*)

—L.B.S.

This discussion is designed to emphasize the self-image and build importance. It would be helpful if small mirrors were available to the class as this story is told. Ask each child to tell what makes him different from anyone else.

## PERSONAL POSSESSIONS

Love is an emotion which some children may not understand. Often there is need to bring in animals or soft toys so that the children can understand the emotion of love as they cuddle them and talk to them freely.

Sometimes a child needs to bring a possession to school—an object which symbolizes a state of security, and which he can call his own. He knows that whatever happens, there is something present that belongs to him alone. Encourage the child to talk about his possession so that the windows of communication may open.

## SOFT TOYS

Soft toys can give comfort and feelings of safety when the child is spending his first days away from home. Teddy bears, Raggedy Ann dolls, and other stuffed toys represent something to cuddle and love—to talk and sing to, and to help alleviate feelings of fear of those first days at school.

## THE CHILD'S PICTURE

Take pictures or slides of children at work and play. Post these photographs or project the slides on a wall. Children will relive these experiences and talk spontaneously about them, sometimes for the first time. If possible, include mothers in some of the pictures.

## SILHOUETTES

Place a lamp at one side of the child; post a sheet of white paper on the wall at the opposite side. The light of the lamp will reflect the shadow profile of the child which can be traced and cut out by one of the teacher's aides.

Ask a child to lie down on a large sheet of wrapping paper placed on the floor. Draw around his head, arms, torso, and legs with a felt tip pen or crayon. Each child will enjoy coloring his own silhouette.

These silhouettes make excellent gifts for parents.

—O.M.A.

## WHAT I WANT TO BE

Cut pictures of workers from magazines and mount them on the bulletin board. The children tell what work they would like to do when grown-up and point out their fathers' occupations. Clothing contributed by parents for the dress-up box may be used by the children to act out and to identify with the workers.

## IDENTIFYING ME

I looked in the mirror and what did I see?
I saw somebody and it was ME.
I looked in the water and what did I see?
I saw my reflection and it was ME.
I stood in the sunshine and what did I see?
I saw a shadow and it was ME.
I looked in an album and what did I see?
I saw a picture and it was ME.

—L.B.S.

Suggest that the children find their reflections around the classroom in a shiny utensil, a toy, or a mirror. Pass around small mirrors to let the children get acquainted with their faces. Be sure that a large mirror is hung low enough so that the child can see and contemplate his whole image.

On the second reading of this poem, the children will enjoy helping the teacher to say it.

Cut two, full-length silhouettes of the same size, one black, and the other yellow. Glue the whole black form upside down at the lower left angle to represent a shadow. Talk about the shapes and lengths of shadows in the morning and at lunch time. Go into the yard on a sunny day and observe individual shadows.

Use this silhouette idea for shadows of animals and objects, also.

### PARTS OF YOUR BODY

There are two little eyes to open and close;
There are two little lips and one little nose.
There are two little cheeks and a tongue shut in;
There are two little ears and one little chin.
There are two little arms and elbows neat;
There are two little shoes on two little feet.
There are two little shoulders stout and strong;
There are two little hands busy all day long.
—Adapted

The children point to each named part of the body as the rhyme is said.

The number concepts of *one* and *two,* and the verb *are* can be emphasized and, possibly, retained by the children.

## TOUCHING

I'll touch my hair, my cheeks, my hand;
I'll touch my feet, and then I'll stand.
I'll touch my nose, my lips, my chin;
I'll touch my arm all covered with skin.
I'll touch my ear; I'll touch my chest;
I'm tired of touching, so I'll rest.
—L.B.S.

The children act out this rhyme. Use before resting time.

## TALL AND SMALL

I live in a real house,
But a playhouse is smaller.
My real house is tall,
But a church may be taller.

I am really quite small,
And my Daddy is taller.
Sometimes I feel tall,
'Cause our baby is smaller.
—L.B.S.

On a second reading of the rhyme, ask the class to supply the last word in each line and to measure tall and small with the hand. Ask children to name things that are small and smaller, tall and taller.

This rhyme affords practice on dimensional parts of speech, and on the suffix *er*.

## HOW TALL AM I?

I am small; (*Crouch down.*)
But now I am tall. (*Stand.*)
I am so little,
I'm nothing at all.
  (*Crouch to floor and hug body.*)
See me grow and grow and grow. (*Stretch.*)
Now I'm a giant with a "Ho, ho, ho!"
  (*Hand on stomach.*)
—L.B.S.

## LEARNING WITH A GLOBE

A globe can provide many learning and language experiences which give the child pride in race and community. Use a flashlight for the sun and turn the globe slowly around so that the children will get the concept of day and night. Tape small paper dolls to the globe to show the city and state where the children live. Discuss where grandparents came from and indicate their countries: Italy, Puerto Rico, Mexico, Africa, Ireland, or Japan.

Locate the capital of the United States and, at Christmas time, the North Pole where Santa has his workshop.

## QUESTION AND ANSWER

The exchange of conversation between teacher and child forms a valuable contribution to the learning process. In this exercise the child is given individual attention, is afforded practice in asking and answering questions, and is given a sense of identity.

TEACHER: Who is there?
CHILD: Can't you guess?
TEACHER: Is it Barry?
CHILD: Yes, it is Barry. I am Barry.

## THE BIG HUNT

With my binoculars
   (*Circle eyes with fingers.*)
I look near and far.
With my telescope
   (*Double fists together.*)
I see a star!
With my magnifying glass
   (*Make circle with fingers of both hands.*)
A big thumb I see.
   (*Wiggle thumb.*)
With my shiny mirror
I find ME!
   (*Hold palm of hand in front of face.*)
—O.M.A.

# CHILDREN ARE POETS

"Poetry is the essence of an insight, a mood, an experience crystalized in language." [6] Poetry is ideas expressed in rhythmic sound. It is the language of children.

> I like my words to dance and sing;
> I like my words to jingle-jing!
> It doesn't matter what they say,
> Just so they fit the game I play.
>
> My words can bounce; my words can swing;
> My words can go with anything!
> And sometimes when I play alone,
> I make up words all of my own!
> 
> —V.S.P.

During the stages of linguistic development, children find pleasure in experimenting with speech sounds and rhythms. Most of these experiments are comprised of sounds, syllables, and word repetitions. Generally, these repetitions, which have definite beats to the rhythm, are accompanied by bodily movements. Children find far more appeal in sound than in meaning. Sound is an integral part of their world.

Dr. Charles Van Riper tells us that children play with words by "rhyming, punning, and distorting their sequences." [7] They have fun isolating word stems and adding different endings and beginnings. Sometimes they will prolong a continuant sound, such as *Mmmmmmm* or *yesssssss*. This vocal play is necessary in learning how to synthesize and analyze words later when the child begins to read and to monitor what he reads back to his own ears. The invented word and the natural rhyme are common expressions of the very young child.

From the child's point of view, there is wonder in everything and he is part of everything that is wonderful. His own output of repetitive syllables, words, and phrases bombard his ears and senses and give him overwhelming elation. Repetition suggests movements of the body and, in turn, movements spur on more verbalization. This circular activity takes place in all normal children.

---

[6] Austin Mills, *The Sound of Poetry*, Allyn and Bacon, Inc., New York, 1963.
[7] Charles Van Riper and Katherine Butler, *Speech in the Elementary Classroom*, Harper, New York, 1955.

A child has such fun putting his feelings into words. Annette, four years old, never doubted her identity as she chanted over and over:

> "Who is me? I am me.
> Me, me, me!
> Here I am! I am me!
> See, see, see?
> Me, me, me!"

The child's world is felt, heard, seen, smelled, and tasted, for he is constantly exploring. One of his most delightful and satisfying ways of expressing these explorations and discoveries is to verbalize them.

A class of five-year-olds discussed mud puddles after the teacher had read them a story about some pigs on a farm. Later, at play time, several children mixed soil and water in shallow coffee cans until the consistency of mud was formed. When they had satisfied their longings to be "messy," they followed the teacher-assistant to the sink where they "cleaned up." Several days later, one of the children sang:

> "I like to feel mud,
> And get it all over my hands,
> And all over my feet.
> I wish I could get it
> All over my body
> Like the little piggy.
> I would squeal and squeal
> Because the mud felt so good."

Kornei Chukovsky describes the verses of young children from two to five as "spontaneous, inspired by movement, melodic exclamations, spoken with accompaniment of clapping and dancing; brief, repetitive, and chorea."[8] These transitory rhythms and repetitive chants are significant parts of the child's growth and preparation for building aesthetic tastes. The child's appreciation for poetry grows through exposure to it in the home and the school. As he shares poetry with others and is well motivated through suitable interpretation, he becomes more skillful in selecting poems that delight him, that appeal to his senses, and that give him personal gratification. The child responds as cheer-

---

[8] Kornei Chukovsky, *From Two to Five,* The University of California Press, Berkeley, California, 1963.

fully and as naturally to poetry as he does to music, for stirring words of poetry *are* music.

A British child of four exemplifies inventive language and rhythm in these expressions:

> "I walk through all the things I do;
> I walk through all the things I do.
> Apopocatepal, acatopotapetal,
> Arranging metal, arranging metal.
> I think she must be using glue.
> I walk through all the things I do." [9]

By the age of four or five, the young child is satisfied not only with his own creations, but also with the poetry of others. He likes poems that:

Tell stories and transport him into a world of imagination.
Give him a sense of movement with skipping and dancing words.
Arouse his sense of humor.
Have onomatopoeic words (words that imitate their natural sounds).
Evoke imagery through figures of speech.
Are close to his own experiences.

We are aware from our own childhood memories that the teacher who ventured along creative pathways was the one who instilled a love of poetry within us. The teacher who critically analyzed, or who forced memorization of poems which often were not understood, stifled our creative imaginations. No standards of perfection can be imposed upon young children. The child first needs the one-to-one rapport with his teacher and sympathetic understanding so that he can feel totally relaxed, dare to be himself, and give free rein to his creative impulses.

As we think back into our early childhood days, we realize that the teachers who won us over were enthusiastic models of good poetry rendition. Although we did not understand at the time why we enjoyed listening to their interpretations, we now know that a particular teacher must have inspired us and fed our senses with beautifully articulated words. She probably forgot that she was "teaching" us poetry. She simply *shared* it, and her own sincere feelings were caught by us as we felt, heard, tasted, smelled, and visualized. She helped us develop

---

[9] Betty Willsher, *School Before Five,* Faber and Faber, Ltd., London, 1959.

appreciation and taste which have molded our standards in choosing good literature today.

Aside from certain intangible and sensitive personality factors which stirred our senses and caused us to think, what characteristics did this kind of teacher have? She had a quiet, well-modulated voice. She created vivid pictures, which she painted with her voice as she highlighted words which brought forth images. She gave us the impression that she enjoyed what she was reading.

We created because she insisted upon our keeping the spark alive. Who can tell if she inspired future scientists, mathematicians, architects, artists, or authors, since creativity and inventiveness are necessary to all such ways of life.

Because children are uninhibited by language forms, they can invent beautifully expressed thoughts almost instinctively. In truth, if given freedom to put their images into words, they may become better poets than will many adults.

Though a young child seems completely unaware of his power to create rhymes, he is extremely sensitive to language, its cadences and movements. When a child expresses himself spontaneously, the teacher can call attention to the fact that he has "made a poem." She shows further appreciation for his efforts by asking the group to repeat his poem. Thus, she keeps alive his natural sensitivity to language.

It is important at this stage that the teacher refrain from suggesting words for his poem or forcing him to think of ideas. His own creativity should be encouraged.

It may be interesting for the teacher to try her hand at composing some verse. This experience, though laborious at first, ultimately can result in gems of expression. Almost any sentence can swing into rhythm if a word here and there is changed. Here are some pointers:

Look around the environment and catch a sparkling idea.
Let the first line come from your experience and imagination.
Touch, hear, see, smell, and taste the words.
Set up a pattern by putting words on paper, in order, so they will express, in some sequence, what you want to say.
Treasure every effort you make and do not hesitate to share your creations with others.

The teacher may be guided in her choices of poetry literature to present to the children by the excellent anthologies available in libraries.

Here are a few examples of enchanting poetry which have kindled imaginations, piqued curiosities, and whetted appetites:

>Aldis, Dorothy, "Kick a Little Stone"
>Bacmeister, Rhoda Warner, "Galoshes"
>Barrows, Marjorie, "Three Little Witches"
>Behn, Harry, "Others"
>Chute, Marchette Gaylord, "My Dog"
>De La Mare, Walter, "The Cupboard"
>Dodge, Mary Mapes, "Snow-Flakes"
>Farjeon, Eleanor, "Mrs. Peck-Pigeon"
>Field, Eugene, "Duel"
>Fisher, Aileen, "Down in the Hollow"
>Fyleman, Rose, "Mice"
>Hood, Thomas, "The Little Piggies"
>Mitchell, Lucy Sprague, "My Bed"
>Morley, Christopher, "Animal Crackers"
>Richards, Laura E., "Little Cat"
>Roberts, Elizabeth Madox, "Mumps"
>Rossetti, Christina, "Fireflies"
>Stevenson, Robert Louis, "The Swing"
>Tippett, James Sterling, "Trains"
>
>—L.B.S.

## WHAT DO RHYTHMS SAY?

On the playground, there are many opportunities for the teacher to encourage a child to express bodily rhythms in words of his own choosing. To help him to become aware of the possibilities of finding words that suit the action, the teacher may, as she swings the child, say:

>"Tommy goes up, up, up!
>Tommy goes down, down down!"

Using Tommy's name will give him a personal sense of the rhyme to which he can add words of his own about himself.

## DRUM SIGNALS FOR YOUR FRIENDS

Select two children whose first names have a different number of syllables. On a soft-toned drum, beat out the name of each child and ask the class to identify the name. Stretch a piece of inner tube over a large popcorn can, a kitchen canister, or small round wastebasket; tie securely with a strip of inner tubing. The children will get a sense of rhythm if their fingers come into contact with what they are beating. Drum sticks are likely to stimulate the children too much. Encourage the children to talk as they tap.

## RHYTHM AT WORK

Usually a certain rhythm accompanies a routine action. For example, washing hands might carry the rhythm of:

> "Rub, rub,
> Swish, swish,
> Shake, shake:
> And now I dry."

Suggest that the children find words to fit the following:

| | |
|---|---|
| Riding a tricycle | Sorting objects |
| Pounding clay | Passing out crayons |
| Sifting sand | Coloring or painting |
| Tearing paper from a pad | Putting blocks in a box |
| Putting on galoshes | Tying shoes and aprons |

## WHAT DO THE PICTURES SAY?

Hold up pictures that involve familiar experiences similar to the following:

Children walking in a puddle of water
A child petting a kitten
A boy smelling a flower
Children eating lunch
A marching band
People using tools

Ask the children what sounds, smells, and tastes they experience as they look at the pictures. Pictures which appeal to the senses are helpful to children who haven't a supply of words with which to express themselves and may serve to enrich vocabulary.

## BOUNCING WORDS

As the child is bouncing a ball on the playground, stimulate word-rhythms by starting him off with a word on each bounce. Stop and let the child continue to "bounce" his own words.

## PICTURES MAKE POETRY

Make a collection of pictures whose names rhyme. As the children match the pictures, they say the names aloud. Often this activity prompts rhyming. Some examples of pictures to include in the collection are:

| | |
|---|---|
| shoe - glue | pig - wig |
| dish - fish | loom - broom |
| coat - goat | cat - hat |
| blocks - socks | bed - sled |
| sun - gun | shop - mop |
| fan - pan | dog - frog |

## WHAT DO OBJECTS SAY?

Bring in a hand egg beater and a sponge for squeezing water into a tin pie pan. Ask the children to tell what the egg beater and sponge are saying as they are being used. Sometimes this device will produce capsule poems.

## NONSENSE RHYMES

Children enjoy nonsense rhymes of any kind. Here are examples of names of foods which go together. The children can supply the second name.

Mrs. Smutter likes bread and _____. (butter)
Mr. Sam likes bread and _____. (jam)
Mrs. Savey likes bread and _____. (gravy)
Mr. Wilk likes bread and _____. (milk)
Mrs. Bunny likes bread and _____. (honey)
Mr. Loup likes bread and _____. (soup)
Mrs. Keese likes bread and _____. (cheese)
Mrs. Neat likes bread and _____. (meat)

The children also will have fun making up rhyming words for the last line of these couplets. Finger ring or stick puppets will be helpful. The child keeps his puppet hidden behind his back until it is his turn to speak.

TEACHER: You have shaggy hair.
CHILD:   I must be a _____. (bear)
TEACHER: Your ears are funny.
CHILD:   I must be a _____. (bunny)
TEACHER: You belong to Bo Peep.
CHILD:   I must be a _____. (sheep)
TEACHER: You lay eggs in a pen.
CHILD:   I must be a _____. (hen)
TEACHER: You found a bone near a log.
CHILD:   I must be a _____. (dog)

## WHAT POEM DOES THE MUSIC MAKE?

Select a record of instrumental music or portions of a rhythm album for playing. Instead of suggesting that the class pantomime or act out the music, ask them to tell what the music is saying. Write down separate impressions and illustrate them with magazine pictures or with children's paintings. Label these impressions with names of the records for which they are intended. From time to time, read the impressions aloud as the music is replayed.

## CLASSICAL POETRY INSPIRES WORDS

All children enjoy "The Gingham Dog and the Calico Cat" by Eugene Field. The class may paint their own gingham and calico designs on poster paper with red horizontal and green diagonal stripes for gingham, and varied colored dots for calico. Use these designs for tracing and cutting dog and cat figures. Then reinforce them with tagboard. Display or show these cutouts as the children make up their own story-poems or episodes about the dog and cat. Paper plates can be made available for the Chinese Plate and the Dutch Clock. A tongue depressor secured with a paper fastener to the center of the "clock" can represent the hands.

One child, with a little encouragement and help from his classmates, made up this poem:

>This is the dog.
>This is the cat,
>And this is where
>The two of them sat!
>The cat scratched the dog,
>"Meow, meow."
>The dog bit the cat,
>"Bow-wow, bow-wow."
>But they are good friends
>Now, now, now!

"Who Has Seen the Wind?" by Christina Rossetti lends itself to rhythmic action and to creative verbal expression as well. After reading the poem aloud and acting it out, ask, "What else sways?"

## TELL US WHAT THE SEASONS SAY

>Tell us what the wind says in the fall.
>Tell us what the leaves say.
>Tell us what the rain says.
>Tell us what the birds say.
>Tell us what gray skies say.

Children's responses about fall may be tape recorded along with other seasonal impressions experienced in the community. Responses may also be written in booklet form to be placed on the browsing table along with some of the seasonal picture-storybooks.

## WHAT COLORS TELL US

One can learn much about a child's feelings and background by holding up a swatch of color and asking, "What does this red color make you think of?" Colors of yellow, orange, brown, green, purple, blue, or pink will remind individual children of wholesome or unwholesome, happy or unhappy experiences. Children can put these thoughts into rhythmic expression.

## TIME SEQUENCE

Watching a bud opening in a vase of water, a plant growing, or a moth emerging from a chrysalis can help children become more observant, help them to understand time, and inspire them to create little poems. Ask:

> How does it look today?
> How did it look last week? (Yesterday?)
> How will it look tomorrow?

The children will need to have experienced these things at least once before discussion can be started or words can flow.

### I WENT TO THE CIRCUS

TEACHER:  I went to the circus and I saw a clown.
CHILD:    The clown said, "_____."
TEACHER:  I went to the circus and I saw a monkey.
CHILD:    The monkey said, "_____."

Continue with other circus or zoo animals; then discuss the farm.

TEACHER:  I went to the farm and I saw a cow.
CHILD:    The cow said, "_____."

The children will have not only a rhythmic experience, but will learn also something about wild and domestic animals.

### SUGGESTIONS FOR USING PICTURE-STORYBOOKS

*A Tree Is Nice* [10] by Janice May Udry has a tremendous, creative language potential. While reading this story to the children, allow them time to contemplate each picture. Then ask the class, "What else is nice?"

"The Sleepy Forest" [11] by Naoma Zimmerman relaxes the children with its sleepy, repetitive words. It presents an ideal poetry activity as the children add other animals to the story and make "lullaby" words.

*A Friend Is Someone Who Likes You* [12] by Joan Walsh Anglund can result in a child's making a small "gem" following the question: "What is being a friend?"

---

[10] Janice May Udry, *A Tree Is Nice*, Harper, New York, 1956.
[11] Naoma Zimmerman, "The Sleepy Forest," in *Listening Time*, Album No. 1 by Scott and Wood, Bowmar Records, distributed by McGraw-Hill, Inc., New York, 1965.
[12] Joan Walsh Anglund, *A Friend Is Someone Who Likes You*, Harcourt, Brace and World, Inc., New York, 1958.

*A Little House of Your Own* [13] by Beatrice Schenk De Regniers appeals to a child who needs possessions and a place for retreat. Questions, such as: "Where would you like to have a house that belongs just to you alone?" or "Why would it be nice to have a house of your own?" may elicit many rhythmic and interesting responses.

Always be sure that a child realizes that a poem can consist of a few words or a spontaneous thought and it need not necessarily rhyme.

—L.B.S. and V.S.P.

## CHRISTMAS RHYMES

December music, such as "Jingle Bells" and "Up on the Housetop," can inspire children to make up additional rhymes that can be accompanied by action. Holiday objects—a sprig of holly, a gift wrapped package, a branch from a fir tree, a candle, a Christmas tree ornament, a stocking, a candy cane, or a picture of Santa—will prompt children to express their ideas. If all of the ideas are put together, a complete Christmas poem originates. This same technique can be used for Thanksgiving or other holidays.

## THE CHILD USES LANGUAGE

The number of grammatical forms which a child has acquired before he enters school is almost incredible. According to Rona Williams,[14] the child of four uses question words, plurals, gender, and syntax amazingly well. Without realizing structure, he is able to place a verb after a noun (*Pepper barks.*), use a noun, verb, and object (*I hear Pepper.*), a noun with linking verb (*Pepper is black.*), and a noun which links a verb to another noun (*Pepper is my dog.*). The child is quite adept at manipulating phrases and clauses. Often, he uses comparative suffixes and superlatives such as *er* and *est*, and the participial *ing*. His words and sounds fall into patterns that rise and fall melodiously.

At one year of age, he has mastered the music of speech and, from this music, flows the words of language. Words bring great satisfaction to him for he has a keen sensitivity to language. For a long time now, he has used it to manipulate his environment, to satisfy his needs and wants, and to express himself emotionally.

---

[13] Beatrice Schenk De Regniers, *A Little House of Your Own*, Harcourt, Brace and World, Inc., New York, 1955.
[14] Rona M. Williams, *Speech Difficulties in Childhood*, George G. Harrap, Co. Ltd., London, 1962.

There are, however, children who come from homes where substandard speech or a foreign language is used. These children must make many adjustments. Sometimes a child knows neither his native language nor English well enough to communicate. Again, he may be able to speak the English language, yet not understand the verbal expressions of his teacher. Her more precise pronunciation and sentence structure may baffle him.

Early childhood education centers are made up of children from varieties of homes and backgrounds. There are the French in Louisiana, the Mexican-Americans in the Southwest, the Indians of the reservations, the Eskimos who have no natural feeling for inflection, Scandinavians in the upper middle states, the Poles and Puerto Ricans in New York, and the Dutch in Pennsylvania. Added to these are the groups from impoverished areas who sometimes appear to have a language all of their own.

Encouraging these young children to acquire more acceptable speech patterns is an important task for the teacher. Since all children need at once to feel adequate in their communication, speech improvement should be planned with use of stimulating activities. All responses of the child should be treated with sympathy and encouragement. This cannot be done if his thoughts are interrupted by comments on his grammar and speech usage. A young child knows nothing about rules of grammar. If he has to stop, think, and try to remember to avoid "ain't," "He done it," or "I seen it," speech will become an interminable process for him. The teacher can be patient with his small errors and welcome his offerings, realizing that direct criticism never helps and perfection cannot be forced.

Language experiences, first of all, must be real, functional, and successful for the child.

There are three reasons for permitting the child to speak freely. The first is to avoid damaging his personality and second, to refrain from blocking his learning which requires oral communcation. The third reason relates to the logical progression of speech and learning. When the child is able to speak easily and unselfconsciously, he can make generalizations for himself about the nature of language. After he has heard correct sentence patterns many times, he can then begin to measure his own expressions against the ones he hears.

Habits are built through usage that becomes established with repetition and practice. Carefully structured questions will evoke correct grammatical usage in a pleasant way. Given a few good patterns, such as those included in the games which follow, the child may eventually tend to reject incorrect ones.

—L.B.S. and V.S.P.

## IS, ISN'T, AND AREN'T

TEACHER: Is the sky green?
CHILDREN: No, it *isn't*.
TEACHER: Are my shoes made of paper?
CHILDREN: No, they *aren't*.

These practice sentences help not only in establishing more acceptable patterns of speech, but provide also humor and pleasant practice. Give individual children opportunities to make up similar questions to ask the class. To provide the additional support for children who may need it, each child may whisper his question in the teacher's ear first. If the child needs help with words or structure, the teacher can lend her support by whispering. When a child responds with "No, it ain't," simply ask the children to repeat the correct response.

## WAS AND WERE

TEACHER: What *were* you doing this morning, Bobby?
CHILD: I *was* making a truck.
TEACHER: What *were* you and Barbara doing this morning, Sue?
CHILD: We *were* playing in the playhouse.

The questions can be used effectively and naturally after free playtime. They can be asked of several children. Add for variety: "Bobby was making a truck" and "They were playing in the playhouse."

## HEAR AND HEARD

CHILD: (*In a whisper*) Did you *hear* me?
TEACHER: I *heard* you.
CLASS: We *heard* you.
TEACHER: Everyone *hears* you.

The children will enjoy taking turns whispering in the teacher's ear. This closeness and personal contact give many children the kind of security and one-to-one relationship which nurture language growth.

## BUY AND BOUGHT

The verb *buy* and *bought* can be used conversationally while playing "store." For all children with poor patterns of English, the time element is vividly illustrated when games are provided for dramatic play.

TEACHER: What will you *buy* at the supermarket today?
CHILD: I'll *buy* (I'm going to *buy*) an orange.
TEACHER: What did Nola *buy*, boys and girls?
CLASS: She *bought* an orange.

## SEE, SAW, AND SEEN

Place three miniature objects on a low table. Ask the children to gather around and tell what they *see*. Then ask them to cover their eyes and name the objects they *saw*.

Vary the game with the addition of the question using *seen*.

TEACHER: What did you *see*, Mary?
MARY: I *saw* a little shell.
TEACHER: Where have you *seen* a seashell, Tim?
TIM: I've *seen* a shell at the beach.

## HAVEN'T—HASN'T, HID—HIDDEN, FIND—FOUND

TEACHER: (*Hides an object.*) What did I *hide*?
CHILD: You *hid* an apple.
TEACHER: Where is the apple *hidden*, Terry?
TERRY: It's *hidden* behind your back.
TEACHER: (*The children look for a hidden object.*)
Haven't you *found* the ball yet, Edith?
EDITH: No, I *haven't*. I haven't *found* it.
TEACHER: Edith *hasn't found* the ball.
LARRY: I *found* it.

## WENT AND GONE

Use a hand puppet for teaching grammatical forms. Ask the class to give the puppet a name.

TEACHER: Where did Pete go?
CLASS: He *went* to the playhouse.

TEACHER: *(Goes to get puppet.)* Let's put Pete back into his box. Where has Pete *gone*?
CLASS: He's *gone* into his box.

## PLURALS

Children from environments where poor speech patterns are exhibited may omit plurals and say, "Three cat" or "Five dog." Draw or paste a picture of an animal onto a card. Paste two or three of the same drawing or silhouette on another card.

TEACHER: What do you see, Esther?
ESTHER: Two *cats*.
TEACHER: Esther sees two *cats*. (Emphasize the sound of *s* on the end of *cats*.)

## POSITIONAL WORDS

Find magazine pictures which will help the children to understand positional words. Dramatize and say sentences similar to the following:

*Among*: "I put this piece of chalk *among* the crayons. Where did I put the chalk?" (*Responses.*)
*For*: "This crayon is *for* you."
*Before*: "Let's put away our puzzles *before* we wash our hands."
*After*: "*After* we all sit down, we will have a story. When will we have a story?" (*Responses.*)
*Against*: "I set the flannelboard *against* the wall. Where did I set it?" (*Responses.*)

Provide other opportunities for using positional words.

| | | | | |
|---|---|---|---|---|
| at | beneath | inside | outside | between |
| behind | over | with | in | into |
| out | near | beside | under | off |
| up | down | below | of | around |

## A GAME FOR USE OF POSITIONAL WORDS

Draw and cut out a large bus shape with windows big enough to fit pictures inside them. Make small animal silhouettes which are in proportion to the size of the bus. Back the bus and animal shapes with outing flannel. Put the cutout bus on the flannelboard; place an animal shape inside the window and ask: "Where is the kitten?" The children will reply: "She's *inside* the bus."

Other positions may be: *behind* the bus, *on top* of the bus, *under* the bus, *in front* of the bus, *outside* the bus, *beneath* the bus, and *in back of* the bus.

## WORDS WHICH HAVE THE SAME MEANINGS

To enrich vocabulary, provide practice with words which have similar meanings. Select pictures which can help the children to understand the concept. Use both words to describe the object or action as follows:

This bear is *big*. He is large, huge, enormous.
Mice run *fast*. They run swiftly, quickly.
We are *still*. We are calm, quiet.

Other synonyms which young children can understand are:

| | | | |
|---|---|---|---|
| small | little; tiny | many | several |
| below | underneath | neat | tidy |
| go | leave | talk | speak |
| begin | start | animal | beast |
| tall | high | glad | happy |

## WORDS WHICH HAVE DIFFERENT MEANINGS

Use words of opposite meanings during daily discussions. For example: "Let's put all of the *wet* papers in the wastebasket. Now put the *dry* papers on the table."

The children who can learn and use the following antonyms will be able to make better observations and more accurate descriptions.

| | | | |
|---|---|---|---|
| open | shut | few | many |
| front | back | big | little |
| out | in | above | below |
| black | white | rough | smooth |
| hot | cold | sunny | cloudy |
| outside | inside | loud | soft |
| asleep | awake | full | empty |

| | | | |
|---|---|---|---|
| east | west | short | long |
| left | right | here | there |
| early | late | first | last |
| down | up | large | small |
| high | low | straight | crooked |
| clean | dirty | warm | cool |
| warm | cool | deep | shallow |
| narrow | wide | top | bottom |
| sad | happy | lost | found |
| no | yes | north | south |

## CONTRACTIONS

Ask the children to repeat words and their contractions with you.

"*I am* a person. *I'm* a person.
*We would* like to paint. *We'd* like to paint."

Use contractions below as suggested and include in daily discussions.

| | |
|---|---|
| didn't | he'll |
| wouldn't | we're |
| shouldn't | doesn't |
| they'll | it'll |
| it's | she'll |
| couldn't | he'd |
| it'll | we've |
| you'll | hadn't |
| I've | she'd |
| won't | can't |
| they've | they're |
| he's | aren't |

## DESCRIBING THINGS

Collect pictures of objects or animals or bring articles to class which the children can use in describing shapes, sizes, and characteristics. Ask: "Can you taste it? How does it taste? Can you smell it? How does it smell? Can you feel it? How does it feel?"

The list on the following page suggests pictures or objects that are easy to obtain for the children to describe.

| | | |
|---|---|---|
| soup | lemons | chair |
| shelf | fish | cotton |
| box | cookie | pencil |
| candy | apples | sandpaper |
| turtle | chocolate | chickens |
| watch | ice cream | salt |

## MYSTERY BOX

Wrap attractively a box containing a "surprise." Leave it on the browsing table to excite curiosity and questioning. Later, call the group together and listen to their guesses of what is in the box. Unwrap it and display its contents. Ask the children to identify the "surprise" and tell its purpose.

## ANIMAL SOUNDS

CHILD 1: Woof, woof! What am I?
CHILD 2: A dog?
CHILD 1: No. I'm not a dog.
CHILD 2: Are you a wolf?
CHILD 1: Yes, I'm a wolf.

The children take turns imitating other animal sounds as the game continues. The child asks questions and uses these particular sentence patterns. He also gains practice in using a variety of voices. Animal sack puppets can be used to "speak" this activity.

## ROLL CALL

After the children have been introduced to voice variety, call the roll using different pitches that place emphasis upon ways in which the voice can be used. This will help children to become aware of the vocal mechanism and its potential. Discuss with them the many ways that the voice can be changed. As a child's name is called, he may respond by saying, "Here," "I'm here," or "Here I am."

## AN IDENTIFYING GAME

Place four or five miniature objects in a box or sack. Take out one, hand it to a child, and say, "What did I give you, Barry?" He replies, "You *gave* me a _____."

Vary the game by asking a child to reach into the sack, feel an object, and identify it.

## FISHING FROM THE FLANNELBOARD

On the flannelboard, make the shape of a fishbowl with yarn. Select small pictures whose names contain specific sounds to be stressed with the children. Back these pictures with outing flannel and place them inside the fishbowl.

The child "fishes" by removing a picture. He names it and tells something about it. In order to get complete sentences without mentioning the word "sentence," ask: "What do you know about this horse?"

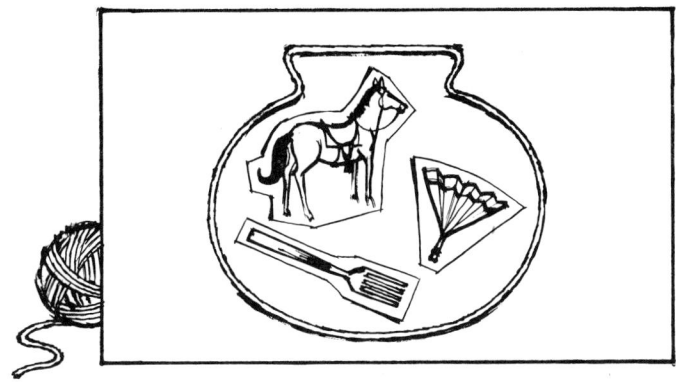

## COMPLETING SENTENCES

Ask individual children to supply the last word in each sentence. Acceptable responses are suggested here; however, recognize any other responses that would make sense. After the game is over, give the children a chance to name other objects or animals and tell what they wear.

I'm a child and I wear _____. (clothes, shoes, a shirt)
I'm a duck and I wear _____. (feathers)
I'm a bear and I wear _____. (fur)
I'm a tree and I wear _____. (leaves, branches)
I'm a cow and I wear _____. (a hide, horns, a tail)
I'm a turtle and I wear a _____. (shell)
I'm a sheep and I wear _____. (wool)
I'm a snake and I wear a _____. (skin)
I'm a man and I wear a _____. (hat, suit, coat)
I'm a house and I wear _____. (a roof, windows, doors)
I'm a fish and I wear _____. (scales)

## WHAT CAN YOU DO?

Use these questions to help develop vocabulary and imagination.

What can you do at the beach?
What can you do on a farm?
What can you do with blocks?
What can you do with sand?
What can you do with snow?
What can you do with crayons?
What can you do at a circus?
What can you do at the zoo?
What can you do with mud?
What can you do when it rains?
What can you do with a cloth?
What can you do with paints?

Additional sentence practice can be provided by asking the class to repeat each response given.

Following are examples of several answers to a question.

TEACHER: What can you do on a hill?
CHILDREN: I can climb to the top.
I can slide down.
I can find rocks on a hill.
I can lie on the grass.

Children will feel flattered if their responses are repeated by the class.

## EXPRESSING FEELINGS

Four and five year olds often express themselves poetically and in amazingly abstract ways. Try one of these topics and see what happens.

What is being happy? Sad? Tired? Afraid? Angry?
What is liking somebody?
What is being unselfish?
What is being naughty?
What is being sleepy?
What is wishing for something?
How would it feel being a puppy? A worm? A bluebird?

## MAKING COMPARISONS

The use of similes stimulates the imagination and increases vocabulary. Ask the children to name something quiet and something noisy.

Responses might be: *As quiet as* velvet; night; an empty room; tiptoeing; bare feet. *As noisy as* crying; a fire engine; glass breaking; a door banging; a drum.

## WORDS THAT DESCRIBE

Ask: "What was the most beautiful thing that you saw today? What is the smallest thing you can think of? The largest? What can you see when you look out the window?"

Read *Look Out the Window*.[15] Then say, "If you had a magic pair of eyes, what could you see that nobody else could see? If you could paint just one picture, what would it be?"

## THE PUPPET WHO LIKES PRETTY THINGS

Draw eyes under the flap of a number three paper sack and eyelids and lashes on top of the flap. Ask a child to insert his hand into the puppet and make the eyes open and close as he goes around the room. Tell him to stop before something and say, "Blinkie sees a _____." Then the child makes Blinkie describe what he sees and the class guesses what **it is.**

The children may use the puppet to praise each other's paintings.

---

[15] Joan Walsh Anglund, *Look Out the Window*, Harcourt, New York, 1959.

Much of the beauty in life is noticing the small things around us. This activity gives practice in observation as well as in talking.

—V.S.P.

## STIMULATING CREATIVITY IN EXPRESSION

The following device gives vent to the imagination, creates an awareness of one's surroundings, and increases the use of language.

How many things can you do with this pail? (*Hold up the object.*)
What can you do with this piece of string?
How many things can you do with this piece of paper?
What could you make from this cloth?
What can you do with this pan?

## INTEREST TABLE

Each day, something new can be added to the interest table so that curiosity will be aroused and questions will be asked. Here are some suggestions of interesting objects that will motivate conversation.

| | |
|---|---|
| broken egg shells | ferns |
| pressed flowers | stones |
| wishbone | fabrics |
| half an apple | wool |
| chrysalis | flowers |
| wood shavings | foil |
| peach pits | snail shell |
| seeds | feathers |
| dried fruit | leaves |
| bark | bottles |

## PRONOUNS AND VERBS

Varying the subjects of the questions requires the children to use *I, he, it, she, we,* or *they* in their responses.

What do people do with ladders?
What did Humpty Dumpty do?
What does a flower do in spring?
What would you do with a hat?
What did Miss Muffet do with her curds and whey?
Why do people carry umbrellas?

## WHAT GOES WITH IT?

The child learns that one object is dependent upon and useful to another. If actual objects are not available, substitute pictures.

A knife goes with a _____. (fork)
A hammer goes with a _____. (nail)
A mitten goes with a _____. (hand)
A chair goes with a _____. (table)
Salt goes with _____. (pepper)
A shoe goes with a _____. (foot)
A hat goes with a _____. (head)
A key goes with a _____. (lock)
Bread goes with _____. (butter)

Encourage the class to name other objects which go together.

## SENSORY WORDS

Say a word and study its effect upon the class. Ask: "What does this word make you think of?" Sometimes children will try to explain the word because it sounds like another word they know, or because it is onomatopoeia. The teacher may want to provide some assistance for the children by indicating her own response to a word. Names of colors may be added to the following:

| | | |
|---|---|---|
| sunny | pebbly | moist |
| cluck | muddy | playful |
| gobble | sweet | merry |

| | | |
|---|---|---|
| jump | proud | peep |
| twitter | clear | soft |
| rough | dainty | splash |
| jolly | scratch | warm |
| cloudy | quack | bright |
| sticky | heavy | cold |

## WORDS WHICH AROUSE EMOTIONS

Sylvia Ashton-Warner[16] describes "organic" words as those which arouse emotions. Here are some examples of "organic" words which will stimulate discussion and arouse the child's interest quickly, since many of the words are close to the child's experience.

| | | |
|---|---|---|
| love | warm | scream |
| tears | win | dream |
| fight | bad | mad |
| sacred | bath | lick |
| ugly | lazy | yell |
| hug | kiss | touch |

Sometimes the children will draw pictures describing organic words and often we can tell through discussion of these pictures what problems and difficulties the children are experiencing.

## THINKING ABOUT THINGS

Ask the following questions to elicit responses which will require reasoning:

How do you know when you are catching cold?
How can you tell an orange from a ball if your eyes are shut?
Why don't you play ball with an egg?
Why can you drink more water than a chicken?
Why does Mother sometimes wear an apron?
Why wouldn't you give a tiny baby an apple to eat?
Why do you water flowers and not rocks?
Why can you hear a fire engine better than Daddy's car?
Why are you hungry at dinnertime?

[16] Sylvia Ashton-Warner, *Teacher*, Simon and Schuster, Inc., New York, 1963.

Why does some music make you feel sleepy and some music make you feel like dancing?
Why does salt taste good on potatoes, but not on ice cream?
How can you tell the difference between a peanut butter sandwich and an egg sandwich?

## WHAT WOULD YOU DO?

The children can give value judgments and respond with critical thinking as they answer these questions individually.

What would you do if you went to the mailbox to mail a letter for your mother and you couldn't reach the slot to drop in the letter?
What would you do if your clothes shrank and became too small?
What would you do if you found some keys on the playground?
What would you do if you broke Grandmother's best cup when she was not in the room?
What would you do if the barber cut your hair too short?
What would you do if Daddy told you that you couldn't go for a ride with a friend on his bicycle?
What would you do if you found a library book on the street near the library?
What would you do if, after you had built a fine tower out of blocks, someone came along and knocked it over by mistake?
What would you do if you were having lunch at a friend's house and you were served something you didn't like?
What would you do if someone went ahead of you in line when you were taking turns at jumping rope?

## BEE VOICES

Descriptive language and vocal expression may be presented through use of striped, black and yellow tagboard, bee shapes. Attach a tongue depressor to each one and use for puppets. Hold up a bee and ask what buzzing sound it might make if it were angry, sleepy, hungry, very young, lazy, happy, sad, excited, or frightened.

## PUMPKIN FACES

Draw pumpkin faces on orange construction paper. Make the mouths and eyes represent moods expressed in the poem. Add a nose on each pumpkin. Cut out the faces and attach to tongue depressors. Hold up one pumpkin puppet at a time as the rhyme is said. The children will enjoy imitating the expressions with their voices.

> Here is a pumpkin who's happy;
> Here is a pumpkin who cries;
> Here is a pumpkin who's sleepy;
> Here is a pumpkin who sighs.
> Here is a pumpkin who's angry;
> Here is a pumpkin who's sad;
> Here is a pumpkin who's noisy;
> Here is a pumpkin who's glad.
>
> —L.B.S.

## THE CHILD SHARES LANGUAGE

By the time the child enters the education center, he has used speech to express his needs, wants, and emotions. He has experimented verbally for the sheer joy of speaking. He may be skilled in his ability to communicate, or delayed in speech development. As explained earlier, the patterns of speech which the child uses are those which he has learned from adults and has developed through interaction and harmony with people closest to him.

In the education center, the child now engages in experiences which require him to share with new adults and with children his own age. Not only does he share the playhouse, blocks, and playground equipment, but he also shares his personal possessions and thoughts.

A special period called "sharing time" gives each child an opportunity to take his turn at this purposeful speaking activity. He speaks freely as he shows a toy or talks about an experience. He projects his own ideas, thoughts, investigations, and observations to those who will listen to him. He comes to a special place in the room and faces other children, who may be sitting on the floor or in chairs placed so that each child can see the speaker plainly. In this setting, it is desirable that the teacher sit beside the child with her arm around him, or, at least, in close proximity, until he feels confident enough to face the class alone.

When speaking, some children may use forty or fifty words, while others will utter only a brief phrase. The teacher should not comment upon the length of the remarks. Instead, she accepts remarks and shows appreciation for each child's contribution. She allows him to feel that *he* is in command of the situation. If needed, she guides and directs his remarks with questions and encourages responses from the group.

During the first few weeks of sharing experiences, emphasis should be placed upon stimulation, verbalization, and attentive listening. Later, standards of speaking may be stressed in a very simple fashion.

During this period, imitation is likely to take place. If one child responds briefly, others often will perform in a similar fashion. Bobby may stand and say, "We have a new puppy," and then sit down. To encourage more detailed discussion, the teacher can give encouragement and assistance by asking, "Who else has a puppy? What questions do you want to ask about Bobby's new puppy?" If the questioning is adept, it is possible to elicit several sentences demonstrating good, logical sequence of thought.[17]

Occasionally the child who is speaking may focus his attention upon the teacher rather than upon his classmates, the audience. This practice can be condoned until the child has acquired more freedom of expression. If a child who wishes to share is rewarded by good listening and questions from the group, he is more likely to give his auditors eye contact. Certainly he is afforded a chance to think that he is making a contribution and to feel confident.

This speech period can be made more interesting by providing inviting things to talk about. A bird's nest will invoke all sorts of questions and conversation. Ask: "What would you like to know about this

---

[17] Elise Hahn, Ph.D., Professor of Speech, California State College at Los Angeles, "Study of the Speech Development of First Grade Children," unpublished master's thesis, Northwestern University, Evanston, Illinois, 1947.

nest? What kind of bird do you think lived in it? Where do you suppose I found it?" These additional questions will open up new avenues of learning.

Encourage the child who seemingly has nothing to say by asking him to tell about his new shirt, socks, or jacket. Inquire about his birthday. Place two or three small objects on the table and find out what he knows about them. Assure him that he has something to say and that others will listen because they *want* to do so.

Evaluation of the sharing period can take place as soon as all children in the group feel secure and can speak freely. Then pose a few questions: "What made the talk interesting? Why did you enjoy listening?" Clarify at times what the child means if he is unable to keep to the subject. Compliment him when he uses good sequence and expresses himself succinctly. Yet, grant recognition to the child who contributes, but who still may need continued direction and support. Commend good listeners and those who take turns speaking.

There are many benefits to be derived from this supervised sharing session. Speech and listening skills are likely to improve. The child gains practice in organizing his thoughts and presenting them clearly. His vocabulary improves through use of words. He experiences critical thinking and learns to see wider, objective meanings. He may discover ways of behaving acceptably, working together more effectively, thinking and planning together, and exchanging ideas.

—L.B.S.

## A TREASURE CHEST

Provide a box, decorated like a treasure chest, where the child can drop his toy or object to share that day. The chest may have a luggage tag with the child's name printed on it. Each time he shares, a sticker may be pasted on the box. If his sharing treasure has a special place, he will not forget to take it home. Each child may construct his own chest from a shoebox with collage paste-ons.

## SHARING SNAPSHOTS

All children enjoy bringing snapshots from home and sharing them with the class. Pictures of the family, pets, and excursions can be passed around so that each child has a chance to look at them closely. After individuals have talked about their pictures, these photographs can be pinned on the bulletin board or projected on the wall. A "homework" envelope may be given each child so that he will not lose his pictures when he brings them to school and takes them home.

—O.M.A.

## BRINGING SOMETHING

In order to avoid a deluge of toys and objects on the same day, the teacher may hold up names of volunteers for the following day and post these names on the bulletin board. The children will then feel more of a responsibility in carrying out their promises and assignments.

## WHAT DID I LIKE BEST?

Ask three children at a time to walk around the room and look at anything they like. At a given signal, they are to come back to the group. Each child then tells his classmates what he saw that he liked best.

The teacher may want to "plant" two or three new items around the room to provide a surprise element.

## FINDING COLORS

Give each child a small, blue, construction paper circle to take home. Ask the children to look for something blue at home that they can share the next day. They can bring either a magazine picture or a real object, or simply tell what they saw and where. Use this same activity for recognizing other colors.

## SINGING TIME

The children take turns choosing an assortment of songs to sing for the day. Children who are reticent about talking, sometimes will sing and even lead the group.

## BRINGING LEAVES TO SHARE

The children bring leaves to the center and put them between newspapers. Place a stack of books on top of the newspapers. After two days, take the leaves out, put them between squares of waxed paper and press together with a warm iron.

Ask each child to tell where he found his leaves. Discuss likenesses and differences in shape and color, and the names of the most common leaves.

—O.M.A.

## SHARING BOOKS

The children enjoy bringing favorite books from home. Each child may briefly tell the story from his own book. Elaborate on the books which have interesting stories and colorful pictures. Show appreciation for each child's contribution.

## SHARING A NURSERY RHYME

After a child has heard a number of nursery rhymes included in this book and has acted them out or has sung them, he will have a favorite. Ask individual children to choose a nursery rhyme, and either say or sing it for the class. If a child is timid, he usually can perform better before a small group. After the children have gained confidence, tape record individual contributions and play them for the class. Mothers will enjoy hearing their children's voices and trying to identify them.

## LETTING A PUPPET SHARE

A child can insert an arm and hold four fingers bent over the flap of a sack puppet allowing it to reply to questions from the group. Such questions might be: "What is your name? Where do you live? What do you like to do at school?"

Many preschool children have difficulty in moving the mouth of a sack puppet to "make it talk," since voice-hand coordination is not acquired easily. After showing the child how it is done, he may, with some practice, accomplish this feat and use his sack puppet to share many of his thoughts and experiences, as well as to answer questions.

## SHARING FACTS ABOUT ONESELF

Make a chart with magazine pictures of a child (or children), a house, and a school glued securely and neatly to a sheet of posterboard. These pictures will give the children clues for sharing this information:

My name is _____.
I am _____ years' old.
I live on _____ Street.
I go to _____ School.

A picture of a telephone can be added to encourage children to learn their telephone numbers.

## BE A NEWS ANNOUNCER

Sharing time can take the form of a telecast. Since most children will have seen and heard announcers on television, they will know something of the procedures of announcing. A few children who have interesting news may plan time with the announcer, so that he can report such items as "Baby's First Birthday" or "A Visit From Grandma." The teacher may help him to remember the events if he should forget them. The children will enjoy getting together to hear their news reported.

## SHARING GENERAL INFORMATION

Here is a list of topics which can be suggested to children for the share and tell time:

  A bus ride taken with the family
  A picture found in a magazine
  A holiday dinner
  A favorite game played with a friend
  A rainy day activity
  A trip to a store
  A building going up

If the topic pertains to an interest of the whole class, write the responses in the form of a continuous story.

## LANGUAGE AS A SOCIAL SKILL

Sometimes a child's home environment may offer him few opportunities to observe simple courtesies and greetings, or, if he knows them, he may feel that social graces belong to special occasions. When a child is socially limited in his experiences, his interaction and contact with others may be met with rejection and hostility.

Children learn how to get what they want and how to handle other people and occasions in many different ways. Even though the child's modes of conduct may satisfy his immediate needs, his behavior may provoke antagonistic feelings in others. He then must necessarily learn other and better ways of controlling his environment. It is not enough for a child to win just approval from adults and his peers. The approval-getting mechanism must be so honest and genuine that the child can respect himself for the means he has used to gain the approbation and good will of peers and adults.

Various cultures have their own greetings and expressions of courtesy. Research indicates that, if a child finds his own culture appreciated, he will contribute more eagerly and will be more likely to appreciate other cultures and customs.

It is well worth the teacher's time to encourage the children to watch for opportunities to say "please" and "thank you." These expressions are easiest to remember and can be practiced during playhouse activities, on the playground, at snack time, and at other times throughout the day. The teacher can find ways of complimenting the children and encouraging them to compliment one another. "I like your new socks, Gary" may not draw a response of "Thank you" until Gary learns a reply which makes him feel comfortable. At first he may smile and his eyes may light up with gratitude, which is his way of saying that he appreciates the attention given him.

Even young children experience embarrassment when they can think of nothing to say in accepting a compliment. Responding to others must be sincere and spontaneous to be of value; therefore, some guidance in practicing courtesies may be necessary.

Songs stressing conversational greetings and thanks are impersonal and pleasant ways of teaching social graces, whereas direct teaching can become perplexing, tiring, and boring for the children. Using the following rhythmic technique may help instill cultural graciousness.

  TEACHER SINGS: Good morning, Mrs. Rowe.
  SALLY SINGS:  Good morning, Sally,

The natural word inventiveness and rhyming talent of young children may be capitalized upon by encouraging the use of song in everyday play experiences:

JOHN SINGS: May I borrow your red crayon, Andy?
ANDY SINGS: Yes, you may. Yes, you may.
JOHN SINGS: Thank you.
ANDY SINGS: You are welcome.

The use of stick puppets engaged in conversation often insures more learning and constructive practice than formal lessons.

The tape recorder also affords a fascinating medium for drill in casual conversation.

"Hello, Tim. I hear you have a new baby brother."
"Good morning, Sally. Isn't it a nice day?"

These comments can invite at least monosyllabic responses. When those reactions are played back, evaluation can be made:

"Jerry said more than 'yes,' didn't he?"
"I like the interesting words Beth used."

Acquiring a few simple social graces helps to build the child's self-image and encourages self respect. When his behavior in a situation elicits friendly and warm responses from others, he develops self respect and feelings of confidence in his ability to relate to others.

In addition to words, there are other simple attributes which the children learn. Personal cleanliness, helpfulness in the home and at school, neatness in possessions, and pleasant facial expressions are all components of social growth and good citizenship. These can be instilled within the group through use of materials in this chapter and in other chapters of this book.

Children withdraw from the didactic approach to the teaching of behavior. They can be particularly sensitive to having their manners and speech criticized, especially when the manners and speech used in the class are different from those used in the home. Therefore, if the given group consists of a sizable segment of children who speak languages other than English, it may be necessary to present models of thanks and apologies in several different languages.

Stories and poems presented in parable fashion often invite discussion on moral values. Spontaneous responses of the children will provide the teacher with insight into their confusions and problems. Here are examples of stories which will provide the group with experience in discussing applied courtesy. The indirect message derived from this type of technique is more likely to be impersonal and more enduring.

—L.B.S. and V.S.P.

## THE LITTLE ROOSTER

Once a little rooster went around bragging about himself.

"Cock-a-doodle-doo! I'm a clever little rooster! Cock-a-doodle-doo! I'm a handsome little rooster! Look at me! Listen to me! Don't I have a beautiful voice? Cock-a-doodle-doo!" he bragged.

Now Mr. Owl, who was a very smart bird, said, "Those are fine words, Little Rooster. But it would be so much better if someone else said them."

Mr. Owl's advice set Little Rooster to thinking, and the more he thought about these words, the more he decided they were true. So right then and there, Little Rooster set about finding ways of saying nice things about others and he stopped his bragging.

As he was walking by the pond one day, he saw Mrs. Goose ruffling her feathers impatiently.

"How are you, Mrs. Goose" said Little Rooster politely.

"I'm angry," said Mrs. Goose. "It is time to go home and I cannot get my babies to leave the water."

Little Rooster was sorry for Mrs. Goose because he knew she was tired and he wanted to help her.

"Why, Mrs. Goose," said Little Rooster. "You are so clever to teach your babies to swim. I cannot swim at all, so you are more clever than I. Your babies seem to be well behaved. I wouldn't worry if I were you. Give them just a few more minutes."

Mrs. Goose felt much better after that sincere and friendly advice. She calmed herself and sat down to wait for her goslings. Soon they saw their mother waiting and they ran to her, shaking the water out of their little wings.

Next, Little Rooster met Mr. Turkey, who was crying.

"Oh, oh," Mr. Turkey sobbed. "I used to be so handsome, but part of my tail was cut off in a mowing machine."

"Never mind," said Little Rooster. "Your tail feathers will grow again. You are still a very handsome turkey!"

Those truthful words made Mr. Turkey feel so good that he began to strut with his head held high.

Finally, Little Rooster met a singing hen.

"It is good to see you so happy, Mrs. Hen," said Little Rooster.

"Cawk, cawk, cawk, cawk!" sang Mrs. Hen. "I am indeed happy, for I just scared away a mean old chicken hawk and saved my chicks."

"What a brave, good hen you are," said Little Rooster.

Little Rooster spent the whole day saying nice, truthful things to others. Soon his heart was so filled with happiness that he completely forgot to brag about himself. In fact, he never needed to brag again.

—L.B.S.

The children may dramatize this story, adding more characters.

Say: "How do you feel when someone says nice things to you? What does *compliment* mean? Look around the class. Do you see somebody you would like to compliment? Why didn't Little Rooster need to brag on himself anymore? Do you think Little Rooster had more friends now? Why? What does sincere mean?"

Be sure to point out that compliments must be *sincere* and *truthful* to be of value. Ask, "What is being truthful?"

## THE LITTLE KITTENS

White Kitten and Yellow Kitten lived inside an old shed where they slept curled up in an old clothes basket.

White Kitten was a dear, purry, furry kitten. But one thing was wrong with White Kitten's behavior. She simply did not know how to manage her claws. If allowed inside the house, it was not long before she was making ugly scratches on furniture, rugs, and drapes.

Yellow Kitten was a dear, little kitten, too; but something was wrong with him, also. He always looked dirty. His fur was scraggly and stood up on end. Because of his appearance, he looked sad. To tell the truth, Yellow Kitten was lazy. He simply wouldn't lick his fur to keep it clean.

White Kitten and Yellow Kitten belonged to Mrs. Murphy, who put up with their bad habits as long as she could. Finally, she made a place for them in the shed. Although Mrs. Murphy could no longer have the two kittens in her neat, clean house, she still loved them and took care of them.

After they were taken to the shed, White Kitten and Yellow Kitten began complaining in loud, yowling voices when it was time for Mrs. Murphy to feed them. To see who could get the most food, they pushed and shoved each other in ways that were unpleasant to see.

Mrs. Murphy shook her head sadly.

"It is no fun to feed White Kitten and Yellow Kitten when they have forgotten to purr a 'please' and a 'thank you,' " she said.

One day, the two little kittens left their clothes basket in the shed and took a walk.

On the street, they met a shiny black kitten who was out for her morning stroll. Black Kitten mewed a polite "How do you do?" and tripped daintily along on her soft little feet.

Now everyone knew that Black Kitten lived in Mrs. O'Hara's comfortable house and slept in a special basket on Mrs. O'Hara's porch.

White Kitten knew this too, and she whispered to Yellow Kitten, "Let's ask Black Kitten why she lives in a house while we must sleep in an old worn-out basket in the shed."

Quickly, the two little kittens hurried to catch up with Black Kitten who, by now, had stopped inside a patch of sunshine by the hedge and was licking her fur with her tiny, rough, pink tongue.

"Excuse me," said White Kitten, who had not quite forgotten *all* of her manners. "My brother and I are very curious. Why do you live in a lovely house and not in a shed as we do?"

Black Kitten finished her bath.

Then she replied, "Mew! It is very simple. First of all, I learned how to keep myself clean so that my mistress might enjoy stroking my fur. When I wanted something to eat, I always purred a 'please' and a 'thank you.' I also learned how to manage my sharp kitten claws so that they would never scratch furniture, rugs, and drapes."

—L.B.S.

Make up an ending for this story. Do you think that White Kitten and Yellow Kitten were ever invited into Mrs. Murphy's house? What did they learn from Black Kitten? Do good manners help? Why?

Kitten shapes may be cut from white, yellow, and black felt and placed on the flannelboard as this story is told, so that the class can follow the sequence easier and attention can be maintained. The tale may be dramatized using three children at a time.

### THE ANIMAL PICNIC
(A Discussion)

One day Mrs. Skunk, Mrs. Squirrel, and Mr. Rabbit decided to have a picnic under the most fragrant pine tree in the woods. Mr.

Rabbit came first and set the table.

What did he use to set the table? (*Responses.*)

Mrs. Skunk came next and she brought a basket of food.

What did she bring? (*Responses.*)

On her way to the picnic, Mrs. Squirrel had bad luck.

What does "bad luck" mean? (*Responses.*)

Poor Mrs. Squirrel dropped her share of the picnic lunch in a mud puddle that had formed after a recent rain. Carefully, she fished out the soggy dirty lunch and put it into a litter can. Now Mrs. Squirrel had no lunch to bring to the picnic.

What should she do? Go home? Go to the picnic anyway? What would you do? (*Responses.*)

How should she apologize to her friends for not bringing her share of the lunch? (*Responses.*) What would they say after her apologies?

Has anything like this ever happened to you? (*Responses.*) Should Mrs. Skunk and Mr. Rabbit give Mrs. Squirrel some of their lunch? Would you? (*Responses.*)

—L.B.S. and V.S.P.

The children may dramatize this story to have direct experience with social skills. Bring in real dishes and silver so that the group may practice setting the table.

Stick puppets or flannelboard figures may be used for retelling the story.

## THE DUCKLING WHO WOULDN'T SAY "QUACK"

Once there was a duckling who wouldn't say "Quack." Nobody knew why. He just wouldn't say "Quack," that's all. He waddled along on his little flat feet looking for bugs that were so good to eat and listening for a better sound than "Quack."

One day the little duckling met a cow.

"Do you know a better sound than 'quack'?" asked the little duckling.

"Of course," replied the cow in a bellowing voice. "MOO!"

It was such a windy *moo* that the little duckling almost fell over backward. He didn't like *moo* at all, but he was far too polite to say so. He thanked the cow anyway and went on looking for bugs and listening for a better sound than "Quack."

—L.B.S.

Ask the children to continue the story as the duckling meets other animals and hears other sounds. Suggest that the class think of an ending for the story.

Ask: "How did the little duck's mother and daddy feel when he wouldn't say 'Quack'? What did they say? What did they do about it? Did the little duckling ever say 'Quack' again?"

## IF YOUR CLOTHES COULD TALK

Wouldn't it be funny if your clothes talked to you? What might your shoes say?

Perhaps they would say, "Stop scratching our toes and sides. Be kind to furniture and to us. We don't like being scuffed. Keep us polished, and don't sit on us!"

What would your socks say to you?

They might say, "Don't throw us around. Wash us and keep us clean. If there is a hole in one of us, please mend it."

What would your coat say to you?

It might say, "Please hang me up. I like to rest on a hanger and not in a heap on the floor."

What would your galoshes say to you?

Maybe your galoshes would say, "Please don't forget us when it rains or snows. We want to protect your feet."

What would your handkerchief say to you? (*Responses.*)

—L.B.S.

Continue the story using other articles of clothing and possessions. Omit the answers in the story entirely and merely ask the questions. Write what the children say. Use real articles of clothing to make the dramatization more vivid.

## THE CRICKET WHO DIDN'T LISTEN

There was once a little cricket who played his fiddle day after day and night after night. He loved his own scrapy, crackly music so much that he forgot that there were other sounds in the world.

"Scrape, scrape, scrape! Crick-crack-crick!" went the little cricket.

Even though the little cricket's ears were below his elbows and not on his head like yours and mine, he could hear just fine with them. But because he listened only to his own scrapy, crackly music day and night, he missed a great many other interesting sounds. He missed hearing lovely melodies around him like the bluebird's song, the bumblebee's hum, and the tree-frog's croak.

One day, the little cricket stopped playing his scrapy, crackly music for a second. And he listened. At first he heard nothing, because, of course, he wasn't used to listening. It was quiet—so very quiet. It was quieter than quiet. Then, from a distance, he heard music. He leaped over to the lake from where the music seemed to come. As he drew closer, the music became louder and he could hear it much clearer.

Now he could *see* who was making the music. All of the insects and frogs were practicing for their evening concert. The little cricket had been left out because he was too busy listening to his own scrapy, crackly music.

The little cricket listened for awhile, but soon he went back to playing his own cricket tune.

Later, on a warm August day when the peaches were ripening in the orchard, the bees had a picnic. They invited their friends to share the sweet peach juices. But the little cricket made such loud, scrapy, crackly music that he didn't hear the invitation and he missed the peach picnic altogether.

—L.B.S. and V.S.P.

Ask: "How do you feel when you are left out of something? (*Responses.*) What else did the little cricket miss because he didn't stop to listen to the sounds around him? Do you think he minded missing those important things? How would you end the story? Did the little cricket ever learn to be a good listener? Does good listening help? Why? What do you like to listen to most of all? Let's listen now. What can we hear?"

## THE GRAY VELVET RABBIT

The "wishing" plot is a common one found in many stories such as "Turkey-Urkey"[18] and "The Cat of Many Colors."[19] Here are examples of dissatisfied creatures who are unhappy with their conditions in life and wish to change. Like "The Little White Rabbit Who

---

[18] Louise Binder Scott and J. J. Thompson, *Talking Time* (Second Edition), McGraw-Hill, Inc., New York, 1966, pp. 130–136.
[19] Louise Binder Scott, *Stories That Stick*, F. A. Owen Publishing Company, Dansville, New York, 1951.

Wanted Red Wings,"[20] they return to their original appearances and realize that their own natural endowments are best for them. This same plot is repeated in "The Gray Velvet Rabbit."

Once upon a time there was a gray velvet rabbit who was the dearest, cuddliest rabbit you ever saw. His small, baby brothers and sisters loved to snuggle up to him because his fur was so soft and silky.

Now the little, gray velvet rabbit was an adventuresome rabbit and, although he was happy with his rabbit family, he still longed to know about the rest of the world. One day, as he went hopping along the road, he saw a farmer's wagon filled with fat, brown burlap bags of potatoes.

"Oh," sighed the little, gray velvet rabbit. "I wish that I had a nice, strong covering like those fat, brown burlap bags."

> So he went to the store
> That had cloth on a shelf,
> And he bought some brown burlap
> To cover himself.

Now the little rabbit was a brown burlap rabbit and he was very proud of himself. But when he went home that night, his little baby brothers and sisters didn't want to cuddle up to him because his coat felt so rough. The little, brown burlap rabbit had to sleep in a corner all by himself.

The next day the little, adventuresome, brown burlap rabbit woke up bright and early. He left his deep burrow-home in the meadow and hopped along, singing a tune about fields of clover in the month of June.

---

[20] Louise Binder Scott, *Tell-Again Story Cards, Level II*, McGraw-Hill, Inc., New York, 1967.

All at once, he came to a playhouse. He stopped and blinked his rabbit eyes for he saw toys, toys, toys, and all of them were stuffed toys. There were big elephants, tall giraffes, and itsy-bitsy dogs. The most beautiful toy of all was a red gingham dog who was sitting beside a calico cat on a table.

"Oh, what a gorgeous color!" cried the little, brown burlap rabbit excitedly. "Red is so much prettier than brown burlap."

> So he went to the store
> That had cloth on a shelf,
> And he bought some red gingham
> To cover himself.

Then the little, red gingham rabbit went hopping down the street, showing off his new, red, rabbit clothes.

Now, because the little rabbit liked stories about the West, he stopped in front of a theater to look at some pictures of cowboys. The cowboys were all wearing blue denim jeans.

"Say," said the little, red gingham rabbit, "blue is a much better color than red."

Then the little rabbit saw a picture of a bad man wearing a red gingham shirt.

"That settles it," said he. "I don't want red gingham any more."

> So he went to the store
> That had cloth on a shelf,
> And he bought some blue denim
> To cover himself.

Oh, he felt so good in his blue denim suit and he sang a tune about meadow flowers in the month of June.

The little, blue denim rabbit was happy, but by now, after all that adventure, he was also thirsty. He hopped along looking for a pond of water where he could get a drink, but he couldn't find a pond. He couldn't find a brook. He couldn't find a river. He couldn't find a lake. But he did find an ocean. Just as the little blue denim rabbit was about to take a drink, he remembered that ocean water has salt in it.

A lifeguard in an orange, terry-cloth robe was resting under a beach umbrella. (Terry-cloth, as you know, is material like your wash cloth and towel; but it is also fine for bathrobes.) The lifeguard had a thermos of water, so he gave the little, blue denim rabbit a drink.

The little rabbit was very grateful.

As he hopped away, he thought, "Orange is such a bright color."

> So he went to the store
> That had cloth on a shelf,
> And he bought orange terry-cloth
> To cover himself.

Then the little, orange terry-cloth rabbit hopped along singing a song about buzzing bees and green leafy trees. All at once, he heard music and there were lots of people all dressed in green, marching down the street to the beat of a drum!

"Why, it is a St. Patrick's Day parade," said the little, orange terry-cloth rabbit.

Men with tall, green felt hats carried their chests high and sang, "The Wearing of the Green."

Of course, you can guess what happened. The St. Patrick's parade gave the little, orange terry-cloth rabbit another idea.

> He went to the store
> That had cloth on a shelf,
> And he bought some green felt
> To cover himself.

"La, la, la la," sang the little, green felt rabbit, for he could not remember the words to "The Wearing of the Green."

By now he felt rather tired so he hopped home to his burrow. Again, he slept in a corner alone because his little baby brothers and sisters would not snuggle up to him.

The little, green felt rabbit woke early with the sun while the dew was still on the grass. After a cabbage-leaf breakfast, the adventuresome, little rabbit hopped away looking for something new.

He hopped up to a restaurant. In the window was a man baking pancakes. He wore a yellow oilcloth apron.

"How nice!" exclaimed the little, green felt rabbit. "Oilcloth is strong and it will protect me when it rains."

> So he went to a store
> That had cloth on a shelf,

>And he bought some yellow oilcloth
>To cover himself.

The little, yellow oilcloth rabbit hopped along thinking how wonderful it would be to make pancakes.

Then he heard music. It was a circus parade with a band, some clowns, elephants, lions, and tigers all making noises like *Om-pah-pah* and *gurrrr* and *yowl* and *whee*.

One clown had a red nose and yellow hair and he wore a big, baggy, purple, shiny satin suit.

"Wow!" said the little, yellow oilcloth rabbit. "I *must* have a big, baggy, purple, shiny satin suit."

>So he went to a store
>That had cloth on a shelf,
>And he bought purple satin
>To cover himself.

But the little, purple satin rabbit couldn't hop very well for his suit was too baggy and his feet got caught in the trousers. Soon he was all tangled up and, after twisting and turning, he landed in some brambles. After twisting and turning some more, he landed in a puddle of mud.

He began to cry, "Oh, oh! I want my mother. I want my daddy. I want my little baby brothers and sisters."

Then along came a patrol car just in the nick of time, and out jumped a policeman.

"Why, you poor, little rabbit," said the kind policeman, lifting the little rabbit out of the mud. "What have you been up to?"

The policeman pulled off the muddy, purple satin suit and wiped the mud off the little rabbit's fur with his handkerchief. And the little rabbit's fur became gray and velvety again. Then the policeman gave the little, gray velvet rabbit a slice of carrot from his lunch box, and set him on the grass so that he could hop away.

Oh, you can bet that the little, gray velvet rabbit was glad to be soft and cuddly again. He hopped home very fast to be part of his very own dear, gray velvet rabbit family again.

—L.B.S.

Cut front-view rabbit shapes for the flannelboard. Glue the colors and fabrics mentioned in the story to the shapes. Back each one with outing flannel or flocked paper so that the figures will adhere to the flannelboard. The children will enjoy arranging them on the board and feeling the textures while the story is being told. Using this approach provides a lesson which stresses discrimination of textures and colors, teaches number concepts, and offers a rhyming experience.

## THE DISH

Once a little girl's auntie gave her a dish. The auntie said, "This is a dish that I have had for a long, long time. My mother gave the dish to me. My grandmother gave the dish to my mother, and the dish has been in our family for many years."

"Thank you, Auntie," said the little girl politely.

What else could she have said about the dish? (*Responses.*)

Truthfully, the little girl didn't like the dish very much. Do you think she should have said so? (*Responses.*)

One day the little girl said, "Oh, dear! This dish is too big to go with my doll dishes. I don't want it."

The mother heard what her little girl said, so she just took the dish and put it into the cupboard with all of the other breakfast, lunch, and dinner dishes.

At noon, the dish was filled with soup. In the evening, it was filled with mashed potatoes. In the morning, it was filled with cereal steaming and hot with lots of sugar and cream. For days and days the dish was filled with all kinds of good food. On Halloween, it was filled with candy for trick or treat. On Thanksgiving, it was filled with turkey gravy. At Christmas, it was filled with all kinds of nuts and at Easter time, it was filled with bright colored eggs.

At the end of the year, the little girl said to her auntie, "Thank you for the lovely, lovely dish. I like it a lot."

And she truly *meant* it.

Whenever there was company, the little girl always brought out that special dish which was used more than any other dish in the house.

—L.B.S.

Bring in an attractive dish in the shape of a small bowl to use while telling the story. Talk about other ways in which the dish could be used.

Discuss kindness to people who give us gifts which we might not like or which we cannot use. Emphasize how a gift can become a prized possession.

# IMPROVING ARTICULATION OF SPEECH SOUNDS

The major speech sounds with which young children have difficulty are included in this chapter in order to help the teacher determine the misarticulations a child may be making, and decide which new articulatory patterns he may need to acquire. The teacher is advised to refer to *Talking Time*[21] for additional information.

## TIMMY TEAKETTLE'S SOUND

Here is Timmy Teakettle's spout. (*Point to teeth.*)
Sss - sss - sss. (*Children repeat.*)
This is where the steam comes out.
Sss - sss - sss.
Timmy Teakettle likes to say: (*Repeat action.*)
"Sss - sss - sss"
Very softly, that's the way.
Sss - sss - sss.

—L.B.S.

The usual mispronunciation for *some* is *thumb*. Pass small mirrors around the class so that the children can see if their tongue tips are hidden as they make Timmy's sound.

## GRAY GOOSE'S SOUND

I am old gray goose; when I say, "Hello,"
I put out my tongue and I blow and blow:
Th - th - th! (*Children repeat.*)
—L.B.S.

The usual mispronunciation for *thumb* is *fum* or *some*. Ask the children to show the tongue tip and blow softly. Use small mirrors so that they can see what the tongue tip does.

## MISTER ROOSTER'S SOUND

Mister Rooster on the gate,
Will you crow for me?

[21] Louise Binder Scott and J. J. Thompson, *Talking Time* (Second Edition), McGraw-Hill, Inc., New York, 1966.

Mister Rooster on the gate,
Please don't crow off key.

"I will crow," the rooster said.
"I will crow, yes, sir!
I will crow for you this way:
Er, er, er, er, errrrr!" (*Children repeat.*)
—L.B.S.

The usual mispronunciation for *rooster* is *wooster*. Ask the children to smile, keeping the lips back as they crow. The tongue tip must be raised toward the palate slightly. Collect pictures containing the "r" sound in initial position and use in naming activities. Always prolong the staccato "rrr" sound slightly as you name words so that the child can hear it plainly.

## THE ELEVATOR'S SOUND

The elevator goes up to the very top floor.
It stops and lets people walk out the door.
"Lllllllllll," up, up to the top;
"Lllllllllll," and now we will stop.
—L.B.S.

Ask the children to raise the tongue tip to make this prolonged "elevator" sound. Ask them to sing "La, la, la" to the rhythm of a favorite tune. The usual misarticulation for this sound is *wamp*, or *yamp* for *lamp*.

## FLUFFY CAT'S SOUND

There was a fluffy cat,
And a cute one at that;
But when she was afraid,
This funny sound she made:
"F,f,f,f!" (*Children repeat.*)
—L.B.S.

The usual misarticulations for *four* are *sore, pour,* or *thour*. Cut a cat's head shape from black tagboard. Include green sequin eyes and an open slit for a mouth. Each time the cat makes the "afraid" sound, protrude the finger tips through the slit.

## MR. CROW'S SOUND

I saw a crow in the yard today.
Caw, caw, caw! (*Children repeat.*)
He flapped his wings and he flew away.
Caw, caw, caw!

—L.B.S.

The usual mispronunciation for *caw* is *taw*. Ask the children to make a quiet "cough" sound in the back of the throat: "K, k, k." Ask them to feel a puff of air on the palm of the hand as they say, "Caw."

## THE FROG SOUNDS

Three little frogs lived in a pond.
Gummm, gummm, gummm.
Of insects they were very fond.
Glug, glug, glug.
The daddy frog made a big loud croak:
Gummm, gummm, gummm. (*Low voice.*)
The mother frog made a middle-sized croak:
Gummm, gummm, gummm. (*Natural voice.*)
The baby frog made a little wee croak:
Gummm, gummm, gummm. (*High voice.*)
*Glug!*

—L.B.S.

Children may substitute "d" for "g" as *dum* for *gum*. Ask the class to say the refrains using the different voices. Select three groups of frogs and dramatize the poem.

## MRS. FLY'S SOUND

Mrs. Fly goes around and around.
Vvvvvvvvvvvvvvvvvvvvv! (*Children repeat.*)
She makes a pretty humming sound.
Vvvvvvvvvvvvvvvvvvvv!

—L.B.S.

Children sometimes substitute "b" for "v" as *balentine* for *valentine*. Ask them to bite the lip gently with their upper teeth and hum.

### CHICK-CHICK'S SOUND

Chick-Chick is a tiny fellow.
Cheep, cheep, cheep. (*Children repeat.*)
He is downy, soft, and yellow.
Cheep, cheep, cheep.

Chick-Chick has two little eyes.
Cheep, cheep, cheep.
For one so small, he's very wise.
Cheep, cheep, cheep.

He likes to hunt things on the ground.
Cheep, cheep, cheep.
And tell you of the bugs he's found.
Cheep, cheep, cheep.

—L.B.S.

Some children may substitute *sheep* for *cheap* and *cheap* for *sheep*. Find pictures of objects which have the "ch" sound in their names as: chair, chimney, and cheese.

### PINK SHELL'S SOUND

The pretty pink shell talks to me.
Sh - sh - sh. (*Children repeat, prolonging the sound.*)
It tells me stories of the sea.
Sh - sh - sh.

—L.B.S.

Find pictures beginning with the "sh" sound for the children to name, such as: *sheep, ship,* and *shelf.* Ask them to push out their lips and blow softly to make this quiet sound. Ask them to talk about their *shoes.*

## THE BELL'S SOUND

This device is used by Miss Frances C. Hunte, Speech Specialist, Garvey School District, California. Children who say *goin'* for *going* will soon learn to enjoy the vibrating feeling in the head as they make the prolonged "ng" nasal sound. As the following rhyme is said, they make big sweeping movements using their whole arms from the shoulders to the finger tips. Soft volume should be used. The *ring - ng - ng* should sound like a vibrating musical tone.

Christmas is coming,
(*Prolong "ng."*)
Ring - ng - ng - ng,
Ring - ng - ng - ng,
Ring - ng - ng - ng.

Other holidays or seasons may be substituted such as: Thanksgiving, Halloween, Easter, or special occasions such as birthdays or vacations.

## THREE BEARS TALK

In substandard speech, often "n" is substituted for "ng" as *eatin'* for *eating* and *sittin'* for *sitting.* Dramatizing "The Three Bears" can give practice in pronouncing "ing" words included in the following questions and other sentences in the story.

Who's been *eating* my porridge?
Who's been *sitting* in my chair?
Who's been *lying* in my bed?

## COPYCAT LOOKING GLASS

Hang a mirror in the playhouse so that a child can talk and observe his speech helpers (tongue, teeth, lips, and jaw) as he names words and makes sentences. All children enjoy learning about the parts of their bodies. This technique can be used to help a child establish a favorable self-image and gain self-confidence.

## MAKING SOUND BASKETS AND SCRAPBOOKS

Ask mothers to help find objects or pictures which begin with the speech sounds listed below (with the exception of the sound of "ng" which is used in final position).

|  |  |
|---|---|
| b—bottle, box, button | t—top, tack |
| w—washcloth, window | n—nail, nut |
| y—yarn, something yellow | wh—whistle, wheel |
| l—light bulb, leaf | ng—ring |
| f—fork, fan | p—pencil, pan |
| g—gum | r—rock, ribbon |
| v—velvet, valentine | j—jar, jelly |
| h—handkerchief, hat | z—zipper |
| k—key, candy, candle | sh—shell, shoe |
| d—dish | ch—cheese, chain |
| s—soap, salt | th—thimble, thread |

Place the objects or pictures in a basket and use them for discussion and to help with pronunciation. This cooperative effort can help parents to understand the sounds of the English language and better guide their children with mispronunciations. Suggest that the mothers help make scrapbooks by finding magazine pictures to cut out and use. Impress upon everyone that speech must be *fun* for the child and that pressure to talk should not be exerted.

SUPPLEMENTARY REFERENCES

Almy, Millie, et al.: *Young Children's Thinking: Studies of Some Aspects of Piaget's Theory*, Teachers College Press, New York, 1966.

Dawson, Mildred, and G. C. Newman: *Language Teaching in Kindergarten and Early Primary Grades*, Harcourt, Brace and World, New York, 1966.

Gray, Susan, et al.: *Before First Grade: The Early Training Project for Culturally Disadvantaged Children*, Teachers College Press, New York, 1966.

Hechinger, Fred M., ed.: *Pre-School Education Today*, Doubleday and Company, Inc., Garden City, New York, 1966.

Heffernan, Helen, and Vivian Todd: *The Years Before School*, The Macmillan Company, New York, 1964.

Jenkins, Gladys, et al.: *These Are Your Children*, Scott, Foresman and Company, Glenview, Illinois, 1966.

Lewis, Morris M.: *Language, Thought, and Personality in Infancy and Childhood*, Basic Books, Inc., New York, 1964.

Rudolf, Marguerita, and Dorothy H. Cohen: *Kindergarten: A Year of Learning*, Appleton-Century-Crofts, New York, 1964.

CHAPTER 2

# Sensory Avenues To Learning

A wealth of color, music, odors, tastes, and tactile experiences pour into the child's emotional and mental life throughout all of his waking hours. Floods of sense stimulation are around him everywhere waiting to be sorted out and identified. The senses, which are stimulated by sound, sight, smell, taste, and touch experiences, are the dispatchers to the nervous system. Perception itself involves the activation of nerves in one or more sense organs. Impulses from these organs travel to the brain and are interpreted there. The child then *hears, sees, touches, tastes,* and *smells.* He experiences pressure, pain, heat, and cold. When the message received by the brain becomes meaningful, perception, thought, comprehension, and expression are set into motion.

The sensory pathways in very young children are open to absorb thousands of impressions. Vivid images are built which are basic to all learning and communication. Therefore, it is important that teaching be concerned with the full development of sensory power so that young children will become alerted to the world around them, and will acquire a firm foundation of knowledge and rich environmental experiences that will be both stimulating and satisfying.

The techniques described in this chapter will enable the teacher to help young children become aware of what their senses can do and how the parts of their bodies can help in learning. The children also will develop language facility in expressing what they see, hear, feel, taste, and smell.

*The new baby is born with a well-developed sense of hearing.* At around five to six weeks in prenatal life, the ears begin to take shape. By the end of seven weeks, parts of the ear, including the auditory canal, middle ear bones, cochlea, and semicircular canals, are formed. Research shows that even babies in the womb react to sound. Within a few weeks after birth, the baby will cease crying at the sound of music or his mother's soothing voice and listen intently. Many biologists believe that young babies react specifically to sound patterns coming from parents. Eventually, as an infant's nervous system matures and aural perception becomes refined, he will be able to imitate speech.

*The new baby sees.* We are not precisely aware of *what* he sees, but no doubt he can note the difference between light and dark. However, not until around four months is the retina developed well enough to enable the baby to distinguish color. Considerably younger than this, however, he can follow visual stimuli like a shiny object and look at it up, down, and sideways. His movements are controlled by six small muscles in each eye.

Finally, the child correlates object with sound. He connects the face of his mother with her voice. He watches her movements and reacts with joy and laughter when he hears her speak.

He begins to observe and learn from these observations when his nervous system has matured sufficiently so that he can move his eyes willfully and can gain complete satisfaction from what he sees. To learn to creep and crawl, he must depend somewhat upon vision because now he is exploring a third dimension.

*The new baby feels.* He may cry with discomfort when a blanket is rumpled under his back, if a pin is sticking him, or if the room is too hot or cold. Eventually, he learns to correlate visual stimuli with bodily actions as he examines things with his hands, fingers, and tongue. These movements give him important help in learning to know himself and his surroundings. The chair may have a far different perspective after he has crawled around it and stood beside it. The child's use of larger muscles in crawling, walking, and standing prepares him for more refined movements of fingers, hands, and feet.

He touches what he can reach and thus gains knowledge of hardness, softness, stickiness, roughness, and smoothness. He organizes this knowledge in ways we are not fully able to explain.

*The new baby has fairly well-developed taste buds at birth.* Since smell and taste are closely allied, the child can identify through the sense of smell many substances before he tastes them. For awhile, he will use his mouth as well as his fingers to discover if things are pleasant, unpleasant, dull, bitter, sweet, sour, or salty. There is simultaneous action in the nervous system for each movement he makes, but development of this process requires time and maturity. Eventually, taste and smell will work together more precisely for him.

Where there is interest, the intellect, as well as the body, functions. The young child must be fed stimulating sensory ideas and materials which he can compare, relate, and classify. All the time he is being fed through his senses, he is experimenting, investigating, and learning. How can the child *know* sound unless an awareness of it is created? How can he *know* beauty unless he becomes sensitive to his surroundings? How can one explain *fur* to a child who has never stroked the back of a kitten or a puppy? How can one imagine the odor and taste of an orange if he has neither tasted nor smelled one?

Within this unit are varieties of listening, observation, tactile, olfactory, and gustatory techniques which the teacher can employ to help the young child discover his wonderful senses as avenues to learning.

### IMPRESSIONS OF THE WOODLAND

What do you see in the woodland
When the sun has gone to bed?
I see the fairies dancing
In gowns of blue and red.

What do you hear in the woodland
When all the world is still?
I hear the fairies singing,
And I hear a whippoorwill.

What do you feel in the woodland
When the fairies dance and sing?
I feel the soft wind touch me,
To tell me it is spring.

What do you smell in the woodland?
I smell the fragrant pines.
I smell sweet wild flowers,
And honeysuckle vines.

—L.B.S.

Read the poem slowly to the children as they close their eyes. Ask the class to make up a song the fairies would sing.

Obtain pine needles, leaves, box-sage, moss, and flowers for the children to smell. Show pictures of trees, streams, and growing plants.

## GENERAL IMPRESSIONS

The following impressions or similar ones can be presented in order to encourage children to submit their own. Present just a few at a time. Ask: "What do you like to hear best? What things do you like to see? Feel? What foods do you like to taste? What smells do you like best of all?"

*Impressions of sound:*

Clatter of rain on the roof
The tune of an ice-cream truck
Ice clanking in a pitcher
    of lemonade

A foghorn
Bird songs
Mother's voice
A train whistle

*Impressions of sight:*

A cat's eyes in the dark
A black and yellow bee
A dog's pink tongue

Clouds floating
A tiny cup of tea
A rainbow

*Impressions of touch:*

The lining of Mother's coat
An ice cube in summer
Bare feet on grass

A fuzzy mitten
Cotton
Rough tree bark

*Impressions of taste:*

Freshly baked bread
Chocolate pudding
Peppermint ice cream

Crunchy celery
Corn on the cob
Turkey dressing

*Impressions of smell:*

A Christmas tree
A dog that has been in the rain
Freshly cut grass
Cookies baking

Gasoline
Soap
Bacon frying
Peppermint

## WHICH SENSES ARE USED?

Hold up an object or a picture and ask: "Can you taste this? How does it taste? Can you smell it? How does it smell? How does it feel with your fingers? Can you see it? Hear it? Does it make a sound?" Here are examples of food and objects that can be presented to the children:

| apple | music box | finger paint |
| cotton | horn | dish |
| sand | felt | candy |
| top | lemon | bell |
| pear | orange | dish |
| toy | grass | soup |

## SENSES AND THE SEASONS

Choose a topic like "A Spring Day" and ask: "What smells good in the spring? What looks fresh and green? What sounds can be heard? What feels nice to the touch? What foods do animals like in the spring? What food do you like in the spring? What games do you play in the spring?" Use this technique for talking about other seasons.

## A FIVE SENSES POEM

My ears help me hear;
My eyes help me see;
My hands help me touch.
They are all part of *me*.

My tongue helps me taste;
My nose helps me smell.
These are called the five senses
And they all serve me well!
—L.B.S.

Cut mouths, noses, eyes, ears, and hands from magazine pictures and mount them on a chart. Discuss how each of these sensory parts helps us breathe, eat, talk, listen, or feel.

Ask: "How do we keep these parts of our bodies clean? How are animals' eyes, noses, and ears different from ours?"

## APPLYING SENSORY STIMULATION

A child chooses something in the classroom and brings it to the sharing area. He tells if it tastes or smells good, if he can hear it, and how it feels in his hand.

## LISTENING AS AN AID TO LANGUAGE DEVELOPMENT

To listen is to become aware of the identity of sounds which the brain receives. In order to hear, sound waves must move to the brain where they are interpreted. This interpretation is listening. Although hearing and listening are related, they are not the same. The act of hearing may require little or no effort; listening demands concentration and thinking, with a deliberate fixing of the mind upon impressions received through the senses, so that images in the brain are recorded.

Listening is an active process. It demands concentration, exploration, elimination, retention, and decision-making. Listening requires energy since one must forcefully and willfully exclude extraneous sounds in the environment in order to concentrate upon what the speaker is saying.

Although listening is the most frequently used communication skill, there was little concern about it until 1928. Even then, not much was done about listening constructively until the late '40's, when Dr. Ralph Nichols from the University of Minnesota advocated teaching it as a skill. He was one of the first pioneers who researched listening problems and offered suggestions for their improvement. Today, many textbooks and curriculum guides for reading and language arts programs contain chapters and whole units on listening.

Through directed listening experiences, the child's senses are alerted and directed toward creativity; his aural discrimination is sharpened; he gains information; and his vocabulary is enriched.

The child's ability to listen depends, in part, upon the listening experiences he has encountered in the home. Loud speech, confusion, and noise sometimes make listening difficult, since the child has not matured enough to tune out the noises around him in order to listen attentively to particular sounds. Adult interrupters, lack of attention given to the child's questions, inconsistent discipline, and rejection by adults are among the factors which can create an inattentive, restless, easily distracted child. As a result, he usually has a brief attention span and lacks social maturity.

The young child enters school and discovers that he must sit, listen, and take turns talking. The abrupt transition from a home where there are poor listening habits to the center may be too much for him.

It is more likely that better listening will take place if:

There is no hearing loss.
There is adequate language development.
There are no disturbed behavior patterns or emotional tensions.
The child's memory span is sufficient for concentration.
His health is good.
The room has an atmosphere conducive to effective listening.

If a child has poor listening skills, it may mean that he needs attentive auditors and probably more individual attention for awhile until he is able to fit more easily into the group. The teacher who realizes that habits of listening develop gradually over a period of time will understand that patience is needed from her and the parents. The teacher in the center should arrange more silent times and rest periods to offset the noise factors in the environment. Children need to rest their minds and bodies through quiet times during brief periods throughout the day.

Here are some suggestions which can help to establish more effective listening skills in the education center:

Regard listening as basic to all learning.
Refrain from *demanding* listening. Children must be motivated to listen through sense appealing materials. Emphasize listening *to,* rather than listening *at.*
Use good phrasing and relaxed, unhurried speech and manner.
Present well-planned experiences.
Provide time for the children to listen to one another.
Strive for sentence responses and an easy, calm atmosphere.
Refrain from direct criticism of responses.

As we consider emphasis on listening, we should note these particular kinds of listening:

*Appreciative listening.* The child finds pleasure and entertainment in hearing music, poems, and stories. It is best to begin with this type of listening because it is passive, but personal for each child.

*Purposeful listening.* The child follows directions, understands announcements, and gives back responses.

*Discriminative listening.* The child becomes aware of changes in pitch and loudness. He differentiates sounds in the environment. Eventually, he is able to discriminate the speech sounds.

*Creative listening.* The child's imagination and emotions are stimulated by his listening experiences. He expresses his thoughts spontaneously and freely through words, or actions, or both.

*Critical listening.* The child understands, evaluates, makes decisions, and formulates opinions. To encourage this critical listening, the teacher may pose such questions as: "What happens when we all talk at once? What if everyone wanted to play in the playhouse at the same time?" The child must think through responses, decide the most logical solution to the problem, and present a point of view. Other questions requiring evaluative responses are included in the section of Chapter 1 entitled "The Child Uses Language."

## MUSICAL BOTTLES

Fill several bottles (all the same size) with different amounts of water. Place them on top of the bookcase, a desk, or even a chair with newspapers underneath to protect the furniture from water rings. Tap each bottle with a pencil and listen to the different tones. Calculate the correct quantity of water needed to form a musical scale. The children may take turns playing the scale.

—O.M.A.

## DISCRIMINATION GAME

Show the devices needed to do each of the following: clap hands, drop a bobby pin, pour water into a basin, and hit two blocks together. Then ask two or three children to turn their backs to the group. Make one of the sounds and ask one of the three to tell what he thinks produced the sound.

—O.M.A.

## LISTENING FOR KITTEN CALLS

Ask the children to close their eyes. Walk about the room and touch one child gently on the shoulder. He mews and the other children guess who made the "kitten" sound. Substitute other animal sounds.

## LISTEN FOR THE LAST NUMBER

Count backward slowly, letting the voice grow softer and softer until it is barely audible. Stop and ask the children to tell the last number they heard you say.

## LISTENING TREASURE HUNT

Read aloud *The Listening Walk*.[1] Ask the class to participate by producing the sounds mentioned in the story. Follow this presentation by taking the class on a listening walk. Later, ask individual children to tell what they heard.

## ECHO

Ask the class to imitate your different vocal inflections, loudnesses, and pitches as you say, "How do you do?" or "Good morning." This exercise is good for vocal practice as well as for discriminatory listening.

## SOUND BOXES

Encourage the children to help with the collection of two small cereal boxes for each of the following objects. Fill each pair of boxes with the same number and size of the objects and seal.

| | |
|---|---|
| grains of rice or corn | chalk |
| ping pong balls | rocks |
| styrofoam balls | tacks |
| paper clips | pencils |
| beans | bells |

Be sure that stubs of pencils or crayons are exactly the same size and length. The children will match boxes that produce the same sounds.

## SOUNDS WE HEAR

Ask the class to tell and imitate sounds they hear in different situations. They will learn that the world is filled with wonderful sounds just begging to be heard.

[1] Paul Showers, *The Listening Walk*, Thomas Y. Crowell, New York, 1961.

Ask the class to listen as individual children make or imitate the following:

*Sounds at a circus:*

| | |
|---|---|
| Feet marching | Music |
| Sacks rattling | Laughing |
| Animals growling | Voices |
| Hoofbeats | Clapping |

*Sounds at school:*

| | |
|---|---|
| The erasing of blackboards | Children jumping rope |
| | A ticking clock |
| Closing of a book | Bells ringing |
| Balls bouncing | Singing |

*Sounds in a storm:*

| | |
|---|---|
| Windows rattling | Thunder |
| Bushes moving | Rain |
| Leaves rustling | Wind |
| Crackling branches | Trees bending |

## NOISE MAKERS

Creating sounds can be fun. Here are some noise-makers which can produce identifiable and interesting sounds:

| | |
|---|---|
| whiskbroom sweeping clothing | triangles hit with a pencil |
| sand blocks rubbed together | oatmeal box containing an object |
| clappers in action | tin pan containing some grains of corn |
| whistles blown | paper clips in a plastic box |
| crumpled foil or paper | spools strung on a cord and rattled |

Before gluing two paper plates together, insert a definite number of beans, grains of rice, or corn kernels. Use these plates to stimulate aural discrimination. You may paint the plates orange, add glued-on buttons for features, and have an interesting rattle for Halloween or other holiday activities.

## LISTENING FOR FOOTSTEPS

Listening for footsteps can be challenging. Ask the class—when they hear footsteps and see nobody moving inside or immediately outside of the door—to try to decide if the footsteps belong to a child, man, woman, dog, or horse, and if the people or animals are near or far away.

## THE MAGIC WHISPER

Use this story to create alertness and increase memory span:

Once there was a fairy who lost her voice. All she could do was whisper. Here is what she said: (*Whisper something into a child's ear; he then whispers what you have said to the next child, and so on. The last child tells the class what the fairy said.*)

Soon the sun came out and warmed everything and the fairy's voice came back. She didn't need to whisper anymore, but she could talk with a sweet voice just like you.

—L.B.S.

## SLEEPING GIANT

Display a tennis shoe, a button, a pencil, and a ball. A child is chosen to be the sleeping giant who sits in a chair placed in front of the class so that the child's back is toward the group. The "giant" pretends to be asleep.

The objects have been distributed to members of the group. At a signal from the teacher, a child tiptoes behind the giant and drops an object on the floor. The children chant:

> "There is someone coming near.
> Giant, giant, do you hear?"

Then the "giant" identifies which object made the sound.

—V.S.P.

## RAINDROP SONGS

Provide a tin pie pan, a deep kettle, and a thin shingle or piece of plywood. With a hammer and a nail make several holes in the bottom of a coffee can. Place the pan, the kettle and the wood on the ground.

Fill the coffee can with water and ask the children to take turns holding the can over each object, letting the "raindrops" fall. Ask: "What sounds did the raindrops make? Which sound did you like best? Why were the sounds different?"

—V.S.P.

## LISTENING TO TAPS

Select three jars or tumblers of different sizes. Tap them gently with a pencil to hear the tones. One child may hide his eyes while another taps a jar. The first child tries to guess which jar was tapped. Choose jars markedly different in size so that the tones will not be similar.

—O.M.A.

## WHERE IS THE SOUND?

The children close their eyes. One child rings a bell in one section of the room, then tiptoes back to his seat and sits down. At a signal from the teacher, eyes are opened and the group tells specifically where the sound came from as: "It came from the easel, teacher's desk, closet."

## METRONOME

Metronomes were invented in the days of George Washington and have fascinated children and adults ever since.

Sock-footed rhythmics encourage good foot development and are especially pleasant to do to the clicking sound of a metronome. The children will learn to run on tiptoes or walk with a strut as the tempo is altered. They will become aware of tempo as part of music expression.

Some tempos are exciting and some are sleepy. This careful listening experience can aid in the development of language skills as children sometimes describe movements inspired by the metronome.

Young children enjoy tapping to music. The "Allegretto" from Beethoven's Eighth Symphony records the fascination with a metronome. The musician wrote this metronomic music to exemplify a variety of tempos. On the first tune, the children may tap on a table with the fingers. On the second tune, they may tap with their feet (removing their shoes to do so). On the third tune, they may walk. At the end of the movement, they may assume a rag-doll stance with feet apart, head down, and arms swinging.

—V.S.P.

## THE STRANGE NOISE

The boys and girls were resting on the floor. They were lying on a rug. It was ever so quiet. It was so quiet that you could hear an insect buzzing on the window sill. It was a very good time to think.

Suddenly there was a noise. It was not a loud noise.

It was a soft noise, a strange, small, noisy noise.

"Listen!" whispered Bobby.

"Listen!" whispered Susie.

"Listen!" whispered Joan.

"Listen!" whispered the teacher.

"Listen!" whispered all of the children.

The teacher said softly, "Let's think about the strange noise. Let's guess what is making the strange noise. Let's find out where the strange noise is coming from."

The children asked questions about the strange noise.

"Can you ask a question about it? (*Responses.*) They tried to guess what was making the strange noise.

"Do you have some guesses? (*Responses.*) Shall I tell you, then?

"It was a shiny black cricket with gauzy wings and strong back legs rustling around in the wastebasket looking for something to eat.

"Can you make up a good ending for this story?" (*Responses.*)

—L.B.S.

## OBSERVATION AS AN AID TO LANGUAGE

"Observation is no magic power. It is simply finding out. To do this, one must open his senses to see, hear, feel, taste, and smell."[2]

Helping the child to develop visual acuity is a significant goal of the teacher in the education center. When puzzles, color concepts, designs, and matching games are provided, the child sharpens his powers of observation by noting likenesses and differences and seeing how things are put together and taken apart. In this chapter are lesson plans and devices designed to develop visual acuity and build attention for the

[2] Robert P. Crawford, *Techniques of Creative Thinking,* Hawthorn Books Inc., New York, 1945.

eventual complicated processes of reading and writing. Many commercial multisensory devices and flannelboard cutouts, which aid in strengthening observation, may be purchased at school supply houses.

## EYES

There are many things that can be said about eyes which will be of interest to young children and which they will understand. Try the following motivation:

"What helps you to see? Look up at the ceiling and then down at the floor. What do you see? (*Responses*.)

"Your eyes are round like a ball. Little muscles move your eyes sideways and up and down. Your eyes sit in your head and they can be different in color from those of someone else.

"What is the color of your eyes? Look in the mirror and tell us. Look at your eyelids and eyelashes. Your eyelashes are like a screen that keeps dust and dirt from hurting your round eyeball.

"Why do you have eyes? (*Responses*.) They help make your face look pleasant. Eyes look at picture-storybooks to see their lovely pictures. Eyes see the first snowfall in winter and the first flowers in spring. Eyes see a cocoon which will hatch into a moth and eyes see bright red and golden leaves of autumn.

"What else can your eyes see? (*Responses*.) They help you tell which coat is yours. Describe your coat." Hold up several coats for children to identify.

## CLOSE YOUR EYES

Say: "Sometimes you can imagine that you can see things with your eyes closed. Close your eyes now. You are in a meadow. What do you see? (*Responses*.)

"You are at the zoo. What do you see? (*Responses*.)

"It is a beautiful summer day. Can you see the hills and birds skimming across the sky? Can you see a newborn colt by its mother?"

## MAGIC EYES

Construct some play eyeglasses from pipe cleaners. The children will have fun wearing them and looking for "magic things." Also, the child who must wear glasses will feel less self-conscious. This activity will help children to observe things they would not see otherwise.

## ANIMALS' EYES

Say: "Owls have big round eyes which cannot move as ours do. Cats have good eyes and they can see up and down and in the dark. Horses can move their eyes from side to side as we can.

> "Cats' eyes are small when it is light,
> But they are round and bright at night.
> Worms have no eyes, but dragonflies
> Can see and catch bugs twice their size."

Hold a mirror behind a candle. Say: "What happens to the light? (*Responses.*) It looks bigger and brighter. Most animals, like racoons, skunks, and cats, have eyes that shine at night."

Bring a cat to school and take it into a dark closet. Ask the class to notice how its eyes shine.

—L.B.S.

## THINGS TO DO

Say: "Count your fingers one at a time. Could you see each finger separately? Look at your hand. Did you see it all at once? Hold your hands out at your sides and look straight ahead. Can you see your fingers? Close one eye and look at me with the other. Can you see me?"

## POEMS ABOUT EYES

> What kind of eyebrows do you wear?
> Are they dark or are they fair?
> And are your eyelashes made of hair
> That keep out dust that's in the air?
>
> A little gland makes teardrops come.
> Tears keep your eyes from getting dry.
> Sometimes there are a lot of tears,
> When you are sad and have to cry.

—L.B.S.

Say: "Why do people cry? Have you ever laughed until you cried? Look in the mirror. Do you see the dot in the middle of your eye? That dot is called the *pupil*."

## MATCHING

Use your eyes, use your eyes;
Quickly look and see.
If your color is like mine,
Bring it here to me.

—V.S.P.

Pass around colored construction paper discs. Keep a duplicate of each one. Say the rhyme as you hold up a disc. The children chant the rhyme, too. If a child has one that matches your disc, he comes forward.

## SEEING SHAPES IN EVERYDAY OBJECTS

Basic shapes used in mathematics can be recognized in things that children see frequently.

*Square*: handkerchief, record, album, sidewalk block
*Triangle*: Cub Scout neckerchief, cracker, cushion, folding rug, napkin
*Rectangle*: Kleenex, chocolate bar, window pane, drawer, flower box, door
*Circle*: plate, bracelet, doily, ring, button, clock

Look for shapes in such objects as wagons, tricycles, chairs, books, and tables.

## FIND ONE LIKE MINE

Make individual flannelboards for the children by covering tablet backs or chipboard pieces of conforming size with dark outing flannel, which will not show soil. Cut triangles, rectangles, circles, and squares from different colors of felt. Give the children an assortment of these shapes. Each child takes a turn at displaying one shape and color on his flannelboard for the other children to match on their boards.

This is an excellent device for teaching color and for providing practice on shapes.

—O.M.A.

## TALKING ABOUT PICTURES

If the children have had few, beautiful, visual experiences, the teacher can usually borrow fine arts pictures from a library.[3] Show a picture, talk about it for awhile, and encourage questions. Turn the picture over and say: "Was there something in this picture that stayed in your mind even though your eyes cannot see it anymore? Do you remember what it was? Tell us."

Be careful that this device does not appear to be an "examination." There are no wrong answers. If a child says, "I saw a horse," and there was no horse in the picture, say to him: "Yes, a horse would enjoy this place."

## IT LOOKED LIKE SPILT MILK[4]

Make pellon cutouts of the objects and animals mentioned in this story and use them on the flannelboard as you tell it. Pictures could also be torn from white paper by the children and backed with bits of outing flannel to make them stick. As you tell the story a second time, the children will be able to join in, and even tell the story in relay singly.

    1. Sometimes it looked
      like Spilt Milk.
    But it wasn't Spilt Milk.
    2. Sometimes it looked
      like a Bird.
    But it wasn't a Bird.
    3. Sometimes it looked
      like a Rabbit.
    But it wasn't a Rabbit.
    4. Sometimes it looked
      like a Tree.
    But it wasn't a Tree.

[3] Alice E. Chase, *Famous Paintings* (Masterpieces), Platt and Munk Co. Inc., New York, 1962.
[4] Charles Shaw, *It Looked Like Spilt Milk*, Harper and Row, Evanston, Illinois, 1947. Used by special permission of the publisher.

5. Sometimes it looked
    like an Ice Cream Cone.
   But it wasn't an Ice Cream Cone.
6. Sometimes it looked
    like a Flower.
   But it wasn't a Flower.
7. Sometimes it looked
    like a Pig.
   But it wasn't a Pig.
8. Sometimes it looked
    like a Birthday Cake.
   But it wasn't a Birthday Cake.
9. Sometimes it looked
    like a Sheep.
   But it wasn't a Sheep.
10. Sometimes it looked
    like a Great Horned Owl.
    But it wasn't a Great Horned Owl.
11. Sometimes it looked
    like a Mitten.
    But it wasn't a Mitten.
12. Sometimes it looked
    like a Squirrel.
    But it wasn't a Squirrel.
13. Sometimes it looked
    like an Angel.
    But it wasn't an Angel.
14. Sometimes it looked like Spilt Milk.
    But it wasn't Spilt Milk.
    It was just a cloud in the sky.

## THE CHILD PAINTS

Every time a child paints, he expresses a bit of his personality. Sometimes, as we look at his work, we realize that childhood is not the happy and untroubled time that we had thought it to be. As we observe the child's splashes, we may learn much about him through his paintings.

If perfectionism and over-cleanliness have been imposed by parents, the child may hesitate to work with paints for fear of soiling his hands and clothes. As he approaches a finger painting experience, the teacher can assure him how pleasant it is to feel the soft paint and encourage him to use all parts of his hand. Some children worry about tackling finger or easel painting when they have had no experience with it. This hesitancy is understandable and these children must be given special assurance to feel that painting is fun and that any experimenting is acceptable.

The teacher encourages self-expression through careful planning so that the child can grow in confidence at whatever he attempts. Anxieties disappear when a child is given interesting things to do and think about. Distressing thoughts vanish as he sees other children enjoying the activity, and talking about their creations.

Usually the child has impressions he wants to paint before he reaches the easel, but this is not always the case. He may feel uncertain and say to the teacher, "What shall I paint?" The answer, "Anything you like" may be worse than no answer at all when a child is asking for help and security. Unless he has something in mind to act as a guide, his power to express may diminish. He should not be left to flounder in a sea of indecision. On the other hand, a teacher may guide too much by handing out butterflies to be colored for follow-the-dot designs to complete. Such tasks defy creativity and merely serve to keep the child occupied. Art is far too important to risk boring a child or using it to fill in time.

From his experimental stages at the easel, the child progresses to identifiable symbols in his painting and he expresses ideas about his work. Day by day, his proportions and lines change and mature. Eventually, his house begins to resemble a house and his tree has a few branches. He begins to produce startlingly good paintings using his favorite subjects, which may be gardens, seas, rainbows, roads, animals, people, skies, trees, buildings, trains, planes, or flowers.

The teacher can help the child if she does the following:

Encourages the child to experiment initially with one color at a time, or, preferably, with not more than two or three colors.
Gives him advice only when he asks for it.
Leads him to talk about his creations and tell, if he feels like it, why he likes them.
Displays his picture while the class is out playing so that it becomes a pleasant surprise and an encouragement to his efforts when he enters the room.

Parents, too, can help their children by providing them with paints and paper and a chance to use them frequently. The activity of easel or finger painting strengthens manual dexterity, improves coordination, helps a child to gain confidence in himself, develops language skills, provides release from tension, and offers the child an opportunity to express himself freely.

—L.B.S.

## EQUIPMENT

Equipment for the painting and art center may include the following:

| | |
|---|---|
| Easels | Construction paper |
| Newsprint | Cans or jars |
| Clay boards | Liquid tempera |
| Smocks | Clay |
| Paint brushes | Blunt scissors |
| Finger-paint paper | Crayons |

## MAKING A FISHBOWL

The children paint with blues and greens to represent water on strips of butcher paper. Help them lay the paper on the floor and splice together several sheets to use to cover all sides of a large cardboard carton.

This "fishbowl" has many practical uses aside from the child's feeling that he is in water and pretending to be a fish. When the fishbowl is not in use, it can serve as a convenient place for storing toys, objects the children have made, or rhythm instruments.

—O.M.A.

## PAINT AND STRING PRINTS

Use a sheet of 12" x 18" drawing paper. Fold it in the center lengthwise and lay it open upon the pages of a mail order catalog. The child dips a piece of string into colored paint and pulls off the excess between the fingers of his free hand. He then lays the string down on the right half of the white paper while still holding one end of the string in his hand. He closes the other half of the paper and shuts the catalog. As the teacher presses firmly on the catalog, the child slowly draws the string from between the pages. The result will be two identical prints. Green paint produces foliage effects, but any color gives satisfying results.

—O.M.A.

## COLORS OF THINGS

Red, red. What is red?
The apple growing overhead.

Yellow, yellow. What is yellow?
A ripe banana, long and yellow.

Blue, blue. What is blue?
My kitten's eyes. She says, "Mew, mew."

Orange, orange. What can it be?
An orange growing on a tree.

Green, green. What is green?
A blade of grass or one string bean.

Purple, purple. Seven, eight, nine.
Sweet grapes growing on a vine.

White, white. What is white?
Fluffy cloud so soft and light.

—L.B.S.

Be sure to read Christina Rossetti's poem, "What is Pink." It can be found in most poetry anthologies.

Discuss the things which have many colors: mittens, rainbows, crayons, pencils. Name things which have only one color: salt, lemons, oranges. Consider what has more than one color: apples, grass, roses, leaves.

## YELLOW, YELLOW

Yellow, yellow duckling swimming in the brook.
Yellow, yellow sunshine, look, look, look!

Yellow, yellow autumn leaves falling from a tree.
I see many yellow things. What do *you* see?
—L.B.S.

Ask the children to name objects in the classroom and at home which are yellow.

## A COLOR IS BLUE

Blue is a color I learned today when I went out to play.
Blue are the skies and blue are your eyes.
Blue is a color I learned today when I went out to play.

Pink is a color I learned today when I went out to play.
Pink is a skirt and pink is a shirt.
Pink is a color I learned today when I went out to play.
—L.B.S.

Continue the rhyme with the following second lines: Red is a clown's nose and red is a rose. Yellow is a sock and yellow is a block. Purple is a plum and purple is a drum. Green is a tree and green is a pea.

Also use words of the children and do not emphasize rhyming aspects. Take a walk in the yard and discover colors of things. Look around the room and name colors. Name colors in clothing.

## SALT AND FLOUR CLAY

Use five parts of salt to three parts of flour and two parts of water. Stir the salt over a very low flame for a few minutes. Mix the flour and water smoothly, then add the mixture to the salt. After this mixture thickens, allow it to cool and store it in a glass jar. Add two drops of oil of wintergreen. This salt and flour clay can be used by the children to mold beads or animal bodies. When dry, the figures can be painted with poster paint.

## MAKE COLLAGES

The children will enjoy pasting bits of wallpaper, artificial flower petals, construction paper shapes, greeting card pictures, macaroni, or dried peas to make designs on a large sheet of paper. These designs will make good wall decorations and stimulate group discussions. While the children are making collages, the teacher may want to play soft music.

## PAINTING COLORS

Slip, slip, slush
Goes my paintbrush!
Left to right and up and down
Painting red and green and brown.
Slip, slip, slush (*Children repeat.*)
Goes my paintbrush!

Slip, slip, slush
Goes my paintbrush!
I paint a road and then a tree.
I can see them; they can't see ME!
Slip, slip, slush
Goes my paintbrush!

Slip, slip, slush
Goes my paintbrush!
I paint a flower and then a sun.
And so my work is almost done!
Slip, slip, slush
Goes my paintbrush!

Slip, slip, slush
Goes my paintbrush!
My brush is cleaned and put away,
And now I can go out to play.
I'll paint again some other day!
And everytime I paint I'll say:
"Slip, slip, slush
Goes my paintbrush!"

—L.B.S.

As the poem is read to the class, they may say the refrain each time it occurs and pantomime it with clean paintbrushes.

Repeat the verses during an actual painting experience.

## WHAT IS A LOVELY SIGHT?

Snow is a lovely sight;
  It is so clean and white.
The sun is a lovely sight;
  It's yellow and makes things light.
An orange is a lovely sight;
  It is orange and it is bright.
Red crayons are a lovely sight;
  They help us draw and write.
The sky is a lovely sight,
  Where bluebirds take their flight.
Purple is a lovely sight.
  Grapes make a tasty bite.

—L.B.S.

Name other foods and objects that have color.

## AN ICE-CREAM CONE GAME

Turn a sturdy shoe box upside down and cut holes in the bottom in which to fit ice-cream cones. Cut the cones from half circles of tagboard. Fold and glue them to form cones. Fill them with colored crepe paper to represent flavors. This idea produces a device for teaching and learning both flavors and colors. Learning can be reinforced as the children play "store" with the cones. Flavors and their color representations may include:

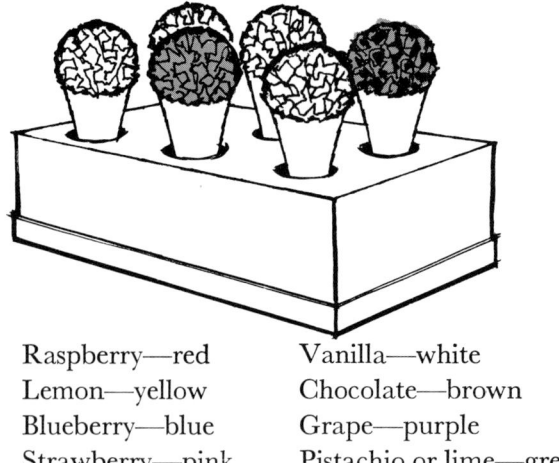

Raspberry—red        Vanilla—white
Lemon—yellow         Chocolate—brown
Blueberry—blue       Grape—purple
Strawberry—pink      Pistachio or lime—green

The children say this as they ask for their cones:

>Yum, yum, yum. Oh, what fun!
>Ice cream, ice cream, yum, yum, yum!

The children may clap the rhythm as the rhyme is said.

## SOMEBODY'S WEARING

>Somebody's wearing a blue, blue dress.
>Somebody's wearing a blue, blue dress.
>Somebody's wearing a blue, blue dress,
>And that somebody is you!

Substitute other wearing apparel and colors as you repeat the rhyme. Ask the children to describe their own clothing and that of other children in the room. Encourage them to paint pictures of themselves and members of their families dressed in their favorite colors.

## BRIAN PAINTS

Brian said, "I want to paint."

So he went to the easel and he found three colors: yellow, red, and blue.

What could Brian paint with yellow? (*Responses.*)

As Brian was thinking and trying to decide what to paint, a fairy whispered in his ear:

>"I can make magic colors
>From yellow, red, and blue.
>And since you like to paint so well,
>A secret I'll tell you."

Brian looked all around but he couldn't see anyone. (That isn't surprising for nobody has ever really seen a fairy.) So Brian dipped his brush into the red paint. He swished the brush around on the paper. Then he rinsed off the brush and dipped it into some yellow paint. He mixed the red and yellow and it came out *orange*.

What did Brian paint with orange? (*Responses.*)

"I need green," said Brian. "I want to paint something green." Then the color fairy whispered:

> "I can make magic colors
> From yellow, red, and blue.
> Just mix some blue and yellow,
> And you'll have a color new."

Brian mixed yellow and blue and it made a beautiful *green*.
Now what could he paint with green? (*Responses.*)
Brian wanted to paint something purple and the fairy whispered:

> "I can make magic colors
> From yellow, red, and blue.
> And now mix colors red and blue,
> And you'll have a color new."

And Brian mixed red and blue and it made a rich *purple*.
What did Brian make with purple paint? (*Responses.*)

—L.B.S.

Use three glass jars of yellow, red, and blue paints or food coloring. Show the children how Brian mixed his colors to make new ones. As this experiment is carried out, the children may join in saying the appropriate verses from the story.

### THE BLUE BEAD

Place large beads in a box. Take out one bead at a time as the story progresses. Ask individual children to complete the thoughts required for the blank spaces. At intervals, count the beads with the class.

Once there was a box of pretty beads which were just begging to be made into a necklace.

Mary Jane and Dolores saw the beads and said, "Let's make a necklace."

So they found a *red* bead. (*The children name the color each time a bead is lifted from the box.*) They found a _____ bead, (continue to select beads) a _____ bead, a _____ one, etc. But Mary Jane and Dolores could not find a blue bead.

Mary Jane said, "A blue bead must be somewhere."

Dolores said, "Let's take all of the beads out of the box. A blue bead must be here." (*Take out all beads and name the colors.*)

But there was no *blue* bead. Where do you think it was? (*Responses.*)

Mary Jane said, "I will look behind the door. Maybe the blue bead is there."

But it wasn't.

Then Dolores remembered. She put her hand into her pocket and there was the *blue* bead. Dolores and Mary Jane finished their necklace and took turns wearing it.

—L.B.S.

## NUMBER AND MEASURING CONCEPTS

Numbers exist in all of our surroundings and they bring order and stability to our lives. The child learns to think more creatively and accurately when he understands number and measuring concepts. Where there is a sense of order, there is number. Numbers and size *are* order. With some concrete knowledge of these concepts, the child builds better, balances more accurately, fits pieces of puzzles together more easily, and gains understanding of the language of how, when, where, how much, or many, which one, and why.

When the child enters the education center, generally he knows that he has two eyes, ears, lips, shoulders, arms, hands, legs, and feet. He knows normally that he has only one nose, mouth, forehead, chin, neck, head, and body; five fingers and toes; many teeth in his mouth and hairs on his head.

The child begins to realize that things sometimes are paired as: socks, hands, feet, glasses, overshoes, and mittens; and that even twin people, animals, or boxes are look-alikes.

He tries to decide if there is room enough on the rug for everyone and whether the doorway to his block garage will allow him to crawl through. These concepts he can understand, especially if he is given a chance to experiment concretely with objects and use them meaningfully with language.

## MAKING COMPARISONS

Comparisons encourage the child to notice how things alike may look different and how things different may look alike. Here are a few words and phrases that may be visually portrayed with objects so that the children will understand the concepts.

| | |
|---|---|
| as many as | deep—shallow |
| a short way | many—few |
| a long way | before—after |
| thick—thin | inside—outside |
| in—out | as much as |
| full—empty | below—above |
| long—short | less—more |

## HOW FAR?

"How far" holds fascination for the young child. He enjoys asking: "How far is it to Grandma's?" Answers "About two more miles" and "Just a short way" satisfy him even though the idea of "miles" or "short" is not yet comprehended.

Opportunities for posing "How far" questions are encountered in daily activities experienced in the education center.

## HOW MANY?

"How many" has a similar appeal. Examples are: How many grandparents, uncles, aunts? How many hours at school? How many legs on the chair or table? How many days until Christmas? How many wings on a bird? How many eggs in a dozen? How many windows in the house? How many crayons in the box? How many thumbs on your hand?

The use of "How many" questions encourages the child to think, reflect, and (as a result) to formulate decisions.

## LEARNING BY TWOS AND THREES

Once the child has learned that there are one or two parts to his body, he is intrigued by the concept *three*. During story time, emphasis can be placed on the Three Bears, three bowls, chairs, and beds; Three Little Pigs and their three houses; and Three Little Kittens who lost three pairs of mittens. Experiences can be planned around other things which go by threes, such as: red, white, and blue; morning, noon, and night; stop, look, and listen; breakfast, lunch, and dinner; red, yellow, and green; knives, forks, and spoons.

The numerals themselves may interest some young children. More mature children will enjoy matching numerals to their word names.

## THE CONCEPT OF PAIR

Though children can understand the term "two," they may have some difficulty comprehending "pair." Refer to "Three Little Kittens" and their pairs of mittens, or "The Shoemaker and the Elves" and pairs of shoes. Ask the children to name the parts of the body that go in pairs: nostrils, thighs, ears, and feet. Ask them to name paired parts of animals: whiskers, wings, paws, fins, antenna, horns. Ask them to name other things that go in pairs: socks, galoshes, and skates.

Early in the exploration of "pair," the teacher should explain the fruit "pear" and help the children to discriminate between the two words.

## WRITING NUMERALS

One is a soldier standing up straight.
1
Two is a swan swimming in the lake.
2
Three is a butterfly yellow and bright.
3
Four is a boat with sails so white.
4
Five is a pitcher with milk to pour.
5
Drink all you like and I'll give you some more.

—V.S.P.

Write the numeral on the chalkboard as you say the rhyme. The second time, ask the children to write the numeral in the air.

## A BOWLING GAME

Cover five empty milk cartons with white wrapping or contact paper. Make large numerals with a felt tip pen on one side of each one. Set the cartons, spaced six inches apart in a line. The children take turns rolling a rubber ball from a distance six feet away and announcing which cartons toppled over. This is a pleasant and easy way to learn numerals.

—O.M.A.

## CLOCKS

All children are interested in clocks which have their appeal in sound and movement of hands. A large commercial cardboard clock is a must for all education centers. Bring in several sizes of real clocks so that the children can watch hour and minute hands and listen to ticks. Suggest that the children act out clocks. Use an imaginary key for winding them as the following couplet is said.

>Take a key and wind the clock.
>Listen to it say "Tick-tock."

The child who is the clock makes the sound, "Tick-tock."

Usually, the young child is interested in time. He learns when it is time for lunch or bed, or when to put aside his work. He wants to know if it is time to paint, have a snack, or go home.

Set the hands of a cardboard clock for a special surprise like a birthday party snack. Be sure that there is a clock with movable hands in the playhouse.

—O.M.A.

## THE ALARM CLOCK

Once there was a little boy who did not like to get up in the morning.

So he said, "I am going to hide my clock. Then I won't know what time it is and I can sleep as long as I like."

The little boy put his clock under some clothes in a drawer where he couldn't see it anymore or hear it tick.

The next morning the little boy didn't get up. He slept and he slept. When he finally woke up, he brushed his teeth, washed his face and hands, and went downstairs. He found that the cereal was cold and his brother had gone to the park without him—all because the clock was shut up tightly in a drawer and couldn't tell him the time.

What else do you think the little boy missed? (*Responses.*)

Then he rushed right back upstairs to the bedroom, opened the drawer, took out the clock, and set it on the table beside his bed.

"I'm sorry, little clock," said the little boy. "I know that you are my good friend and I'll never, never hide you again."

—L.B.S.

This story helps the child to understand family cooperation and responsibility. Ask: "What sometimes happens when we are not on time? What would happen if buses or airplanes didn't run on time? Were you ever left out of something because you were not on time? How does a clock help us? Do you have a clock at home? Tell about it. Let's count the numbers on the clock. Is there a number that tells how old you are?"

## THE LITTLE CUCKOO

A noisy, little cuckoo lived inside a clock. Every hour he popped out through a little door and sang, "Cuckoo." At one o'clock he sang, "Cuckoo." At two o'clock he sang, "Cuckoo, cuckoo." (*Continue until the cuckoo has sung five or six times and ask the children to participate.*) On the half hour, the noisy, little cuckoo always made one cuckoo to let folks know he was on the job.

One day the children decided to practice on their musical instruments. But when they were right in the middle of their tune at three o'clock, the little cuckoo popped out and sang, "Cuckoo, cuckoo, cuckoo."

"Our music is spoiled," said the children.

They could not be angry with the little cuckoo because it was his duty to sing the time. They just started their tune all over again, and finished it before the little cuckoo had a chance to come out again.

The next day when the children began their orchestra practice, out popped the little cuckoo at two o'clock, "Cuckoo, cuckoo." This time the children had a plan. They loved the little cuckoo and they knew how important it was for him to do his work, so they wrote a special part for him in the orchestra. From that time on, the little cuckoo could help whenever the children played their music.

—L.B.S.

Ask the children to make up a special song for the little cuckoo. Bring in a cuckoo clock to demonstrate its action.

## CALENDARS

Children can understand the concepts of yesterday, tomorrow, day after tomorrow, and next week through activities involving the calendar. The class can begin to comprehend the passing of time as the days are marked off.

Children are interested in what day they will go to the zoo, or go on a picnic, or what day they can send valentines. This interest creates a real reason for having a large calendar available in the center.

A pocket chart type calendar and a set of numerals from one to thirty-one can provide the flexibility needed for many kinds of activities. This calendar can be used easily for each month.

A calendar drawn on large construction paper or a real calendar is useful. The teacher can attach to it a flower or some interesting object when a child has a birthday. Children can draw or paste on weather symbols such as: umbrella, clouds, sun, snowflakes, raindrops, or wind.

Calendars can be drawn on the chalkboard.

—O.M.A.

## LITTLE MOUSIE MONDAY

Little Mousie Monday washed all day;
Little Mousie Tuesday ironed, they say.
Little Mousie Wednesday made the bed.
Little Mousie Thursday baked the bread.
Little Mousie Friday swept the house
Just like any neat little mouse.
Little Mousie Saturday went to town
And bought herself a pretty Sunday gown.

—L.B.S.

Use the rhyme to teach the days of the week and to teach about work in the home.

From construction paper cut out seven mouse puppets like the one shown and fold on the dotted lines. Make the whiskers out of pipe cleaners. Be sure to have the puppets large enough so that they can be seen by the group. Choose seven children to hold them. Each child clasps and moves the mid-part of the puppet with thumb and forefinger to simulate movement in talking. The manipulation of this puppet helps the child to attain rhythmic speech and improves his hand coordination.

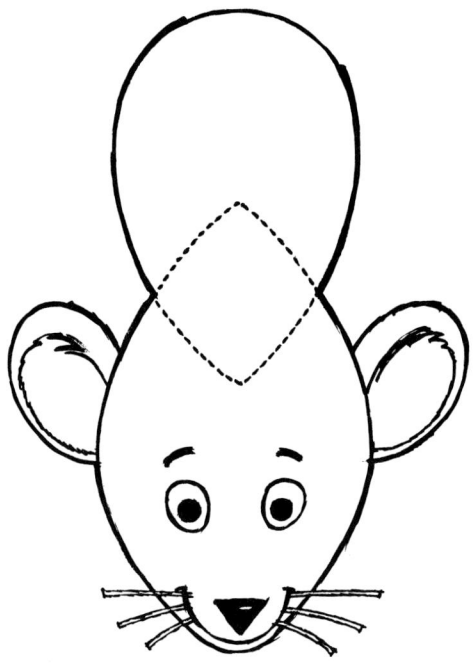

## IF YOU'RE GLAD IT IS MONDAY

(Tune: "She'll Be Comin' 'Round the Mountain")
    If you're glad it is Monday, clap your hands.
      (*Clap twice.*)
    If you're glad it is Monday, clap your hands.
      (*Clap twice.*)
    If you're glad it is Monday,
    If you're glad it is Monday,
    If you're glad it is Monday, clap your hands.
      (*Clap twice.*)

—V.S.P.

Continue with other movements: stamp your feet, turn around, show your thumb, nod your head, blink your eyes, slap your knees.

## THE LONESOME LITTLE PENNY

A lonesome little penny lived in a pocket. Now a penny couldn't buy very much, so it just stayed in the pocket, and finally another penny came to join the lonesome little penny.

How many pennies were there? (*Responses.*)

Then another penny came, and another, and another, and another one. Soon one more penny came, and another, and another, and another one. (*Children count the pennies as they are displayed.*)

How many pennies were there in the pocket? (*Responses.*)

What did the pennies buy? (*Responses.*)

Show the pennies. Show five pennies and a nickel. Show ten pennies and a dime.

—L.B.S.

## USING A TELEPHONE

The telephone dial gives the child an early experience in recognizing numerals in everyday life, yet we do not teach the child to dial these numerals. However, using toy telephones is an important language activity for it encourages one-to-one verbalizations as well as imaginary conversations and self-talk.

A tin can telephone can be made easily. Take two soup cans, joined together by a length of string that has been waxed with paraffin. One child speaks through one end, while another child listens through the other. The sound will travel along the line when it is held taunt. The children alternate talking and listening.

Be sure the edges of the cans are smooth.

—V.S.P.

## MAKING A TELEPHONE DIRECTORY

On large lined paper, write the last and then the first name of each child in alphabetical order. Place his address and telephone number beside his name and add a small snapshot of the child. Leave the "telephone" book on the browsing table so that each child will become familiar with his own name, address, and telephone number.

## THE THERMOMETER

Discuss thermometers and measuring temperatures. Bring in some thermometers for the children to examine, such as: room, oven, fever (clinical), roast, freezer, and aquarium. Cardboard thermometers can be purchased at school supply houses. Keep a large room thermometer displayed where the children can see it and observe the changes in temperature.

## MAKE YOUR OWN THERMOMETER

1. To show the principle of a thermometer, use a medicine bottle filled with water. Add red food coloring. Insert an eye dropper so that the narrow end is below the liquid. Then seal the tube with play dough. Red liquid will rise inside the tube when this "homemade thermometer" is set in a pan of hot water. As you add ice cubes, the water will go down.

2. Cut a piece of heavy cardboard 12" x 40". Near each end, cut a slit 1/4" wide and 3/8" long. Purchase red satin ribbon 1/4" wide and white elastic 1/4" wide. Sew the red ribbon to one end of the white elastic and thread this strip through the slits of the cardboard so that the strip fits smoothly, but not so tightly that it can't move around. Mark the sides of the path it takes in tens to give the appearance of a real thermometer. Add fives in between if desired. Include 32 degrees, since this is freezing temperature. Turn the thermometer over and sew the two ends of the strip together. As a temperature change occurs, pull the strip until the top of the ribbon is even with the appropriate degrees. The children can begin to learn about what happens to a thermometer when there is a change in temperature.

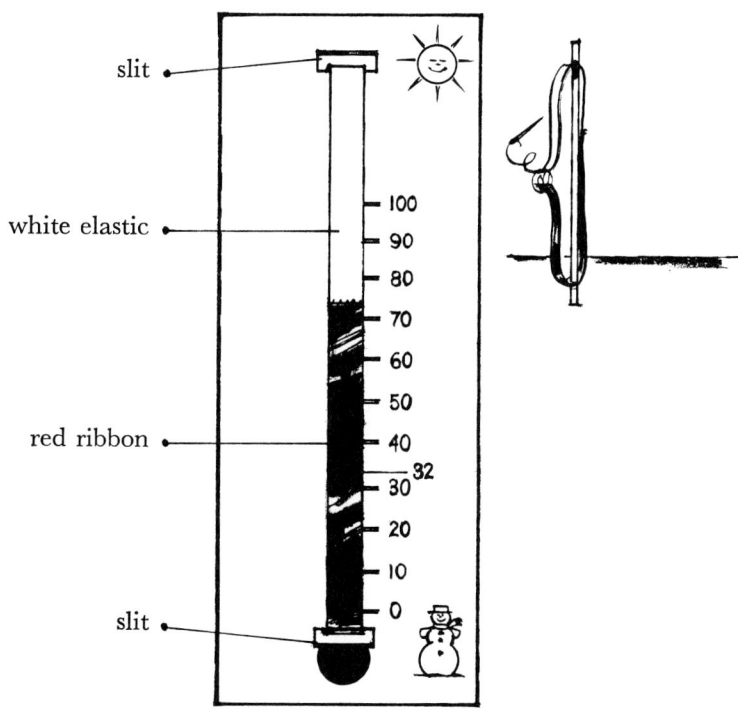

## WEIGHTS AND MEASURES

Bring in a kitchen and a bathroom scale. Let the children experiment by weighing books, scissors, crayons, erasers, or pencils on a kitchen scale. Suggest that they weigh each other on the bathroom scale.

## USING LINEAR MEASURE

The children enjoy using a tape measure to see how big arms, waists, necks, wrists, and heads are. Draw a tree that is taller than the tallest child in the class. Add names of children who are the same or different heights so they may compare measurements and note growth.

Cut a strip of heavy paper about six inches wide and about twelve inches longer than the height of the tallest child. Mark the strip off in inches and attach it to the wall for the children to measure themselves and each other.

### A POEM FOR MEASURING MYSELF

I measured my arm, I measured my toes,
I measured my fingers, I measured my nose.
I measured my neck, I measured for fun,
I measured my waist, and now I am done.
—L.B.S.

As you say the rhyme, the children pantomime it.

### OBSERVING THICKNESS AND THINNESS

A mouse's tail is long and thin;
So is a pencil and so is a pin;
So are the whiskers on a cat;
So are the feathers on a hat.

Mud is thick to make mud pies;
You can make them any size.
Thick is the jam upon your bread.
Thick is a pillow for your head.
—L.B.S.

Ask the children to name other things that are thick or thin. Find objects in the room that are thick or thin, such as paper or a book.

## OBSERVING TALLNESS AND SHORTNESS

> My thumb is short and so is my nose.
> My legs are long, but short are my toes.
> Short is the tail on a little dog.
> Long are the jumping legs of a frog.
> —L.B.S.

The children name other things that are tall and short. Ask: "Which finger is longest? Shortest? Which crayon is shorter?" Use a piece of chalk and a pencil to show which is thinner or longer. The children will learn the use of comparative parts of speech.

## OBSERVING ROUNDNESS

> Round is a circle; round is a ball;
> Round is a button, large or small.
> Round is a snowman made of snow.
> Round is your mouth when you say "Oh."
> —L.B.S.

Discuss other things that are round. Bring in an apple, an orange, and a ball. Ask the children to feel and smell them. Look for round shapes in the room: clock, dish, ball, or wheel.

## THE SENSE OF TOUCH

A baby of seven months has only to see an object in order to want to grab it. Gradually, as he begins to move about, seeing becomes insufficient. Now he must touch everything that looks exciting. His fingers with their sensitive nerve endings help him to "see" each object more accurately. When we think of a blind person reading and identifying through use of the fingertips, we are not surprised that a baby needs and uses this touch sense to find out about his world. As his mind and body coordinate, his small muscles are stimulated and strengthened. Now he is fascinated with anything bumpy, fluffy, sticky, slippery, hard, or soft. Feeling a smooth egg, a bristly brush, a splash of water, sand running between fingers, or a gooey lollipop delights him. The warmth of a hug and the touch of a kiss let him know that he is loved. A warm blanket, a billowy pillow, and a furry panda comfort him.

Touch experiences in early childhood prepare the child for perception of spacial relationships and the eventual eye-hand skills of handwriting. Also he is provided with visual memory experiences.

Many suggestions in this unit encourage children to work independently. Remember, however, that many children need guidance and help even with tasks they have chosen themselves.

## TOUCHING

My fingertips help me to touch
A bunny's fur I like so much.
I feel the trickle of warm sand,
Or sticky jelly in my hand.
I like to touch my Daddy's face,
Or feel a bit of dainty lace.
I like the hardness of a rock,
Or softness of a woolly sock.
I like to hold a cube of ice,
And soapy water is so nice.
Oh, I can feel and learn so much
If I just use my sense of touch.
—L.B.S.

Read this poem to the children and ask them what they like best to touch. Take the class on a "touching spree" and later ask each child to tell about his touch experiences.

## THE SOFTEST THING

"I know something that is very soft," said Christopher.

Tall-eared Bunny asked, "Is it I? My fur is like cotton—soft cotton."

"No, it is not you," said Christopher. "Your fur *is* soft, but I know something softer than your fur."

"Is it I?" asked Purry Kitten. "My fur is soft as velvet—soft velvet. Is it my fur?"

"No, it is not you. It is not your fur," said Christopher. "Your fur *is* as soft as velvet, but I know something softer than your fur."

"Is it I?" asked Fuzzy Duckling. "My feathers are as soft as flower petals—soft flower petals. Is it my feathers?"

"No, it is not your feathers," replied Christopher. "Your feathers are soft to touch, but I know something softer."

"But what is softer than cotton, or velvet, or flower petals?" asked Tall-eared Bunny, Purry Kitten, and Fuzzy Duckling. "What is softer than fur or feathers?"

So Christopher led them to the nursery where Baby Brother was asleep.

"See?" said Christopher.

He touched the baby's hair.

"See?" said Christopher. "A baby's hair is softer than cotton or fur, or feathers or velvet or flower petals. A baby's hair is softest of all."

"Amazing!" said Tall-eared Bunny, Purry Kitten, and Fuzzy Duckling.

—L.B.S.

The children will enjoy saying the refrain, "Is it I?" After reading this story, ask them to name other things that are soft. If possible, obtain a piece of fur, some feathers, cotton, velvet, and flower petals for the browsing or science table so that the class can have the experience of feeling and describing these objects. Use these materials in dramatizing the story.

## TALKING ABOUT YOUR SKIN
(A Discussion)

Your skin covers all of your body and protects it. It lets you perspire (sweat) when you get too warm. Your skin has millions of little nerves that tell your brain that you have felt something when you touch it with your fingertips.

> When you were a tiny baby,
> Your hands helped you so much
> To explore the world around you,
> And learn through your sense of touch!

How do you keep your wonderful skin clean? (*Responses.*)

> Some skins are dark and some are fair.
> Your hands have skin. (You have a pair.)

And tell me—are they dark or fair? (*Responses.*)

There are exciting things to feel:
A piece of fur, an orange peel.
You can feel seeds inside your hand;
And the yellow sun that makes warm sand.
You can feel a fly upon your nose;
You can feel soft mud between your toes.

What do you like to feel? (*Responses.*)
—L.B.S.

## HOW DOES IT FEEL?

Encourage complete sentence responses as you ask these questions?

Is a mouse furry or fluffy?
Is a lollipop sticky or sandy?
Is a rock hard or soft?
Is an apple rough or smooth?
Is a brush smooth or rough?
Is a stove hot or cold when it helps cook something?
Is lemonade hot or cold when it has ice in it?
—V.S.P.

## HOW YOUR HANDS HELP YOU

Your hands can make a puppet walk
And move the mouth to make it talk.
  (*Bring fingers and thumb together to imitate talking.*)
Your hand can bend down at the wrist,
Or double up to make a fist.
  (*Children imitate your actions.*)
Your hand can wave when you say "Hi!"
Or flutter like a butterfly.
Your hand can hold a lump of clay.
Your hand salutes the flag each day.
—L.B.S.

Suggest that the children show what their hands can do after they have pantomimed the poem as it is read. Have them take turns making a stick or a sack puppet walk and talk simultaneously. These movements are good for coordination of speech and muscle action.

## HOW YOUR FINGERS HELP YOU

Your fingers help you to paint and draw;
Your fingers help you to hammer and saw.
Your fingers help you to put on a sock;
Your fingers help you to wind a clock.
Your fingers help you to play in the sand.
How many fingers are on your hand?

—L.B.S.

Ask: "What do your fingers help you to do? Can they do the things in the poem? I'll read it again. Tell me if your fingers help you paint, draw, hammer, saw, put on a sock, wind a clock, and play in sand."

Bring in a run-down clock and let two or three children help wind it.

## FEET

Feet can dance and feet can skip;
Feet can run and feet can trip.
Feet can hop and feet can climb;
Feet can jump rope to a rhyme.
Feet can tiptoe very still;
Feet can help you slide downhill.
Feet can skate upon the street;
What can you do with *your* feet?

—L.B.S.

Ask the children to tell and show what they can do with their feet.

## FEELING WITH FEET

Ask the children to take off their shoes and step upon these objects to get the feeling of textures. Ask them to describe how the objects feel.

| | | |
|---|---|---|
| rug | velvet | towel |
| pillow | rubber | table |
| bean bag | sandpaper | cotton |
| newspaper | sand | leaves |
| cardboard | fur | grass |

## USING THE HANDS

Children who have used their hands frequently in making mud pies, working with clay or dough, building with blocks, cutting out things, coloring, and scribbling, are better prepared generally for reading and writing skills presented in the first grade.

Children are fascinated with water. Taking clothes out of a washing machine, blowing bubbles, and playing with water toys that float give the child experiences with both large and small muscles.

## PLAY DOUGH

One speech therapist gives the nervous child a handful of play dough so that he can have something to manipulate in order to work off tensions while the speech session is in progress. Play dough for the young child provides not only emotional release in working off excess energy, but it also affords material for creativity.

Following is a recipe for play dough which stays moist if kept in plastic bags or capped in wide-mouthed jars. In a refrigerator, it will keep for months.

2 cups of flour
1 cup of salt
1 tablespoon of powdered alum
3 tablespoons of mineral oil
1½ cups of cold water

Mix the dry ingredients and combine water and oil. Cook in a double boiler, stirring constantly until the mixture is thick like bread dough. Remove from the heat and when it is cool enough, knead the dough thoroughly. Add food coloring and oil of wintergreen for fragrance.

## HAND PRINTS

Trace two flat hand shapes on red and green construction paper, red for left, and green for right. These colors provide association with traffic lights. Mount the handprints on white construction paper and post on the bulletin board. Use as an aid for helping children to learn left and right.

Ask the children to mold whole left and right hand prints in finger paints, wet sand, or in moist flattened play dough, or clay.

Read *Good Day! Which Way?*[5] for emphasis on left and right.

---

[5] Charlotte Steiner, *Good Day!—Which Way?* Alfred A. Knopf, Inc., New York, 1960.

## A BOOK OF FEELS

Paste configurations made of varieties of fabrics and textures inside a scrapbook and lay the book on the browsing table for the children to feel the shapes and surfaces. Shapes may be circles, squares, rectangles, triangles, ellipses, or any animal shape, or object shape. Textures may be silk, fur, velvet, sandpaper, cotton, foil, oilcloth, or nylon.

## FEEL AND SAY

Here are some objects to put into a basket or box for the children to try to identify by parts or textures.

| | | | |
|---|---|---|---|
| pencil | cup | key | bulb |
| ring | rose | ball | valentine |
| spoon | quarter | crayon | clothespin |
| salt shaker | button | leaf | lock |
| watch | mirror | gum | toothbrush |
| penny | flower | eraser | sandpaper |
| sock | candle | necktie | top |
| purse | nut | fork | zipper |
| glove | pan | box | jar |

## SOFTIE TOYS

Cookie-cutter-like animal shapes with short legs are good for patterns. Select two pieces of corduroy, gingham or velveteen for each animal shape and mark the lines for sewing. Cut out the shapes leaving a half inch just outside of the sewing line. Sandwich the foam stuffing, slightly smaller than the pattern, between the cloth pieces and hold in place with a large pin. Using a darning needle with strong thread or embroidery floss, start a simple running stitch on the underside of the figure; continue stitching on the sewing line until complete. Ask the mothers to sew on buttons for eyes. These animals are very popular with young children.

—V.S.P.

## FEELING SHAPES

Look for objects which have these definite shapes and which may be placed in a box to be felt by the children.

| | | |
|---|---|---|
| round | wide | triangle |
| half of circle | straight | thin |
| rectangle | circle | crooked |
| curved | narrow | egg-shaped |
| quarter of circle | pointed | thick |

Discuss terms: edge, line, whole, part, piece, and center.

## AS SMOOTH AS ———

Start the children with one comparison and encourage them to continue with others.

As smooth as an ——— (egg).
As sticky as a ——— (lollipop).
As fluffy as a ——— (feather).
As rough as ——— (sandpaper).
As slippery as ——— (finger paint).
As soft as ——— (skin).
As hard as ——— (fingernails).
As wet as ——— (water).
As thin as ——— (string).
As heavy as a ——— (table).
As deep as a ——— (hole).
As empty as ——— (this cup).

Bring in actual objects which the children may feel and explore to understand the concepts. Read to them: *Find Out by Touching*.[6] Give the children the touch experiences described in this book.

## FRUITS AND VEGETABLES

Some young children are not familiar with all fruits or vegetables. Bring in the least perishable ones, such as: lemons, oranges, bananas, grapefruit, apples, carrots, potatoes, and peas in the pod. Pass them around for each child to feel, smell, and tell the colors. Choose the ones you wish the children to taste and cut into small sections. Ask a child to close his eyes and try to identify a fruit or vegetable by the smell as well as the shape. Ask him to describe it in terms of being long, round, big, or small.

[6] Paul Showers, *Find Out by Touching*, Thomas Y. Crowell, New York, 1961.

## CLOTHESPIN APRONS

Place small toys or objects in the pockets of a clothespin apron or shoe bag. The child will identify an object through touch, describing it before he removes it. For variety, use objects that have similar shapes so that the child will need to recognize it through texture or other differences.

To aid in the teaching of colors, sew eight different colors of pocket sections to the bottom of the apron, using plain percale, or unbleached muslin. The child names a color pocket and identifies the object contained within it. Within each pocket, include a piece of fabric or a toy of the same color, but not necessarily of the same shade.

## TELL WHAT IT IS

Cut circles, squares, rectangles, and triangles from stiff cardboard or linoleum. The children form a circle with hands behind them and one child is chosen to be *It*. He goes to the box of shapes and chooses one, holding it so that the others can't see it. He then places the shape into the hand of one child in the circle who must guess by touch what the shape is. If he guesses correctly, it is his turn to be *It*.

## FELT MATS

Felt makes wonderful place mats which give the children a feeling of comfort and security. The mats are far easier and more restful to work on than a hard-surfaced table. Cut a felt rectangle large enough for each child. Often, felt pieces can be purchased reasonably from fabric manufacturing companies or those that make felt products.

## EXPERIMENTING

Children enjoy almost anything that is done in a sensory way. They discover that work with sand, blocks, or clay can be fun. Pounding, pouring, patting, feeling, filling, stirring, winding, moulding, sifting, and blowing are all activities that create delight and satisfaction. "We are experimenting" should be a sentence which the teacher uses often during these activities. In this way, the idea is transmitted that everything done is purposeful and a part of learning.

All activities develop talking points and concepts and parts of speech are taught readily as the children are "experimenting."

*Wet or dry sand* gives the feeling of rough texture. The concepts empty, full, half full, dry, wet, heavy, light, different, and alike can be learned as the children use different shaped containers to hold amounts.

Both outdoor and indoor sandboxes can be secured. Since many children cannot go to the beach, a sandbox is quite an important piece of equipment for the room. The class may be involved for hours making roads and tunnels and digging ditches and holes. Jelly molds, sieves, plastic cups, bottles, funnels, ladles, teapots, brushes, eggbeaters, and pitchers can inspire a variety of sand activities.

*Water play* is excellent for experimentation. A pitcher for pouring rice and sand is a must, for it teaches muscle control. The concepts empty, deep, full, shallow, hollow, sink, and float can be learned.

The children enjoy using a sponge or large brush and painting with water. At one center a group of children "painted" the fence back of the school. The same group watched a pan of ice melt and steam coming from a teakettle.

*Block building* brings in concepts of thick, thin, tall, long, short, narrow, and wide. Seal the ends of milk cartons, cover them with contact paper or let the children paint them, and use them for blocks.

*Clay* provides muscular experience in pounding, patting, kneading, and moulding. The child expresses himself in something he considers useful and beautiful. He may make pies, cakes, candy, vegetables, dishes, snakes, fruit, cats, pumpkins, eggs, beads, marbles, or nests.

## WINDING ACTIVITIES

Save large spools, such as those from typewriter ribbons, adhesive tape, or Scotch Tape, for winding string or yarn. Winding develops both large and small muscles and improves coordination. Children like to accompany this activity with words.

> Wind, wind, wind, wind,
> Around, around I go.
> I wind the string around, around,
> Slowly, slowly ⎯⎯⎯⎯⎯ Slow!

## RECOGNITION OF OBJECTS

Place a small object in each toe of five brightly colored socks. Ask the children to guess what is in each sock by feeling the shape of the object. Change the objects often.

## SORTING OBJECTS

Cover cigar boxes with contact paper and fill them with a mixture of supplies such as beads, buttons, ice cream sticks, paper clips, and crayons to be sorted into categories according to color, use, material, or size. This activity improves small muscle coordination and sharpens observation. Cut a rectangular felt piece for each child to work on and make his sorting activities easier.

## PAINT PRINTING

Mix powdered paint with water and a little liquid starch. Spread it on butcher paper with a brush. Ask the children to create their own designs by stamping with empty spool ends, cookie cutters, bottle caps, jar lids, corks, carrot sections, or potato pieces that have been cut into a variety of shapes. The children will experiment with these shapes and experience pleasure from reproducing the repeated shape quickly and satisfactorily.

—O.M.A.

## PLAYING JACK FROST

Beat suds made from soap flakes until a fluffy mixture is obtained. The children pretend to be Jack Frost and dab the mixture on the windows. The designs can be sponged off easily.

## SPONGE PAINTING

Dip a small sponge into water, squeeze it so that there will be no dripping, and let the children express pictures by making designs on the chalkboard. Amount of space determines the number of children who can work at a time. Permanent painting with sponges can be achieved with tempera or newsprint.

## DROPPING ONE BY ONE

When a child picks up one article at a time and drops it into a can or box, his finger dexterity is improved. Show him how to use beads, grains of corn, small pebbles, or blocks. The child enjoys the sounds made when there are different sizes of boxes or cans.

The children may take turns dropping several of the same objects into a container and then shaking it for others to guess the objects used.

## EXPERIMENTATION WITH DROPS

Ask the children to take turns dropping water from a medicine dropper to improve finger-muscle control. Note that each drop which falls will be the same size. For variation, add food coloring to the water.

Discuss tiny baby animals that are fed with medicine droppers.

## BEAN BAGS

Some children are afraid of a hard ball. Nearly all can catch a bean bag. The bean bag should not be stuffed too full because the looseness makes it easier to catch. Six to eight-inch squares of durable cotton scraps doubled and sewed round the edges make good bean bags. Stuff them with beans to make a fine toss game.

## PEELING AND SPREADING

Tangerines are easy for the child to peel if he is shown how to start at the stem end. Oranges can be quartered by the teacher so they may be peeled easily. Demonstrate peeling an apple or a potato.

Bring in jelly, butter, or whipped cream. The children will enjoy spreading their own crackers at snack time with an ice cream stick, tongue depressor, or a small plastic spatula.

## BALANCING

Ask the children to "be black Halloween cats walking along a fence," as they hold their arms out from their sides and step with one foot directly in front of the other. You may want to draw a line with chalk on the floor for this activity.

## CARRYING WITHOUT SPILLING

The children can get experience in carrying a small pan half full of water across the room. With practice they will carry the pan without spilling any water. On their own, they will fill the pan with more and more water to challenge their own balance systems.

## BALANCING ON THE HEAD

Carrying light boxes or small baskets on the head is an experiment which develops the concept of balance. This activity stresses the need for balance and gives the child an opportunity to have a successful coordination performance.

## MAGNET FUN

Large magnets can keep young children happily occupied in a learning situation for hours. Keep a box of objects which magnets will pick up and one which magnets will not attract. Occasionally mix all the objects in one box. Magnets will develop a new field of interest, keener thinking ability, and improved finger dexterity.

Bags of small, magnetized steel bits can be bought at a hardware store. Glue them to the backs of flat pieces of cork. These cork magnets can be used for many purposes. Attach pictures to them with pins and let the children move them about the magnetic board. You may also glue the small magnet bits to small toys and use them for storytelling.

## MAKING A MAGNETIC FLANNELBOARD

Attach a thin sheet of metal or piece of screen to a piece of heavy cardboard. Both materials should be the same size. Cover the metal side with outing flannel drawn tightly and secured to the opposite side with tape. A different color of flannel, cut with pinking shears, may be attached to the back for both utility and neatness.

## MOUNTING

Once a child feels comfortable in the center, he begins to gain confidence and is able to play freely and enjoy working at various activities. A set of pictures cut from magazines and mounted to tagboard may be one of his first activities. The child names what he sees, then tells a story about the pictures. Later, the teacher can cut the pictures apart so that they can be used as puzzles. Mounting his own pictures in a scrapbook will prove a most enjoyable activity for him.

## BRAIDING

Carpet warp, rug yarn, and candlewick make excellent braiding materials. Sheeting cut in two-inch wide strips may be used as long as there are no ravellings. This can be avoided if cutting is done with pinking shears. Attach strands at the top of a chair or ask one child to hold the strands as another braids.

## ZIPPER PURSE

Small zipper purses can be purchased at a five and ten cent store. The children will enjoy zipping and unzipping these purses and filling them with small articles.

## BUTTONING

Bring in discarded coats or dresses for the "dress-up" box. The children can gain experience in buttoning and unbuttoning the buttons as they dress up.

Cut slits in an eight-by-eight inch piece of felt. On another piece, sew on buttons which will fit into the slits so that the children can get additional practice in performing this activity.

## PACKING A SUITCASE

Show the children how to fold clothes and pack them into a suitcase. They will enjoy packing and unpacking garments and will engage in this activity untiringly.

## PRESCHOOL DRAWING OR SCRIBBLING AS A PREPARATION FOR WRITING

Educators have long recognized that practice on large surfaces with chalk or crayons prepares the child for writing. Between the ages of two and four, scribbling is often a favorite activity. If given writing instruments, a child of three will cover a newspaper or chalkboard with scribblings intelligible only to himself, yet scribbles show that the child is beginning to gain motor coordination. As he gains the power to express himself, a resemblance to something he knows can be seen in his drawings. Uncontrolled lines start to take more definite shapes through repetition just as babblings of the infant eventually become intelligible speech.

The child enjoys the movement which crayons and chalk afford him for he can move them any way he likes, making up and down or left and right movements across a page or chalkboard. Sometimes his movements are controlled and sometimes not.

This is a period of experimentation where often ellipses and circles emerge. It is an important part of the tactile stage, so it becomes the task of the teacher to plan scribbling experiences that will be conducive to growth in oculomotor skills.

Scribbles encourage language. Many children organize stories about their scribblings and sometimes use amazing sequence both in scribbles and in the telling. Others make up rhymes as they scribble. Playing a recording will often encourage the child and suggest to him what to draw.

## SCRIBBLING TO NURSERY RHYMES

Spread newspapers on the floor. The child scribbles with crayon as he sings or says a nursery rhyme or listens to a recording of one. Rhymes suggested for scribbling are: "Little Jack Horner," "Little Miss Muffet," "Little Bo-Peep," or "Rain, Rain Go Away."

## SLATES FOR SCRIBBLING

Paint an artist's board, heavy tagboard, or a tablet back with blackboard paint, which can be purchased at any hardware store. Let the paint dry thoroughly, then give it two more coats. The children may have their own scribble slates and wipe their chalk scribblings off with a damp sponge.

## SCRIBBLES

This little wheel goes around and around,
As it runs along the ground.

I swing up high, I swing down low.
Oh, why do I love swinging so!

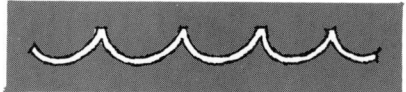

See-saw, see-saw, go up and down with me.
See-saw, see-saw, higher than a tree.

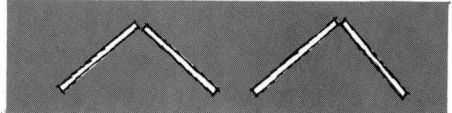

Up-slide, Up-slide! I do this with my hand.
Up-slide! Up-slide! Be careful how you land!

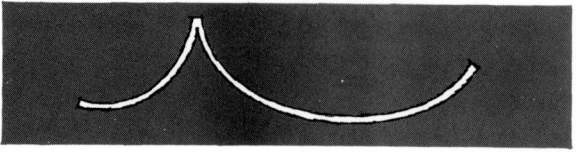

—L.B.S.

The teacher scribbles on the board as she says the verses. She then asks the class to trace the movements in the air with the pointer fingers as they say the rhymes with her. Many children will imitate these scribbles on paper and make up their own verses for others.

### THINGS TO DRAW

Can you draw hills?
Or mountain peaks?
Can you draw heads
With funny beaks?
Can you draw a fence?
Or a lollipop?
Can you draw a tent?
Or a spinning top?
—L.B.S.

Draw these figures very slowly on the chalkboard as you say the rhyme. Do this with sufficient pause between each picture. Ask the children the second time to draw the pictures in the air with the pointer fingers.

### ARTISTS

"I am going to work," said Mr. Thumb.
 (*Hold up thumb.*)
"Now, who will go with me?"
Said Mr. Pointer, "I will go.
 (*Hold up index finger.*)
You need my help, I see."

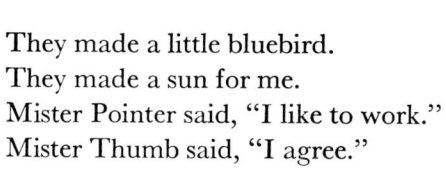

So they worked together
  (*Scribble in air.*)
As happy as could be.
And they made a lovely apple
On an apple tree.

They made a little bluebird.
They made a sun for me.
Mister Pointer said, "I like to work."
Mister Thumb said, "I agree."
              —O.M.A.

Draw the pictures on a chart with crayon, rather than on the board. The rhyme helps the child to understand how to hold his crayon correctly and encourages him to start a picture. Turn over your pictures so that the children will use their own ingenuity and will not copy what you have done. Ask the children to draw pictures in their own creative style.

The poem helps to create an awareness that the thumb and forefinger are important in writing.

## WHAT IS IT?

I made a little circle,
And four times cut it through.
Tell me now what I have made.
Just what did I do?
Do you see a wheel?
Do you see a pie?
Do you see a half an orange?
Or a little birdie's eye?
              —O.M.A.

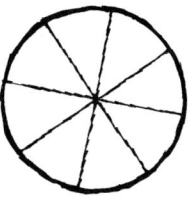

Draw very slowly as you say the rhyme. The children will decide individually what the drawing might be. All answers are acceptable.

## DRAWING AROUND HANDS

Suggest that the child draw around the fingers of his hand. This activity will demand precise coordination. However, the four and five year olds can perform this activity over and over and can become quite skillful at doing it. Write the child's name inside his drawing and post it on the bulletin board.

## SOMETHING TO DRAW

Humps for camels,
A curved snake,
A half a cookie
I can make.
A lightning flash,
A kitten's tail,
A circle,
A stick,
And a boat with a sail.

—L.B.S.

## A SORTING BASKET

This experience combines the brilliant array of colors with the pleasure afforded by feeling soft textures.

Variegated yarn may be purchased in most dime stores. Cut the colors apart into separate pieces. These will be about ten inches long. Two or three skeins will make a generous quantity. Place different colored pieces of the same length in a basket or an attractive box.

The children can work in little groups at a table. Direct them to make piles of the different colors. One child may wish to collect yellow, while another may select all the blue, and so on. After this color discrimination activity, mix all the yarn together again so it will be ready for use another day.

—O.M.A.

## YARN PICTURES

Children enjoy creating their own colorful designs. Lay an 18″ x 24″ black flannelboard on the table. Provide each child with a large spool on which he has wound a generous amount of variegated yarn; he makes his own picture from this yarn. If one end has been secured to the spool, the yarn may be rewound and used again by other children. The vivid colors against the black flannel are very effective.

—O.M.A.

## PERMANENT YARN PICTURES

On ditto paper make large designs of simple objects such as an apple, a house, a leaf, a boat or a balloon. Each child dips a length of colored yarn into a bowl of liquid starch. He squeezes the excess starch through his finger and thumb down to the end of the strand. Then he outlines the picture with the piece of yarn. Allow his picture to dry so that he may take it home.

—O.M.A.

## SMELLS AND TASTES
(A Discussion)

Say: "Your nose has two nostrils. They have little hairs inside. The hairs are nose sweepers that sweep the dust in the air away so that it will not get into your throat. Your nose warms the air you breath so that icy-cold winds won't hurt your lungs.

"Here is a mirror . . . Look at your two nostrils. Take a breath. Feel the air go inside and through your nose. Make it come out your mouth.

"What if your nose were all stopped up and you couldn't breathe well? Has this ever happened to you? Tell about it."

> What if your nose were all stopped up,
> And the smells could not get through?
> What if you couldn't smell apple pie?
> Now just what would you do?

> You couldn't smell a violet,
> Or a cake with nuts and spice.
> You couldn't smell your favorite soap,
> Or an orange that tastes so nice.

Ask: "What is your favorite smell? Tell about it. What do you like to taste best?"

—L.B.S.

## WHEN YOU HAVE A COLD

> When you have a cold, your nose swells inside,
> And that is the place where the germs like to hide.

Ask: "How do you take care of yourself when you have a cold? Go to bed? Drink plenty of water and juice? Blow your nose properly?

"Hold your nostrils and then try to talk. Say *me, new, sing.* How does your talking sound? If you hold your nose, these pretty nose sounds cannot get through." (*These sounds are* "m," "n," *and* "ng.")

## NOSES OF ANIMALS

Say: "How does your pet's nose feel?" If there is a schoolroom pet, have the class to observe it, touch it, and describe its nose.

Compare people's noses with noses of animals. Ask a child to describe his pet's nose. Cats have a good sense of smell that protects them from eating bad food. A hippopotamus has two big nostrils that stick out of the water when he is underneath. An elephant picks up things with his nose. He uses it for a hand. Discuss other animals.

## A SMELLING SESSION

Use several small jars with screw-on covers. Keep waxed paper in the lid covers. Corks may also be used. Place a label on each jar and number it. If the content is liquid, insert a bit of cotton which will prevent evaporation. This "smell" exhibit will be popular with the class. Identification can be a protective measure, since some children are allergic to foods or smells, and if they learn them, they can avoid them. Collect other things relevant to the lives of children, and those they like to smell. Here are some suggestions for contents of the jars.

| | | |
|---|---|---|
| perfume | chocolate | coffee |
| mustard | vanilla | orange peel |
| licorice | bar of soap | bath powder |
| banana | flower petals | lemon extract |
| sage | piece of onion | celery |
| witch hazel | pine cones | wood shavings |
| apple slice | vinegar | peppermint |

Ask: "Which of these do you like to smell?"

Bring in several objects or foods for the class to feel and smell: pine tree branches, soap, bark, candy, flowers, new shoes, ferns or leaves, egg shells.

## TASTE
### (A Discussion)

Say: "Your nose and tongue are good friends. Your nose tells your tongue that something may not taste good and then you may not eat it.

"Your tongue has little taste buds. At the end of your tongue are taste buds for sweet tastes. What are some sweet tastes? (*Responses.*)

"Look at your tongue. (*Supply mirrors.*) The sides of your tongue have little taste buds for things that are salty or sour. Name something salty. Name something sour. (*Responses.*) Look at the sides of your tongue.

"The back of your tongue has taste buds for bitter foods like chocolate. Think of something else that is bitter. (*Responses.*) Look at the back of your tongue.

"Your tongue pushes food into the back of your mouth so that it can be swallowed and go down the tube into your stomach."

## YOUR TONGUE
### (A Discussion)

Say: "Your tongue is important. Why? (*Responses.*) It helps you taste, chew, swallow, and talk. It lies on the floor of your mouth. It is pink and velvety-looking.

"Look at your tongue in the mirror. You can move it all around inside your mouth. Imagine that your mouth is a room and your tongue is a broom. Sweep the ceiling. Sweep the walls. Sweep the floor. Shake the dust out of your broom. Now say *loo, loo, loo.* What did your tongue do? Say *gah, gah, gah.* What did it do? Say *thumb, thumb, thumb.* What did your tongue do? Did it peek out between your teeth?

"Do you use your tongue when you say your name? Say your name. Did your tongue move?"

Creating an awareness of the tongue in speaking is important, particularly if some of the children are having difficulty in talking. Ask the child to say his name and tell what his tongue does.

## TASTES

Ask: "What do you think tastes good to a cow? A horse? A dog? A kitten? A frog? A squirrel? A rabbit? Do we all eat the same foods? Do we eat any foods that animals eat?

"If you could have only one thing to eat, what would it be?" As a surprise, bring in one or two of the favorite foods mentioned for the children to taste.

## MAKING GINGERBREAD AND POPPING CORN

Bring in an electric oven or roaster. Buy two packages of gingerbread mix. Help each child to stir about two tablespoons of mix with a teaspoon of water. Grease some small muffin tins. Ask the children to pour their own mixtures into the tins for baking. Surprisingly enough, each child will remember his own muffin. Ginger cookies also can be made by adding just enough water to make thick bread dough, rolling it with a rolling pin, and cutting it with a cookie cutter.

Use a small electric stove and bring in a couple of packages of "popcorn-in-skillet." The class takes turns shaking the skillet. When the popcorn is ready, each child may have some on a napkin.

### Supplementary References

Aliki: *My Five Senses*, Thomas Y. Crowell Company, New York, 1962.
Borten, Helen: *Do You Hear What I Hear?* Abelard-Schuman Ltd., New York, 1960.
———: *Do You See What I See?* Abelard-Schuman Ltd., New York, 1959.
Gay, Zhenya: *Look!* The Viking Press, Inc., New York, 1952.
Gibson, Myra: *What Is Your Favorite Thing to Touch?* Grosset and Dunlap, Inc., New York, 1965.
Schlein, Miriam: *Heavy Is a Hippopotamus*, William R. Scott, Inc., New York, 1954.
———: *Shapes*, William R. Scott, Inc., New York, 1952.
Shapp, Charles and Martha: *Let's Find Out What's Light and What's Heavy*, Franklin Watts, Inc., New York, 1961.

CHAPTER 3

# The Wonderful World of Play and Make-Believe

Childhood is a time of wonderment, curiosity, and investigation. Every day, a secret gate leading into a garden of sensory challenges opens to glorious adventure with things and with words.

Friedrich Froebel stated that "play for the young child is not mere amusement seeking, but the means by which he gathers information of the world around him."[1] Froebel believed that children are like young plants. If the seed is deposited in rich soil, it takes root. If it gets sufficient moisture and sun, it puts forth leaves, flowers, and fruit. But if the seed falls upon stony ground, and is left without light or moisture, it will grow stunted or die.

If resources for play are meager, or if the child has been restricted in his play activities, there will be little chance for him to observe, gain insight, and grow through that insight. Deprived of play experiences, he may reach adolescence completely unprepared to assume adult roles in life because he has lacked activity where he could pretend and "play" the people of a grown-up world. It is a widely accepted theory that favorable play conditions in childhood foster initiative and creativity in adult life. The significance of play in early childhood education is recognized by educators *as a means of self-teaching,* if it is properly motivated.

*What is play?* Play is conducted generally for its own sake, for the absorbing pleasure of the activity itself. Work is performed for the future good of the individual. The work of an architect, a musician, an artist, or an author, however, may *feel* like play since it expresses the personality and comforts the individual, giving him a sense of well-being and accomplishment. Winston Churchill, for instance, considered

[1] Friedrich Froebel, *Mother Play and Nursery Songs,* Lee and Shepard, Boston, 1878.

brick laying a form of relaxed play, whereas this activity to someone else could be sheer boredom and hard labor. Actually, there can be no line of demarcation between many forms of work and play. To a child especially, work and play can be synonymous.

In the early part of the 18th century, play was considered by many proper and exacting people to be a waste of time and "sheer folly." An American minister expressed this thinking in a published sermon: "We prohibit play in the strongest terms . . . let this rule be observed with the strictest nicety; for those who play when they are young, will also play when they are old."

Fortunately, the succeeding century brought forth many changes in philosophy. With the establishment of the kindergarten came the realization that play was of serious and deep significance. Parents discovered that when play-pleasures were provided, babies stopped crying. When toes were tweaked as the mother chanted, "This little pig went to market," the baby crowed and gurgled with delight. Many mothers employed the "Mother Plays" of Friedrich Froebel; these were the beginnings of finger plays, which are used widely in nursery schools and kindergartens today.

Studies have been made of the play habits of animals. The young kitten and the puppy are playful, while the young guinea pig and the chicken are settled. Generally, the higher the species stands in intelligence, the more it appears to indulge in play. Each animal has its own play behavior. The young kitten teases a ball of string in the same manner that its mother teases a mouse. This suggests that play for the sake of play diminishes as the creature matures and more constructive forms of play enter in to prepare the animal or individual for functioning productively in the future.

*Everything is play to a young child.* Everything is a laboratory where he finds places to climb and crawl, where he builds bridges, plants seeds, and puts challenging puzzles together. Everything is expansive, dramatic, and marvelous!

It is through informal play that the child learns best. He acquires more knowledge quickly, however, *if he chooses his play* activity since personal involvement insures interest. It is through motor acts of play that the child works off temper and aggression, channels anger, and exerts self-control. It is through play that he gains a self-image, grows, expresses his feelings freely, and carries through his ideas in constructive ways. It is through play that he develops judgment, speed, strength, and coordination. It is through play that a little child comes to trust and rely upon friends, and prove his own worth to them. As he earns their respect, he gains satisfaction in his own abilities. Eventually, through play, he attains a basis for abstract thinking and spacial relationships.

Play must involve that necessary stage of make-believe, formlessness, and random experimentation—with unique expressions of them—before a child can weave together his experiences and knowledge into a creation which is *his alone*. Play is valuable for the learning it involves, for self-expression, and for the pleasure it gives.

Children of four and five, unless they have had nursery school experiences, engage mainly in solitary or parallel play which is unrelated to a group. This kind of play takes place alone or alongside another child. Even as a teacher works with a group, a child may leave the situation and return to solitary or parallel play, indicating that he is not yet ready for a larger, cooperative venture. The teacher, however, must continue to encourage group activity so that the child has those experiences necessary for self-sustained and cooperative play activities in the school yard and classroom.

Most play occurs when a child is alone, but gradually he learns to share with a peer and finally with a small group. Eventually, he may enter into some larger group activities for singing, listening to a story, or playing a rhythmic game. This socializing process occurs as soon as the child is ready to give, take, and share graciously. But until the child has experienced parallel play and play with a small group, he will operate on his own.

Anyone who watches a little child at play can observe a day-by-day unfolding process. The child puts a puzzle together which previously was too difficult for him to master, or paints a picture of a rainbow because now he is aware of color. Reaching out with his muscles and senses, he gains power and understanding of things he can or cannot do for himself. Nobody has to tell him how to build a garage. He is the architectural authority. The blocks provide an expression for his thoughts, and represent a self-imposed challenge which he meets with satisfaction. Thus, he gains a buoyant sense of accomplishment. Next, there may be an airport or a fire station where he becomes a pilot or a fireman. As he plays this role, he gains insight into the character and function of the person he emulates.

The progressive playing of adult activities helps the child to unfold and find his identity. In short, the young child experiments with a bit of life every time he arranges a situation in his mind and brings his creation to fruition. The teacher is a mere observer who offers encouraging comments or questions now and then as she senses that the child welcomes her interest. She may verbalize what he sees, hears, and does, and thus give impetus to his development and use of language.

A child from an environment of limited experiences and resources must learn to play since he may find no place for it in the home setting where play patterns should begin. The child's world may be barren and may present relatively few opportunities for expression or even imagination away from the street or the fire escape. One child from an impoverished climate entered the education center, found a corner, and sat in it, claiming it as his own. For the first time, he felt that he could assume ownership of something, so he said repeatedly, "This is my place." Eventually, he established a one-to-one relationship with the teacher, made friends with one peer, then another, and discarded the corner since he no longer needed it to feel safe and comfortable.

The child's world may be so empty of enrichment that he cannot function at a level which starts with simple, normal experiences. Therefore, it is desirable to begin with those people and experiences he knows best. If there is a fruit vendor or a garbage collector in his neighborhood, emphasis on community workers can begin here. If Daddy drives a truck, the child can be encouraged to build one from blocks and *be* a driver.

The child tells much about himself through play. One teacher made a list of observations on behavior patterns as she watched the children move in and out of the playhouse. She noted that certain children acted out situations, while others were passive. She heard them communicate ideas to one another, and listened to them convert fantasy to realism, solve playhouse problems, and indulge in self-talk.

"No doubt," the teacher said, "the child was happiest when he was doing something constructive like building or painting. His inimitable creations gave him strong feelings of self-worth and the only properties he needed were blocks or a paintbrush."

Children who have had the advantages of play are more likely to love, to become sensitive people, and to develop standards of behavior and principles of moral conduct. A child who can attend an early childhood education center is, indeed, fortunate in respect to these early, character building experiences.

## TOYS ARE MAGIC

Toys are the magic instruments through which young children learn. They provide the tools for intellectual, emotional, social, and aesthetic development.

According to Dr. Elizabeth Lodge Rees,[2] toys are universal and every toy has a history. The ball and the doll are used in every culture and in every country in the world. Yo-yos, kites, and tin soldiers are also extremely old.

Joseph Lee's book, *Play in Education,* which was published in 1915, contained these statements: "Play to the child is what work is to man. Toys to children are what tools are to grownups." At the end of World War I, the United States was busily engaged in manufacturing toys. One toy manufacturer in 1921 advocated that toys should be a means of stimulating growth and thinking processes. By 1939, 95 percent of all toys in the United States were made in this country. "Toys for learning" have been improved upon and wide varieties are manufactured so that now, one can buy toys for almost any specific learning experience.

Since there is a plethora of toys flooding the market, educators should evaluate toys and equipment carefully before purchases are made. Each toy should be judged by such authorities as curriculum specialists, professors of education, psychologists, safety councils, and, of course, the children themselves. Often toys are labeled to show that they have been tested and approved by a recognized and qualified organization that specializes in evaluation.

Emma D. Sheehy notes in her book, *The Fives and Sixes Go to School,* that "a room must talk to children."[3] To create this warm, personal feeling, educators must provide toys and equipment which enable the child to achieve a healthy, creative development so that his physical, psychological, and intellectual needs are met. Thought provoking equipment is needed to meet individual and group interests.

A few toys and educational materials used widely with young children are listed here.

| | |
|---|---|
| Blunt scissors | Clocks |
| (also left-handed ones) | Play dough and clay |
| Water toys | Crayons |
| Crawling-through apparatus | Playhouse |
| Toy suitcases | Playhouse furniture |
| Push and pull toys | Telephones |
| Doll carriages and dolls | Blocks |

[2] Elizabeth Lodge Rees, *A Doctor Looks at Toys,* Charles C. Thomas, Springfield, Massachusetts, 1961.
[3] Emma D. Sheehy, *The Fives and Sixes Go to School,* Holt, Rinehart and Winston, New York, 1954.

| | |
|---|---|
| Family dolls | Wagons and tricycles |
| Large balls and beanbags | Stick horses |
| Magnets and magnifying glasses | Painting materials |
| | Hopscotch games |
| Large cartons | Wooden and stuffed animals |
| Color games | |
| Musical instruments (cymbals, triangles, etc.) | Calendars |
| | Number wheels |
| Matching games | Peg boards |
| Music boxes | Globe |
| Stereoscope with a box of pictures | Beads and peg boards |
| | Cages for pets |
| Puzzles | Hand puppets |

### MAKE A TOY SCRAPBOOK

Staple sheets of sturdy wrapping paper together to make a scrapbook. Ask the mothers to find large pictures of toys in magazines, discarded books, or mail order catalogs and send them to school to be pasted into the toy scrapbook. Place the book on the browsing table.

### BRINGING TOYS TO SCHOOL

Plan a unit on toys and encourage the children to bring favorite toys to school. The purposes of this unit are to increase the children's appreciation and enjoyment for toys, to help encourage safety in the use of toys, to encourage children to care for toys properly, to provide occasions for conversation and sharing, and to give opportunities for creative growth. To help guide this activity and achieve constructive purposes, ask the following questions:

What is this toy made of?
Does it move? How?
How do you play with it to keep from breaking it?
How do you and your friends play with it?
What would you do if something went wrong with it?

### A TABLE PLAYHOUSE

Turn a small table upside down. Lay a twin-sized sheet over it so that the sheet will hang down evenly on all sides. Cut the material from the floor to the top of the table and overlap it at the four corners. Attach snaps, pin with safety pins, or sew the corner edges together. The children will enjoy playing in this make-believe playhouse. Read *A Little House of Your Own*[4] to the group.

## BLOCK PLAY

Blocks provide rich experiences in dramatic play. Shoeboxes can be converted into building bricks. Tape each lid securely to the box and glue on bits of wallpaper or pictures to make an attractive design. Cover the box completely and shellac it for durability. The children can help with the covering and designing.

## ODDS-AND-ENDS BOX

This box will serve many areas involving creativity. Cover the sides with brightly-colored contact paper containing an interesting design, or let the children make and paste on their own designs from scraps of wall paper. The mothers can help fill the box with these suggested odds and ends:

| | |
|---|---|
| Spools | Pie tins |
| Large beads | Pipe cleaners |
| Foil | Cancelled stamps |
| Wheels | Salt boxes |
| Sacks | Scraps of paper |
| Bells | Bottle tops |
| Feathers | Drinking straws |

[4] Beatrice Schenk de Regniers, *A Little House of Your Own*, Harcourt, Brace, and World, New York, 1954.

| | |
|---|---|
| Spoons | Paper plates |
| Sponges | Egg cartons |
| Clothespins | Felt, silk, and gingham |
| Apothecary bottles | swatches |
| Buttons | Ice cream sticks |
| Small blocks | Milk cartons (½ pint size) |
| Wallpaper | Berry boxes |
| Broom straws | Shirt cardboards |
| Velvet pieces | Corrugated paper |

The children may choose items to experiment with, to make a collage or a picture, form a three dimensional, or make something original. The materials can be used for dramatic play or creative dramatics.

## NEW THINGS FROM OLD

Discarded articles can be solicited from parents and used in many ways to serve the needs of the children and the center.

*Cans*—Banks, paint containers, birdhouses
*Old calendars*—Number games, numerals for clocks
*Shirt bosom cards*—Puzzles, backing for mounting pictures
*Nylon stockings*—Material for braiding activities, stuffed dolls
*Spools*—Devices for stringing or winding, for dipping in paint to stamp designs on paper
*Newspapers*—Scribbling, tearing, cutting
*Chicken feathers*—Indian play, trimmings
*Bottle tops*—Play money, dishes, wheels
*Boxes*—Baskets, peep shows, puppets, card files, drawers (stacking boxes all of the same size together and using buttons for knobs)
*Buttons*—Eyes for puppets, counting and stringing devices
*Socks*—Puppets, bags for small treasures, containers for marbles and jacks

## DRAMATIC PLAY

Dramatic play is an unstructured, spontaneous interpretation of real-life situations performed in solitary or parallel fashion. It is a creative activity involving both movement and oral language. It begins with the child's interest: his home, people in the environment, and inanimate things. As he imagines himself to be a veterinarian, a pilot, or a carpenter, the child imitates people and reenacts what he thinks they say and do. He realizes how it feels to be someone else through his performance. He uninhibitedly projects himself into situations, develops sensitivity and understanding toward others, and enriches his own personality.

What a child does in dramatization is wholly exploratory and experimental since he hasn't yet acquired the experience nor the background to bring full knowledge to the situation. Through this make-believe enactment, he plays a supermarket clerk from what he understands of the clerk. Playing the clerk brings him one step closer to an understanding of the worker and how he functions in the community.

In dramatic play, the child conceives an idea, plans his own dramatization, and then performs. To give his ideas concrete form, he may need the "dress-up" materials, the playhouse, blocks, boxes, or other properties which will help him to put his ideas together and produce something that will give him gratification.

There are several stages to be considered in this creative expression which help the child to progress from one idea to the eventual concrete and satisfying conclusion:

1. He must prepare for the enactment. Experience, a feeling that it is the right time to proceed, oral facility with language, and an ability to interrelate knowledge and imagination are the tools he needs.

2. He must use creative and critical thinking when deciding upon possible procedures.

3. He must blend together judgment, perception, discovery, information, experience, and imagination as he sets up his properties. During this third stage, he may come to the conclusion that everything is working out well for him and he will proceed to another constructive step.

4. He has worked out a problem and its solution; now he is confident to try again at another time. If the progress is not satisfactory, he will end the activity of his own accord, and proceed to something else. He will eventually see his efforts completed. There is actually no one beginning or end to dramatic play.

The teacher's role is one of *observing and guiding*. Guidance may be a smile of approval, an affirmative nod of the head, or a verbalization of the child's procedures. This latter form of guidance is called parallel talk and it encourages the child to engage in self-talk as he plays. Self-talk is important to language development. Actually, the teacher must allow the child complete freedom in planning and working. She refrains from giving unasked advice as to "what might be better" or "what could be changed." She is an onlooker and a subtle commentator who feels the spirit of play and adventure with the child, and reacts favorably and encouragingly to his verbal expressions and his procedures.

The teacher tries to help the unsure child establish confidence, realizing that creative play will not take place until he has faith in his own abilities. Her ability to effect a one-to-one relationship, her tone of voice, her relaxed speech, and her sensitivity will win over the most timid, unsure child and calm down the most hyperactive one.

The teacher does not consider whether a child *can* build an airport out of an old box. She simply makes such an activity possible by providing a box that he can feel belongs to him; he can demolish it through pounding, sitting, or climbing without evoking censorship. However, when a child demonstrates an interest, the teacher may make a few comments to spur on the play, such as, "We are all looking forward to seeing what you make." At no time does she give an impression of hurry or impatience.

Sometimes the teacher may feel self-conscious at "letting go" and dramatizing a poem, story, rhythm, or situation with the children. Although it would be in her favor to become more expressive, she still can motivate creativity in her children. With experience, practice, and conscious effort, she will eventually acquire a naturalness in these situations.

These things a teacher should keep in mind in providing the climate for dramatic play:

Recognize and accept individual differences.
Awaken the mind of the child through use of picturesque words.
Encourage creative expression.
Study the child's potential and help to develop a positive self-image.
Plan for painting, play, poetry, and story times with enthusiasm.
Be warm, dynamically interested, and sensitive to the child's needs.
Realize that individual differences in teachers help the child to adapt to different people in an adult world.

To awaken creative responses, both teacher and children will enjoy a period designed to evoke critical thinking and bring out creative verbalization. The teacher may use such questions and statements as:

What would happen if there were no more pilots in the world? Chickens? Cows?

What would happen if the garage you just made became real?

How would you feel if everything in this room were blue?

Close your eyes and tell me what you see when I say, "Policeman."

What would you do if you couldn't get into a supermarket you built?

Think of some different ways this box could be used.

Dramatic play can be motivated and can grow out of the discussions that occur during this creative language period.

The values of dramatic play are many:

The child feels the need for oral language to express his thoughts. His ability to verbalize is facilitated if he is permitted to express his thoughts freely.

The child uses both cognitive and creative thinking.

He learns better how to arrive at conclusions and make decisions.

He develops a better understanding toward himself and others through listening, sharing, taking turns, and cooperating.

He explores, plans, and make events come to life.

## EXPRESSING WITHOUT WORDS

Pantomime is a language of movement through which the individual conveys who he is, where he is, what he is doing, and how he feels. Its intrinsic purposes are to create imagery and to encourage children to communicate when they have no words with which to express themselves. Pantomime makes situations come to life. The young child needs only head, torso, arms, fingers, legs, and feet to express his thoughts and feelings when "Dance of the Reed Flutes" by Tchaikovsky is played. His thoughts find an outlet in movement as all parts of his body respond to the music. When the teacher reads "The Swing" by Robert Louis Stevenson, the child will catch the feeling intended as the voice paints this vivid picture of movement.

Pantomime is an aid to growth and development of all children, but particularly of the young child whose senses radiate and respond naturally and uninhibitedly to stories, poetry, and music. Even the most shy child will join with a group when he feels secure and ready. As he notes the whole-hearted enjoyment of other children, he gradually gains confidence and finally adjusts to the animated activity with his peers.

The emotionally disturbed child releases his frustrations and tensions, for the rhythmic movements help instill harmony and peace within him. A gift for this type of physical expression is often shown in children who seem to have few abilities. It is desirable to let each child succeed somewhere, and free expression allows him to do so. For the child with many gifts, each medium of expression is another enrichment to his life.

Pantomime is an excellent way of introducing the class to the poems which normally are included in children's literature anthologies and in books of poetry. Many of these selections are easily pantomimed as the teacher reads them. The poems listed at the end of the unit "Children are Poets," page 19, are excellent for this purpose.

Music with movement sometimes can reach a child who cannot be approached in any other way. If a child has experienced pressures and severe conformity at home, here at least is one place where he can try his wings without fear of censorship. He can improvise and *be a child*. In fact, he can be anything he likes as he communicates in a non-verbal way and feels safe in an environment which allows him to express himself and win approval.

It is best to begin pantomime with music that paints pictures in the mind, arouses imagination, and tells a story. Encourage a child to tell the story through movements which the music tells *him*. There is no "right" story; *his* story is an honest reaction to what he has heard or felt.

The teacher can help the children to comprehend an idea by associating it with their familiar experiences. After reading Christina Rossetti's "The Wind" to the class, she may ask: "Have you felt the wind on your face? What can a strong wind do? If you were a wind, show how you would move?" Ask the child to listen to a dripping faucet, a whirling lawn mower, or any other familiar and easily available sound. Say: "What does it seem to be saying? What do those sounds make you feel like doing?" Encourage the child to act out the words or mimic the action. He may "sing" the story as he would a nursery rhyme.

Traditional stories and nursery rhymes may be pantomimed without music as the teacher reads them.

## ACTING OUT NURSERY RHYMES

To the chanting of a rhyme, children may make up their own movements. Spontaneous dialogue and participation in saying the rhyme should be encouraged. Though concentration is intrinsically upon movement, words inspire movement and movement stimulates free verbalization. Rhymes which lend themselves readily to pantomime are:

Little Miss Muffet     Little Boy Blue     Jack Be Nimble
Little Jack Horner     Jack and Jill     Pat-a-Cake

Further suggestions for acting out nursery rhymes may be found on pages 139–147.

## ACTING OUT FAMILIAR TRADITIONAL TALES

Traditional folk and fairy tales are easy for children to pantomime because these stories contain a development of plot which uses repetition of ideas and events. A teacher who has watched a group act out "The Three Billy Goats Gruff" realizes the values of the experience provided by this activity.

"Chicken Little,"[5] another of the favorite tales, can be pantomimed easily by a group. The children may decide what movements to use after the following portion of the story is read:

One day Chicken Little was in the garden.
A pea popped out of its pod and hit her on her teeny-weeny, feathery tail.
"Oh, oh!" cried Chicken Little.
"The sky is falling. I must go tell the King."
So Chicken Little hurried away to tell the King.

Continue the story and have groups of children take turns pantomiming the different parts.

## LITTLE DUCK
### (A Group Pantomime)

The group acts out this story by imitating the movements of the teacher. Suggested actions for pantomiming:

*Run*—Slap thighs quickly.
*Walk*—Slap thighs slowly.
*Big steps*—Thump fists on chest.
*Swim*—Rub palms of hands together rapidly.
*Bang*—Clap hands once.

---

[5] Louise Binder Scott, *Tell-Again Story Cards, Level I,* McGraw-Hill, Inc., New York, 1967.

Little Duck was scolded for eating too many bugs, so he said to his mother, "I am going to run away. Then I can eat anything I like."

So Little Duck left the barnyard and his own dear mother who loved him. He walked down the road on his little flat feet. (*Action.*)

Little Duck met a cow who was munching hay.

"Have some," offered the cow.

Hay was much too rough for Little Duck to eat because he had no teeth to chew it. He thanked the cow for her thoughtfulness and walked on. (*Action.*) Suddenly, he heard a big BANG. (*Clap.*) Little Duck trembled with fright.

"Oh, oh, that must be a hunter with a gun," he cried.

Little Duck ran away from there fast. (*Action.*) Then Little Duck heard some BIG, LOUD steps coming toward him. (*Action.*) He hid in some bushes until the big steps went by.

"Why, that was only a HORSE," said Little Duck happily.

Little Duck met a dog with a bone.

"Have some," said the dog.

"No, thank you," said Little Duck as he walked on. (*Action.*)

Little Duck came to a pond. He jumped into the water and swam across the pond. (*Action.*) He climbed out of the water and walked on. (*Action.*)

Suddenly Little Duck heard a fierce sound, "Grrrrrrowl, Rrrrrrruff." Right in front of Little Duck sat a fox!

"Yum, yum," said the fox, smacking his lips. "Duck for dinner!"

"Oh, oh!" cried Little Duck as he began to run. (*Action.*)

He ran and ran faster and faster. (*Action.*) He came to the pond and swam across. (*Action.*) The fox was right behind him.

Suddenly there was a loud BANG. (*Action.*) When the fox heard the big noise, he turned and ran away. (*Action.*)

Little Duck felt safer now, but he kept right on running. (*Action.*) He passed the horse—and the cow—and the dog with a bone. Soon he was back in the barnyard with his own dear mother who loved him.

He said:

"I'm a little duck as you can see,
And this barnyard is the best place for me."

Little Duck knew that being scolded was for his own good, and he never ate too many bugs again. He never ran away again, either.

—L.B.S.

Ask: "What made the big bang?"

## ELF IN THE RAIN

Once there was an elf who lived under a toadstool. One day, the elf went for a walk. (*Slap thighs gently.*) All at once, it began to rain. (*Tap fingers lightly on table or floor.*)

Now out in the meadow a little, bumpy, lumpy toad came hopping and jumping along. (*Make hopping motion with arms.*) He saw the toadstool and crept under it to get out of the rain. (*Hands on top of head.*)

The elf was dancing around a rosebush when the rain came, and he skipped very fast to get back to his toadstool. (*Slap thighs rapidly.*) When the elf reached the toadstool, there sat the bumpy, lumpy toad.

"Oh, dear," sighed the bumpy, lumpy toad. "I didn't know this toadstool was your home. I'll go away at once."

But the elf wouldn't hear of such a thing.

"Please stay, little toad," he said. "This toadstool is big enough for both of us."

So there they sat side by side, the elf and the bumpy, lumpy toad. (*Repeat action of rain.*) Soon the rain stopped and each went his own way. Then the sun came out. (*Make circle with arms.*) A big rainbow came into the sky and many beautiful colors could be seen. (*Children hold colored scarves above heads.*)

—L.B.S.

Read the story slowly, phrasing carefully to give the children time for movements. For variation, choose children to act out the elf, toad, rain, sun, and rainbow. Six children may hold blue, orange, red, green, yellow, and purple scarves to make the rainbow. On subsequent readings, encourage children to demonstrate other actions for the story or act it out adding episodes.

## BEATING RHYTHM

A tom-tom can be used to supply simple rhythms for children to respond to with movements. The teacher may use a soft tom-tom or construct one by stretching a piece of inner tube over a coffee can and tying the tubing with shoelaces or a strip of the rubber to hold it in place. Either one of these instruments will provide a gentle, soothing rhythm.

A drum which produces a louder sound may be over-stimulating or distracting, especially to very young or nervous children. When the sound is muted, the drum calls attention to the rhythm of the music and not to the instrument itself.

A good way to begin is to beat out children's names: *Shir-ley, Car-o-line,* or *Mar-y Belle.* Ask: "Is the drum calling someone? Who can it be?" Sometimes young children will learn to beat the syllables of their own names and of other names as well.

After a child has identified the syllables of his name, repeat the rhythm several times so that a small group of children can beat out the pattern.

## AROUND THE HOUSE

Ask the children to show how they would perform these actions around the house:

Brushing teeth         Washing hands
Combing hair           Dusting furniture
Winding a clock        Eating cereal
Taking a bath          Beating eggs
Drinking milk          Sweeping the floor

## PANTOMIME ALL THE YEAR ROUND

These following pantomimic ideas tie in with the months and seasons:

*September*: Raking the yard; walking to school.
*October*: Pretending to be falling leaves, a scarecrow coming to life, a witch riding a broom.
*November*: Pretending to be an Indian; strutting like a turkey.
*December*: Trimming a Christmas tree; hanging up stockings.
*January*: Rolling and throwing snowballs; pretending to be whirling snow.
*February*: Walking like polar bears; pretending to be a melting snowman.
*March*: Flying a kite; whirling like the wind.
*April*: Planting seeds; wading through puddles.
*May*: Pretending to be growing flowers; performing a Maypole dance.
*June*: Picking flowers; packing a suitcase.
*July*: Marching in a parade; saluting the flag.
*August*: Swimming; having a picnic.

## FOLLOW THE LEADER

The leader makes simple movements which the children can **imitate** easily. Play "The March of the Toys," by Victor Herbert as background music to stimulate such movements as:

| | |
|---|---|
| Bow from the waist | Touch the knee |
| Twist the hands | Flop like a rag doll |
| Jump up and down | Swim like a fish |
| Walk like a soldier | Gallop |
| Hop on one foot | Nod the head |
| Turn around | Skip, step, and hop |
| Fly like a bird | Sway like a tree in the wind |

## WHAT CAN I DO?

I can spin around like a top.
    Look at me! Look at me!
I have feet and I can hop.
    Look at me! Look at me!
I have hands and I can clap.
    Look at me, look at me!
I can fold them in my lap.
    Look at me, look at me!

—L.B.S.

The children say the refrain and act out the other lines as the teacher reads them. This selection can be used to prepare children for an immediate listening activity.

## THE TRADITIONAL NURSERY RHYME

Though the nursery rhyme entered the door of the child's literary experience over 200 years ago, it has always been an integral part of the speech experiences of the young child in both home and classroom. Speech sounds which many young children have difficulty pronouncing within words are contained in many of the poems. References to some of the speech sounds are made in the instructions accompanying the rhymes presented in this chapter.

Memorization is easy so that many of the rhymes provide an opportunity for the children to engage in immediate verbal participation and dramatic activity. At the same time, attention span seems to increase. Intonations and emphasis upon rhyming words provide help, especially for the child who has first learned to speak another language.

The memorable language of the Mother Goose or nursery rhyme has its appeal in rhythm, imagination, humor, surprise, and nonsense. Children derive untold pleasure from the primitive repetition, chanting, and suggestions for body action which these rhymes afford. The musical quality, cadence, and acceleration of these classics have prompted many musicians to write tunes for them.

## HUMPTY DUMPTY

Humpty Dumpty sat on a wall.
Humpty Dumpty had a great fall.
All the King's horses and all the King's men.
Couldn't put Humpty Dumpty together again.

With folded arms and crossed feet, the children sit in small chairs and rock from side to side in rhythm to the verse. On the line, ". . . had a great fall," the children lean forward and touch the floor with their fingertips. On the line, "All the King's horses and all the King's men," thighs are hit alternately to suggest galloping. Hands are held out for the last line of the rhyme.

Cut an oval piece of pink outing flannel for the flannelboard. Cut eyes, nose, mouth, arms, and legs from the scraps. The children will enjoy putting Humpty together again after the fall.

## HICKORY, DICKORY, DOCK

Hickory, dickory, dock! (*Partners swing arms from left to right.*)
The mouse ran up the clock. (*Partners exchange places.*)
The clock struck one. (*Clap.*)
The mouse ran down. (*Partners return to their original positions.*)
Hickory, dickory dock! (*Repeat swinging motion.*)

Accentuate the "k" sound in *dock* and *clock* for a ticking effect.

## SING A SONG OF SIXPENCE

Sing a song of sixpence,
A pocketful of rye.
Four-and-twenty blackbirds
Baked in a pie.

When the pie was opened,
The birds began to sing.
Wasn't that a dainty dish
To set before the King?

The children join hands and form a large circle. The teacher chooses from two to six "birds," depending upon the number of children in the group. The "birds" squat in the circle (pie) and the children walk around them saying or singing the rhyme. As they say, "When the pie was opened," they raise their hands and "birds" jump up and say, "Tweet, tweet." Let different children be "birds."

Another idea is to ask the children to sit in small circles with their feet together. "When the pie is opened," the children jump to their feet.

A slight stress on the sound of "s" in *sing, song, set,* and *sixpence* will help the children to hear this sound.

## LITTLE BO-PEEP

Little Bo-Peep has lost her sheep,
  (*Shade eyes with hand.*)
And doesn't know where to find them;
  (*Extend hands.*)

Leave them alone and they will come home,
Wagging their tails behind them. BAA!
  (*Place one hand behind the body and move it
  back and forth to simulate tail movement.*)

The children are provided with practice on the verb form *doesn't*.

Trace a large sheep figure and color the head and feet black. Mount it on a low bulletin board and let the children take turns pasting on bits of cotton for wool. This device can be used also for "Baa, Baa, Black Sheep." Draw sheep outlines on ditto and run off a copy for each child so that either bits of cotton or popped corn can be glued to the form. This makes an excellent take-home picture.

## LITTLE BOY BLUE

TEACHER: Little Boy Blue, come blow your horn. (*Imitate.*)
CHILDREN: The sheep are in the meadow;
The cows are in the corn. (*Children make the animal sounds.*)
TEACHER: Where is the little boy
Who looks after the sheep? (*Hands shade eyes.*)
CHILDREN: He's under the haystack fast asleep! (*Whisper.*)

Ask the class to select a child to represent "Little Boy Blue." He pretends to sleep under a desk or table. On the last line Boy Blue awakens, yawns, and stretches. Ask the children: "Does anyone ever depend upon you for help? What happens if you fall asleep and forget to take care of your baby brother?"

Place emphasis on: sheep *are*, cows *are*, where *is* the little boy and *He's*.

## I'M A LITTLE TEAPOT

I'm a little teapot short and stout.
(*Stand.*)
Here is my handle. (*Left hand on hip.*)
Here is my spout.
(*Bend right elbow and open palm.*)
When I get my steam up, hear me shout,
"Tip me over, (*Bend body to right.*)
And pour me out!"

For variation, the children may draw and cut their own teapots from construction paper, and then use them to dramatize the rhyme.

The "sh" sound is presented in *short* and *shout*. The sound of "s" is used in *stout, spout, steam*.

## TWO LITTLE BLACKBIRDS

Two little blackbirds were sitting on a hill.
(*Hold up thumbs.*)
One was Jack; (*Wiggle one thumb.*)
And the other was Jill.
(*Wiggle other thumb.*)

Fly away Jack;
  (*Put thumb behind back.*)
Fly away, Jill.
  (*Put other thumb behind back.*)
Come back, Jack;
Come back, Jill.
  (*Hold up thumbs again.*)

Practice for the "j" sound is provided in the words *Jack* and *Jill*.

Cut two bird shapes from black construction paper; mount them on tagboard; cut around the shapes and glue them to tongue depressors. Use these stick puppets for dramatizing this rhyme.

On a rainy day ask a child to stand behind his chair. As the rhyme is said, he taps with his pointer finger on the back of the chair in order to experience the rhythm of speech. On each bird's name he taps with the right and then the left finger. On "Fly away," he tucks in his finger and points his fist over his shoulder. On "Come back," he taps with his pointer finger again.

For variation, substitute the words "Two little butterflies" and let the children use colorful butterflies cut from gummed paper. Moisten the paper butterflies slightly and apply to the index fingernails. "Two little dragonflies or houseflies" may be used also.

## PUSSY CAT AND QUEEN

CLASS: Pussy Cat, Pussy Cat, where have you been?
CHILD: I've been to London to visit the Queen.

CLASS: Pussy Cat, Pussy Cat, what did you there?
CHILD: I frightened a little mouse under her chair.

Children will want to take turns being the Pussy Cat and the questioner. Use large, cat puppets made from paper sacks that cover the head; attach pipe cleaner whiskers. Leave holes for the eyes and nose.

Here is another version of this rhyme:

Little girl, little girl, where have you been?
Gathering roses to give to the Queen.

Little girl, tell me, what did she give you?
She gave me a diamond as big as my shoe!

## WEE WILLIE WINKIE

Wee Willie Winkie runs through the town,
Upstairs, downstairs in his nightgown,
Rapping at the window, rattling the lock.
"Are all the children in their beds?
For it is nine o'clock!"

Set a clock at six and move the hands as the song proceeds until nine o'clock is reached. The children can do what the lines suggest. On the last two lines they can hurry to their tables, put their heads down on their arms, and pretend to sleep.

## PUSSY WILLOW

I have a little pussy. (*Kneel on floor.*)
Her coat is silver gray. (*Rise very slowly.*)
She lives down in the meadow (*Put left foot down.*)
Not very far away. (*Stand on both feet and bend over like a rag doll.*)

She'll always be a pussy. (*Stand tall.*)
She'll never be a cat. (*Head bowed.*)
She is a pussy willow.
Now what do you think of that?
   (*Raise arms.*)

Meow, meow, meow, meow,
Meow, meow, meow, meow.
               Scat!

## A MUSICAL FLANNELGRAPH

Singing the scale helps the children to listen for pitch and, when accompanied by a visual activity, they become aware that some tones are higher than others.

Using black yarn, stitch a musical staff of five lines, a treble clef, and a measure line to a piece of white outing flannel. Notes and little gray flannel kittens may represent the scale. The children may put them in place and "read" their music with the teacher's help. In this way, the children will feel as well as hear the notes of the song.

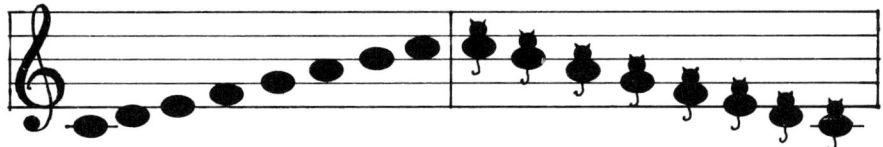

Each of the first eight lines of the poem, "Pussy Willow," is sung with each of the ascending notes of the scale. Sing a "meow" for each descending note. All the children may say *scat* in unison.

## TO MARKET, TO MARKET

> To market, to market to buy a fat pig.
> Home again, home again, jiggety-jig.
> To market, to market to buy a fat hog.
> Home again, home again, jiggety-jog.

Use a clapping or galloping rhythm. A child may put a doll on his foot, and hold its hands as if it were riding horseback. The lines can be said as the child jiggles the doll on his knee.

## LITTLE MISS MUFFET

> Little Miss Muffet sat on a tuffet
> Eating her curds and whey.
> Along came a spider,
>   (*Say slowly.*)
> And sat down beside her,
> And frightened Miss Muffet away.
>   (*Say quickly.*)

The class may act out the rhyme, half of the class taking the part of Miss Muffet and the other, the spider. Explain: a tuffet is a footstool or a low seat; curds and whey are cottage cheese. Bring a milking stool for the demonstration.

Place a pan of sour milk on the lowest heat setting of a hot plate. The children may watch the thickening process at intervals until it is time to pour off the whey. Add salt to the curds and give each child a small portion on a cracker.

The sound of "s" is emphasized in *sat, spider,* and *Miss.*

## JACK AND JILL

Jack and Jill went up the hill
   (*Swing hands.*)
To get a pail of water.
Jack fell down and broke his crown
   (*Get down on knees.*)
And Jill came tumbling after.
   (*Repeat Jack's motions.*)

The children may choose partners and act out the rhyme. Craft or construction paper crowns and round cardboard cartons with handles of string can be used for this activity.

## HEY DIDDLE, DIDDLE

Hey diddle, diddle!
The cat and the fiddle!
   (*Pretend to play fiddle.*)
The cow jumped over the moon.
   (*Curve left hand to form a half moon. Move right hand in a jumping motion over top of "moon."*)
The little dog laughed to see such sport,
   (*A child barks.*)
And the dish ran away with the spoon.
   (*Two children hold hands and run around the room.*)

## LITTLE JACK HORNER

Little Jack Horner sat in a corner
Eating his Christmas pie.
He put in his thumb and pulled out a plum,
And said, "What a good boy am I!"

Let individual children take turns acting out the rhyme. Ask: "Would you eat pie with your fingers as Jack Horner did? What would you use? Why did Jack think he was a good boy? What is a plum? What color is a plum? Why do you think Little Jack Horner was eating his pie in a corner?"

## PEASE PORRIDGE HOT

Pease porridge hot,
Pease porridge cold,
Pease porridge in the pot
One day old.

The children choose partners and alternate clapping their own hands, and then the hands of their partners as each line is said. Increase the number of days until the number ten is reached.

## HOT CROSS BUNS

Hot cross buns, hot cross buns.
(*Clap rhythm.*)
One a penny, two a penny,
Hot cross buns.
If you haven't any daughters,
Give them to your sons.
One a penny, two a penny,
Hot cross buns!

This rhyme may be used during the Easter season.

Buy some roll mix and make rolls according to directions. When the dough is ready to shape, give each child a small portion and a few raisins to knead into it. After the rolls are done, squirt instant icing on each one. Here is a chance to teach the children to wash hands and fingernails. Plan other activities while the rolls are baking. Each child will remember his own roll when the pan is taken from the oven.

## ACTION RHYMES

"What the child imitates," said Friedrich Froebel, "he begins to understand. Let him represent the flying of birds and he enters partially into the life of birds. Let him imitate the motion of fishes, and his sympathy with fishes is quickened. Let him reproduce the activities of farmer or baker, and his eyes open to the meaning of work. In one word, let him reflect in his play the varied aspects of life, and his thoughts will begin to grapple with their significance."[6]

---

[6] Friedrich Froebel, *Mother Play and Nursery Songs,* Lee and Shepard Publishers, Boston, 1878, pp. 6–7.

From their beginnings in babyhood, children have delighted in using fingers as effigies and as an expression of free activity. It was Froebel's first purpose to create parental understanding of the subconscious play of the child. He felt that then mothers and fathers would become more sympathetic and companionable toward their children. He thought that parents would begin to understand the meaning of sensory perception, and the motivation that hastens the development and progression of the child's spiritual, creative, physical, and educational growth. Froebel's teacher trainees, who learned the psychology of guiding the young child at the turn of the century, developed insight into the values of play which required use of parts of the body. They realized that young children gained early, character training in intellectual and social skills where play methods were used extensively.

The finger play or action rhyme provides first steps in play for the very young child. This activity becomes a part of the necessary stages of random manipulation which leads to concrete experiences and expressions of them and provides a basis for abstract thinking. When a child projects himself into an effigy (the finger) or uses his body to act out a situation, he takes another step in the process of adjusting to his environment.

Ego expression causes the child to use his fingers and hands more frequently than any other parts of the body for investigative purposes. These tactile experiences help him to become more aware of himself as a person and to feel a sense of control over his surroundings.

The finger play or action rhyme is a dramatic device which leads young children along many avenues of learning.

*It helps to develop language* which is the basis for all learning. The rhythmic appeal of simple verse, expressed in musical form, fulfills a primitive need. Each rhyme depicts a complete story which has a strong dramatic element. The child hears his own verbal output and becomes aware of what he is saying as he speaks. He becomes vibration conscious as he listens to the variations in pitch and volume of his own voice and the voices of others. Rhythm gives him a sense of pleasure in speaking (a valuable step in speech development), a chance to put words together in complete thoughts, and opportunities to recall a sequence of rhymed words and to extend the range of his vocabulary. Rhythm motivates verbal expression.

*The action rhyme serves as an auditory stimulus* in helping to establish more effective listening skills and forces concentration upon directions, specific sounds, words, phrases, and rhymed words.

*The action rhyme facilitates self-expression* enabling the child to find an emotional outlet where he may freely act out the situation described in the verses.

*The action rhyme provides for the use of muscles.* The young child acts out simple stories in rhyme with fingers, arms, and body. Muscle movements, both large and small, are coordinated in progressive muscle action. Thus, the action rhyme helps physically handicapped children.

Children delight in any kind of bodily action: crawling, kicking, running, jumping, pushing, pulling, and climbing. All are activities by which young children gather information of the world around them. The sensations the child feels take form as he uses his muscles to create and express. One child in nursery school was heard to chant as he pretended to be a carpenter and pantomined building movements:

> Wood, wood, nail, nail!
> Hammer, hammer, bang, bang!
> Make a door, make a wall,
> Make a window, make a floor!
> Bang, bang, bang!

This rhythmic self-talk, described here and in the two preceding chapters, is to be encouraged.

*The action rhyme lays a foundation for the understanding of mathematical concepts.* Finger plays usually include numbers from one to ten. Thus, addition and subtraction might take these forms: "Along came another, then there were three" and "One flew away, then there were two." The concept of *number rather than routine counting* is always emphasized. The digits on the hand furnish the child with a ready-made aid in which the elements can be related to one another in a semblance of order to form a schema.

*The action rhyme helps the child to discover abstractions and concepts of position, time, size, place, and dimension.* The vocabulary of this type of rhyme includes such words as *tall, small, little, big, high, low, in, out, up,* and *down.*

*The action rhyme helps the child to learn about people and things* in the environment. Flowers, seashells, vehicles, workers, animals, foods, and toys are subjects of many of the poems.

*The action rhyme helps the slow learner.* Many children are stimulated to participate in this activity because the fear of making mistakes is lessened.

*The action rhyme increases attention span.* Young children cannot attend for long periods of time unless the teacher uses a wide variety of techniques and concrete visual aids. The finger and action rhymes included in this chapter and in other sections of the book make use of a number of techniques and aids. Using these rhymes as suggested will help to maintain group interest and help the children to adjust more quickly to the warm, friendly atmosphere of the classroom.

Actions are suggested for many of the rhymes; yet the teacher should feel free to adapt them to fit the needs of her group. In many cases, the teacher will want to use flannelboard cutouts or stick puppets to vary the dramatizations.

## TEN FINGERS

I have ten fingers on my hand;
   (*Hold them up.*)
They all belong to me.
My fingers can do many things,
As you can plainly see.
   (*Wiggle fingers.*)

My fingers stand up straight and tall,
   (*Demonstrate.*)
And now they open wide.
   (*Open and spread apart.*)
My fingers close up in a ball,
   (*Make fists.*)
And then behind me hide.
   (*Place behind back.*)

My fingers wiggle in the air,
   (*Raise and move them.*)
And now they tap, tap, tap.
   (*Tap on palm.*)
My fingers reach and touch the floor,
   (*Touch floor.*)
And rest right on my lap.
   (*Fold hands.*)

—L.B.S.

## TWO LITTLE FINGERS

Two little fingers wiggle in the air;
Two little fingers run everywhere.
Two little fingers spread far apart;
Two little fingers point to my heart.

Two little fingers walk up the hill;
Two little fingers stand very still.
Two little fingers scratch in the sand;
Two little fingers hide in my hand.
—L.B.S.

The children may pantomime the actions suggested in each line of the poem.

## FINGER FISHES

Some funny fishes went out to play
In the kitchen sink not far away.
They found the soap and they scrub, scrub, scrubbed.
  (*Motion of washing hands.*)
They found a towel and they rub, rub, rubbed.
  (*Motion of drying hands.*)
What kind of fishes could they be?
Why, finger fishes, don't you see?
  (*Hold up ten fingers.*)
—L.B.S.

## TORTILLITAS (tor - tee - YEE - tahs)
(Spanish Pat-A-Cake)

Tortillitas para Papá, (Little tortillas for Papa)
Tortillitas para Mamá. (Little tortillas for Mama)

On the first line, pat the right palm with the left hand. On the second line, give a twist of the wrist and pat the left palm with the right hand. Note that *Papa* and *Mama* are accented on the second syllables in the Spanish rendition. Do not use the "z" sound in the plural "tortillas."

## WIGGLE YOUR FINGERS

Wiggle your fingers, one and two. (*Wiggle a finger on each hand.*)
Wiggle your fingers; I see you. (*Circle eyes with fingers.*)
Wiggle your fingers just for me.
   (*Repeat first action.*)
Wiggle your fingers, one, two, three. (*Clap.*)
Wiggle your fingers; wiggle some more.
Wiggle your fingers, two, three, four. (*Clap.*)
Wiggle your fingers; look alive. (*Show palms.*)
Wiggle your fingers, three, four, five. (*Clap.*)
   —L.B.S.

## OPEN, SHUT THEM

Open, shut them, open, shut them; (*Pantomime action suggested.*)
Give your hands a clap.
Open, shut them, open, shut them;
Lay them in your lap.
Creep them, creep them, creep them, creep them.
   (*Fingers of right hand move up opposite arm.*)
Climb them up so high.
Creep them, creep them, creep them, creep them.
   (*Move fingers down arm.*)
Let your fingers fly. (*Wiggle fingers rapidly.*)

## FEE, FIE, FOE, FUM

Fee, fie, foe, fum!
   (*Raise four fingers, one at a time.*)
See the fierce giant run!
   (*Thumb behind back.*)
Fee, fie, foe, fum!
Four fingers having fun!
   (*Repeat action.*)
Fee, fie, foe, fum!
My giant is a little thumb.
   (*Show thumb.*)
   —L.B.S.

## FIVE LITTLE FINGERS

Five little fingers standing in a row.
   (*Hold up fingers.*)
Look out! Look out! Down they will go!
Down goes thumbkin,
   (*Bend down one finger at a time.*)
Down goes pointer,
Down goes middle-man,
Down goes ring man,
Down goes little man.
Five little fingers are closed up tight.
Five little fingers say, "Good night."
               —Adapted

## A JUMP-ROPE RHYME

Teddy bear, teddy bear, turn around.
Teddy bear, teddy bear, touch the ground.
Teddy bear, teddy bear, say your prayers.
Teddy bear, teddy bear, go upstairs.
Teddy bear, teddy bear, tie your shoe.
Teddy bear, teddy bear, that will do.
               —Old rhyme

Provide individual ropes for the children to use, or they may take turns turning one long rope for the others to jump.

## DOLLS

Here is a dolly asleep in her cradle.
   (*Fingers lie in opposite palm.*)
Here is her chair.
   (*Cup palm, fingers held straight up.*)
Here is her table.
   (*Lace fingers of both hands.*)
Open her cupboard and you will see
Cups and saucers,
   (*Cup palm; straighten palm.*)
And a pot of tea.
   (*Make fist and extend one finger.*)
      —MARY L. HALL, 1917

## FLYING SOUTH

Ten little birdies are ready to fly
   (*Hold up fingers of both hands.*)
Up in the sky where the clouds are high.
   (*Raise fingers.*)
Ten little birdies are ready to go
   (*Spread fingers.*)
Away from the cold and the ice and snow.
   (*Spread arms.*)
Ten little birdies fly far away.
   (*Motion of flying.*)
Ten little birdies will come back some day.
   (*Fold fingers.*)
                                —L.B.S.

## USING BOTH HANDS

Here is a starfish; (*Place one hand
   on table, fingers spread apart.*)
Here is a shell. (*Show palm, hand
   slightly cupped.*)
Here is an octopus; (*Place two palms
   together, fingers spread.*)
Here is a bell. (*Lock fingers with one
   finger down.*)
Here is a fishnet; (*Interlace fingers.*)
Here is a fish. (*Make swimming motions.*)
Here is a birdbath; (*Two hands cupped.*)
And here is a dish. (*One hand cupped.*)
                                —O.M.A.

## SOLDIER DRILL

One, two, one, two,
Stand up straight as soldiers do.
Three, four, three, four,
Crouch way down upon the floor.
Five, six, five, six,
Nod your head and give two kicks.
Seven, eight, seven, eight,
Hold your arms and hands out straight.

Nine, ten, nine, ten,
Stand like soldiers once again.
—L.B.S.

Place felt cutouts of soldiers on the flannelboard for each of the lines containing number words. Have the children provide the action for the other lines. The children may understand number concepts through acting out this poem and the following two rhymes.

### TWO LITTLE REDBIRDS

Two little redbirds sat on a stone.
Tra-la-la, la-la-la, la-la.
One flew away and then there was one.
Tra-la-la, la-la-la, la-la.
One little redbird sat on a stone.
Tra-la-la, la-la-la, la-la.
He flew away and then there was none.
Tra-la-la-, la-la-la, la-la.
And so the stone was left all alone.
Tra-la-la, la-la-la, la-la.
—Old rhyme

The children say the refrain. Use fingers or stick puppets.

### FIVE LITTLE BOYS

Five little boys ran out to play.
It was a bright and sunny day.
One little boy said, "I can't stay,"
So four little boys were left to play.

Five little boats sailed out to sea.
Their sails were white as white could be.
One little boat came back to me,
So four little boats were left out at sea.
—L.B.S.

Repeat the first verse and change the numbers, eliminating one boy at a time. This selection can be acted out with fingers, stick puppets, or five children.

For the second verse use paper boats in a dishpan of water, or cut out felt boat figures for the flannelboard, or let children demonstrate in five large boxes.

### CABALLO (Horse)

Cah - BAH - yoh, (*Clap hands and stamp
  to imitate hoof beats.*)
Cah - BAH - voh,
Trot, trot, trot.
Rest in the shade, (*Clasp hands
  beside head.*)
When the day is hot. (*Fan self.*)

Note: The Spanish *b* and *v* sounds are not pronounced as they are in English. Pretend the lips are chapped and you cannot quite bring them together as you enunciate these two sounds.

### ARDILLA (Squirrel)

Ahr - DEE - yah,
Ahr - DEE - yah,
Run up a tree.
  (*Fingers move up opposite arm.*)
Ahr - DEE - yah,
Ahr - DEE - yah,
Come down to me.
  (*Fingers move down arm.*)

### MARIPOSA (Butterfly)

Mah - ree - POH - sah,
  (*Arms outstretched.*)
Mah - ree - POH - sah,
Flying in the sun.
  (*Motion of flying.*)
Fold your wings above your head
  (*Clasp hands above head.*)
When the day is done.

Children may join in saying this poem at the beginning of a rest period or after a play activity.

### GUAJOLOTE (Turkey)

"Gwa - hoh - LOH - teh, (*Tap thumb
and forefinger in opposite palm.*)
Gwa - hoh - LOH - teh,"
Says the turkey brown.
Here is water, Gwa - hoh - LOH - teh,
See him drink it down.

### CONEJO (Rabbit)

Coh - NEH - hoh, (*Forefinger and
middle finger to form ears.*)
Coh - NEH - hoh,
Hop, hop, hop. (*Move hand up and down.*)
Coh - NEH - hoh, (*Clap rhythm.*)
Coh - NEH - hoh,
Stop, stop, stop!

—Collection written by
V.S.P and L.B.S.

## THE STORY

Storytelling is an ancient art. It began when there were no books to read. People told and retold true and fanciful tales around the fireside, adding their own episodes and expressions each time the story was repeated.

Storytelling is a medium by which the narrator provides color, form, movement, and language for a series of events or episodes. Usually there is a problem to be solved, although an episodic story like "The Sleepy Forest"[7] is common. The story character may solve his own problem, as in the case of the Little Red Hen who decided that the animals that did not work should not share. The character may have help in solving his problem, as happened when the owl advised the Little White Rabbit who wanted Red Wings[8] to "wish off" his unwanted wings. He does so, and the plot is solved.

---

[7] Naoma Zimmerman, "The Sleepy Forest" in *Listening Time*, Album No. 1 by Wood and Scott, Bowmar Records, distributed by McGraw-Hill, Inc., New York.

[8] Louise B. Scott, *Tell-Again Story Cards, Level II*, McGraw-Hill, Inc., New York, 1967.

All stories woven from the imagination of an author or narrator are designed for a particular audience. For the young child, stories are written and told for many purposes: for widening experiences, for providing a variety of listening skills, for discovering moral truths, and for sheer, genuine fun.

The story should be one that allows the young listener to feel that he, too, can tell it. Because of his short attention span, he is easily distracted. Therefore, the story should be brief, strong on sensory appeal, and forceful in capturing immediate interest. It should include familiar people, animals, or events with which the child can identify. It should also contain repetition of words which will enable the young child to participate at once in the telling and to follow the sequence of events.

Patterns of repetition like "I think I can, I think I can" as the engine pulls cars over a mountain, and "I thought I could, I thought I could" delight the child. Nonsensical rhyming, such as "Goosey Loosey, Ducky Lucky, and Henny Penny" or "Jack, Lack, Mack, Quack, Pack, and Quack" found in Robert McCloskey's *Make Way for Ducklings,* repeats the natural repetitions and experimentation with sounds which the child has initiated often in his play.

Sensitive authors are well aware that words have power as they weave them into their stories. Appealing, vigorous, yet simple-to-understand words play a vital part in making it easier for a narrator to paint pictures with her voice. The narrator, therefore, must be concerned with the spoken language of a story for she enunciates the words, gives meaning to the patterns of sounds, and, like the orchestra leader, guides, directs, and motivates the young listeners in participating verbally.

In selecting stories to be told, the teacher should find those which are appropriate to the age group. Also, individual differences in children must be considered, since interest is an important consideration. Stories told over the heads of children or in a condescending manner are a waste of time. Following are other considerations to help guide the teacher in making a selection:

1. *The stories should have strong emotional appeal.* The child must be able to identify with the characters and understand their feelings and behavior.

2. *Stories should have more conversation than narration* and depict characters who do believable things.

3. *Stories should reinforce positive attitudes,* yet one must be cautious of "preachiness," "moral booby traps," or symbolism which builds fear, anxiety, or guilt.

4. *Stories that make minority groups feel inferior,* stories which ridicule stupidity or handicaps, and those which contain sarcasm, slang, or coarse language *should be avoided.*

Young listeners delight in acting out stories, adding their own endings, participating in refrains, and telling stories from a sequential set of pictures. Of course, most children like stories with or without visual aids. Children also enjoy what is known as the "switch" technique where animal and object sounds get turned around. The cow says, "Tick-tock;" the clock says, "Moo." This play with words is a natural phase of speech development and is used by many children's authors.

The rewards of storytelling are tremendous. As the imagination of the group is awakened, there is a spell-binding silence as the children await an old favorite that they feel belongs to them. Sparkling eyes are filled with wonder, and hands and bodies move rhythmically as a familiar phrase or sentence is repeated. These refrains give the child a chance to experiment with sounds, syllables, and words and to gain aural satisfaction from the activity. It is for this reason that a child can listen to the same story over and over, anticipating its events, though he knows quite well what those events will be.

*The fairy tale* probably has the widest and strongest interest for the young child. Fairy tales have had enduring popularity and universal appeal down through the ages. They are easy to recall and dramatize because of their simple plots, their brief descriptions, and their repetitive phrases. They excel in their lasting effect and fascination or they would not be in existence today. They are part of a child's world. They bridge the gap between fantasy and reality. As the child's experiences and knowledge widen, he will come to recognize fact, but now he needs the fanciful tale to enrich his world of imagination.

A little child can experience dismay if forcefully removed from his world of fantasy too soon. This incident took place as Melinda was listening to her dolly talk one day.

"Aw, that doll can't talk," four-year-old Bill said scornfully to Melinda.

Melinda's face fell for a moment.

Then she collected herself, turned to Bill, and said vociferously, "She can *too* talk. *You just don't know how to listen!*"

The scoffers of fantasy, who want children to face reality and who would rob the child of his natural talent of expression, prompted Virginia Snydor Pavelko to write this stanza:

> The people I feel sorry for
> Have never heard a dragon roar.
> They've never looked out on the lawn
> To try to find a leprechaun.
> They've lived their lives all by themselves,
> By never knowing sprites or elves.

Just what is there about the classical fairy tale, then, which has kept it alive for so many generations? The fairy tale has dramatic excitement which all children love. It is based upon simple emotions which everyone understands, such as the reward for Cinderella's patience and faith, or the value of a kept promise to the Frog Prince. It has simplicity and directness which make the ideas in the tale easy to follow. It gives comfort in describing loneliness, rejection, and insecurity since children can identify with these feelings. The terror of trolls or giants, of obstacles, of danger is overcome without complicated references to reality. Usually these forces which obstruct are thwarted by constructive forces.

The fairy tale presents problems to be resolved. Young children enjoy the challenge of solving simple problems even though they do not have sufficient skill nor experience yet to cope with the perplexities of life. There is always a chance for discussion if the story is brought to a close before the final denouement. One group of children decided that the Gingerbread Man should not be eaten by a fox, but rather by a child. They agreed that the Gingerbread Man was supposed to be eaten and accepted this fact, yet they did not want an evil force like the fox to win.

Children delight in all of the make-believe aspects of the fairy tale. Giving animals personalities fascinates young children and the animals become their true friends. Authors and interpreters of the fairy tale, therefore, have woven a magic of belief into creatures by endowing them with mortal traits.

Telling stories to children is a constant experimentation. One must study the children as well as the literature to determine whether the story would be more effectively presented with or without text. There is no doubt that telling a story results in better audience contact, but a story may lose some of its flavor if not presented precisely as the author conceived and wrote it. However, when reading, the teacher must learn to "cut" portions of description particularly when she finds that she may be losing the attention of her class.

Most primary and preschool teachers are adept at the art of storytelling if not from training, then from trial and error, and experience. All teachers, however, can profit from reviewing some techniques.

1. Sit on a low chair. Children need to feel the nearness of you as they group themselves in small chairs around you, or sit informally on the floor. This is a special time and children should feel that you are talking to each one personally.

2. Know the tale through memorizing the orderly chain of events if the story is told and not read. Skip the parts which may create boredom.

3. Read the story aloud before presenting it to the class. You will need to become accustomed to your own voice and should practice controlling it.

4. Be deliberate. Never give an impression of hurry. Children need careful and slow articulation that is easy to follow. Use frequent pauses, remembering that generally the tempo must be slow for the young.

5. Use a variety of tones as you highlight important words.

6. Hold the book with the left hand about a foot from the body, and with the right hand, turn the pages. Allow a brief time to elapse before continuing the reading to give the children a chance to think. If pictures of the story are shown to the class, move the book slowly from one side to the other.

7. Keep the volume of your voice soft, yet not monotonous, so that the mood of the story is set. Be sure not to over-dramatize the characters or use meaningless or distracting facial expressions and gestures.

8. Talking down to the children or using a lecture-type voice should be avoided.

9. Handle all distractions with poise, tact, and calmness.

A major purpose of storytelling is to entertain, yet lives are enriched as children find new places to visit, new bridges to cross, new meanings to absorb, and new stars to view. Within the structure of a good story, the child can be helped to understand, to face his own feelings, and to learn much of the world around him. Through storytelling a child can begin to discover something about attitudes and social relationships. There is no doubt that many good stories help to mold ideals.

Stories of excellent workmanship have a way of arousing a sense of wonder akin to awe and reverence which Edna Mellor describes as "spiritual awareness." [9] This awareness comes through sensitivity to beautiful words.

---

[9] Edna Mellor, *From Education Through Experience in the Infant School Years*, Basil Blackwell Publishers, Ltd., London, 1959.

There are many visual aids which can be used to support this "spiritual awareness," give graphic meaning to words, and capture the imagination of children at any age. These aids can hold the children's interest in a story, help them to remember sequence, and help them to evaluate characters, action, and plot. To accomplish these purposes, visual aids should be seen easily, be interesting, and useful to the story. Not all stories benefit from their use, however. The teacher must be the judge of whether the aid will in any way detract from or actually augment the visualization of events.

*The flannelboard* is one of the indispensable aids used in telling stories to the very young. It can be made by covering a piece of cardboard, Celotex, plywood, or artist's board with outing flannel. Fasten the flannel securely with masking tape on the other side of the board. Both sides may be covered, one with light-colored flannel and one with dark. Either an easel or the chalkboard tray is suitable for supporting the board. A flannelboard can serve as a magnetic board if a thin sheet of metal or window screen is inserted underneath the flannel before fastening it to the board.

*Pictures* cut from magazines and backed with outing flannel or flocked paper adhere easily to the flannel. Be sure to glue the entire area to this backing; otherwise, edges may curl or become torn by the children as they use the pictures to tell the stories. Sandpaper usually is too heavy for backing.

*Felt cutouts* for the flannelboard can be purchased at most school supply houses. Felt is most durable; however, many teachers make their own figures and shapes out of white pellon, a lining fabric which adheres easily and is reasonably priced.

Shapes can be traced on pellon, colored with crayons or oil pastels, and cut out. If the figures wrinkle, turn them over on waxed paper and press with a steam iron.

Shallow, flat boxes make excellent containers for the figures. Select boxes to fit the size of the flannelboard characters and line each one with a single piece of felt or flannel. This material holds the characters in place and prevents wrinkling. Envelopes to contain the story figures may be made by taping manilla folders at the sides.

When telling a flannelboard story, place the appropriate pictures on the board as each character or scene is mentioned. Remove the pictures no longer needed for sequence so that the board will not appear cluttered. Pause to allow the class to think about each event as it occurs, then continue with the narration. Encourage shy children to place pictures on the board so that they will feel they are helping to tell the story.

*Puppets* are quite simple to construct.[10] A sack puppet, for instance, can be made by stuffing a number five paper sack with tissue paper or newspaper and tying it securely at the top, leaving a small opening for inserting the finger. Use a felt tip pen to draw the features and staple on strips of paper for arms and legs. Glue on bits of heavy yarn for hair. The child inserts his index finger into the neck when manipulating the puppet.

Stick puppets are probably easiest to handle. Back the pictures with tagboard, cut them out, and glue them to tongue depressors.

A styrofoam ball about the size of the child's fist makes a most attractive puppet. Dig a hole in the ball. Insert an apothecary plastic bottle or a cardboard cylinder into the hole to form the neck. Attach a garment to the neck with thread and glue. Add construction paper features and cover the head with a cap or strips of yarn. Styrofoam can be painted with poster paint mixed with a small bit of detergent.

Fist puppets can be drawn by the child. With a crayon he sketches a face upon his doubled-up fist and tucked-in thumb, using the space between the thumb and forefinger for a mouth, and draping a piece of cloth over his arm.

*Vegetable puppets* can be constructed by inserting a tongue depressor into the end of a potato, turnip, or carrot. Glue on construction paper features and yarn for hair.

## A SURPRISE WINDOW

Fold a three-sided piece of tagboard to form a shuttered window. Find an interesting magazine picture containing action. Fasten the picture inside the "window" with photo-tabs. Open the window each time there is a new picture, and encourage the children to talk about it or make up a story.

Use the following questions to guide the telling of a story:

Who is in the picture? (Main characters.)
How are they dressed? (Describe them.)
Where are they? (Place of action.)
What is the problem? (Plot.)
What is happening? (More action.)
How does the story end? (Conclusion.)

---

[10] Louise Binder Scott, *Puppets for All Grades,* F. A. Owen Publishing Company, Dansville, New York, 1961.

After this guide or a variance of it has been followed for a few times, the children will begin to tell or make up their own stories, showing some awareness of sequence of plot.

## USING A TAPE RECORDER

Children enjoy hearing their favorite stories repeatedly. Record several of these stories and play them in the audio-center where a small group of children can listen. Use stories and nursery rhymes the class has dictated. When the children have become used to the tape recorder, individuals may want to record. Their tapes may be played for mothers and fathers who visit the program at the education center.

## BRINGING YOUNG CHILDREN AND GOOD PICTURE-STORYBOOKS TOGETHER

The warm glow of joy and the sparkle in the child's eyes as he browses among colorful picture-storybooks is a treasured sight to remember. The child's picture-book of today represents a combination of dedicated, creative, and talented authors and artists, and sensitive, capable editors. As children approach the rich treasures of picture-storybooks, they stand before an open door to learning through enriching and creative experiences.

The teacher in the education center recognizes the picture-storybook as a resource which can help the child:

To develop a love for literature and an interest in learning to read.
To develop positive attitudes about schools and libraries.

To grow in language skills.

To become sensitive to the ways in which language functions.

To appreciate creative art through observation of colorful pictures.

To grow in his own techniques of art expression.

To respond to humor, and to share fun and laughter.

One of the first steps in planning for the successful use of book resources is to provide a library area in the education center. There should be appropriate equipment in this area and a continuing circulating supply of high quality picture-storybooks that meet the needs of the children. Careful thought should be given to the setting. A pleasant, comfortable, and inviting location for a library should be set apart from the noises of other busy areas. One way to accomplish this is to use room dividers. The setting should suggest relaxed browsing and quiet concentration and the atmosphere should promote feelings of pleasure and discovery. There should be a low table with chairs to fit the heights of young children.

Display racks may be used since they are more functional than shelving, and because picture-storybooks have a wide variety of shapes and sizes. Also, the racks present a full view of the cover designs of an entire collection for the child's quick survey. When books are readily accessible, children find it much easier to return them to the library shelves or racks in an orderly way. Displays of interest, such as a stuffed toy representing a storybook character, will provide an additional motivating factor in the library area.

When this center is equipped and ready to function, it moves into action at once with Mother Goose collections and traditional favorites such as "The Three Bears." Gradually new titles may be added as they are introduced during storytelling time.

As the children are introduced to the library area, some stress should be placed upon the care of books. Basic ideas which can be discussed with the class regarding the handling of books may include the following suggestions:

Clean hands are necessary to preserve the beauty of books.

Both hands help to hold a book comfortably.

The best way to turn a page is to lift it gently at the upper right hand corner.

Those who use the books are responsible for returning them to their proper places.

As the children explore and become interested in the library, they begin and should be encouraged to "read" pictures. Illustrations should, of course, explain and amplify the words of the author so that the child can be invited to "walk into the picture" and become a part of the scene as he involves himself in the action. Picture-reading may begin with simple enumeration of what the child observes in the picture. He can then proceed to a description of characters, action, and mood. Eventually he progresses to an interpretative level where he grasps the main idea and projects his imagination into what may have preceded or followed the action of the picture.

Recently, a number of picture-storybooks which have no printed text have become available. *A Cat Story*[11] by Elliott Gilbert and *Birds in Wintertime*[12] by Allan Eitzen are examples of picture-books without words. Since these books have no language structure and cannot be read to the class, the child uses his own vocabulary in telling the stories.

"Reading" picture-books is a creative experience involving observation and imagination. The children will become aware of their own language skills as the teacher records their verbal responses on chart paper and later reads them aloud. Children will then realize that their ideas can be written down and read. Thus, children are introduced to reading in a very personal way.

After the teacher has read a story, many opportunities for conversation and discussion will arise. The children may then explore the pictures further after the book is placed upon the browsing table. As the child follows sequentially the pictures in his favorite storybook again and again, he masters the story and actually imagines that he is reading. To say that he learns a story by "heart," is literally true since he cherishes these favorite stories with his heart and emotions.

Selected functions of picture-storybooks are presented here with examples for quick reference: Picture-storybooks can touch the spirit so that the story is recalled long after the title has been forgotten. Dubose Heyward's *The Country Bunny and the Little Gold Shoes*[13] with pictures by Marjorie Flack delights all children as it depicts the warmth of living through shared responsibilities as portrayed by a rabbit family.

---

[11] Elliott Gilbert, *A Cat Story,* Little Owl Reading Time Library, Holt, Rinehart, and Winston, New York, 1963.
[12] Allan Eitzen, *Birds in Wintertime,* Little Owl Reading Time Library, Holt, Rinehart, and Winston, New York, 1963.
[13] Dubose Heyward, *The Country Bunny and the Little Gold Shoes,* Houghton-Mifflin, Boston, 1939.

Picture-storybooks can help children feel the warmth of home security, and love. *Curl Up Small*[14] by Sandol Stoddard Warburg, illustrated by Trina Schart Hyman, helps children to feel that it is wonderful, as the sun sets and shadows darken, to curl up small and safe, strengthened by love and welcomed by sleep.

Picture-storybooks can help young children to accept change and adjust to new situations. Virginia Lee Burton's *The Little House*[15] tells of rural to urban settings and suggests the feelings that accompany the drama of skyscrapers that overshadow the little house, and subway trains that shake its foundation. The escape of the little house to the beauty of the countryside provides a satisfying ending.

Picture-storybooks lead children to explore, learn about, and appreciate the natural world around them. *Gilberto and the Wind*[16] by Marie Hall Ets presents the experience of a small Mexican boy as he responds to the changing rhythm and tempo of the wind. The artist portrays many moods of the wind by combining colors of black, brown, gray, and white.

Picture-storybooks stimulate visual imagery and descriptive vocabulary. Margaret Wise Brown's *The Runaway Bunny*,[17] with pictures by Clement Hurd, has a delightful repetitive quality that suggests old nursery rhymes and songs.

Picture-storybooks enrich the beauty and enchantment of the classics from the "world of make-believe" through artistic and sensitive illustrations. *Cinderella*,[18] translated and illustrated by Marcia Brown, and *The Shoemaker and the Elves*[19] by Brothers Grimm, illustrated by Adrienne Adams, are tales of high quality in translation combined with sensitive, creative pictures for motivation in listening.

Picture-storybooks can bring fun and laughter that delight the young child. *Dandelion*[20] by Don Freeman provides listening pleasure. The child's imagination is stimulated as he learns how to manipulate words to achieve humor.

---

[14] Sandol Stoddard Warburg, *Curl Up Small*, Houghton-Mifflin, Boston, 1964.
[15] Virginia Lee Burton, *The Little House*, Houghton-Mifflin, Boston, 1942.
[16] Marie Hall Ets, *Gilberto and the Wind*, The Viking Press, New York, 1963.
[17] Margaret Wise Brown, *The Runaway Bunny*, Harper & Row, Publishers, New York, 1942.
[18] Marcia Brown, *Cinderella*, Charles Scribner's Sons, New York, 1954.
[19] Brothers Grimm, *The Shoemaker and The Elves*, Charles Scribner's Sons, New York, 1960.
[20] Don Freeman, *Dandelion*, The Viking Press, New York, 1964.

Picture-storybooks enable the child to travel to many interesting places. Robert McCloskey's *Make Way for Ducklings*[21] transports the child to Boston where he follows the mallard duck family across the common and to a thoroughfare, as friendly people help the ducks in their crisis.

Picture-storybooks help children to experience good times and enrich their enjoyment of special days. *Come Again, Pelican*[22] by Don Freeman depicts life in a trailer at the beach. The story appeals to the children's interest in natural life at the seashore.

Picture-storybooks foster creative oral expression, provide oral experiences with sentence structures, and stimulate appreciation for language. *Tell Me, Mr. Owl*[23] by Doris Van Liew Foster, illustrated by Helen Stone, provides a setting for spontaneous discussion on Halloween.

Mark Taylor, noted columnist and authority on children's literature, has enunciated the new dimensions we are seeking for the role of books in the lives of today's children with this summary: "In a world whose problems seem to multiply and grow complex beyond measure, one great aim for most of us is to help children grow up whole and happy on a rapidly shrinking planet in a rapidly expanding universe. We believe that through books we can help children find their way to the very thresholds of this universe, ready to face its dazzling facts and accept its awesome challenges. In one way or another, we try to see that children are given not only factual knowledge and technical know-how, but even more importantly, the small store of man's dearly gained wisdom, and a sufficiency of aesthetic and spiritual insights and ideals. Books for children, besides providing delight, can open children's eyes to the splendors of the world and fill out their minds with great ideas and strengthen their hearts with great feelings."[24]

—CHRISTINA R. MCDONALD

## USING PICTURES

Pictures are effective teachers for they can be employed in many ways as aids to learning in every area of the curriculum. They can initiate an activity, supplement a program, and serve as substitutes for

---

[21] Robert McCloskey, *Make Way For Ducklings*, The Viking Press, New York, 1941.
[22] Don Freeman, *Come Again, Pelican*, The Viking Press, New York, 1961.
[23] Doris Van Liew Foster, *Tell Me, Mr. Owl*, Lothrop, Lee & Shepard Co., New York, 1957.
[24] Mark Taylor, "Writing for Children: A Challenge and a Vision," *Elementary English*, XXXIX, No. 8, December, 1962, p. 800.

live experiences. Whatever the purpose, care and forethought should be utilized in the selection of pictures.

Pictures containing only one object or character can serve purposes of vocabulary building, sentence building, and speech-sound discrimination. Simple, uncluttered pictures enable the child to concentrate upon one thought unit at a time.

Pictures which instill quiet and calm within the child are those that depict scenery, sleepy animals and toys, and relaxed people. *The Sleepy Little Lion*[25] by Margaret Wise Brown with photographs by Ylla creates instantaneous effects of both interest and calmness. The young lion cub moves slowly and sleepily through one episode after another in quiet adventure.

Pictures which contain insects, plants, and animals are useful for nature study.

Pictures portraying members of a community enrich the social studies program. *Workers in Our Neighborhood*[26] is designed to help children learn about people and their services; at the same time many oral language experiences are derived.

Pictures portraying people or animals in action can motivate storytelling. There should be sufficient detail and expression of meaning so that a child can visualize and interpret events that are taking place or are about to happen. The action depicted should be familiar to the young observer so that imagination will be aroused.

When using a picture to encourage storytelling, the emphasis initially should be on free conversation with no thoughts of plot in mind. After a child has related details in a picture and has described what he sees, then he can begin to think in terms of *who, what, where, when,* and *why*. From this point, he can move into problem solving by telling the conflicts he thinks the character has and how he believes they may be resolved.

One teacher found a picture of a small boy helping a kitten who was caught in a wire fence. Beside the boy on the ground was a lunch box. The sky in the picture contained dark, ominous clouds. The teacher displayed the picture to the class as she asked questions which stimulated and guided the discussion. Following is the story which was developed then by the children:

---

[25] Margaret Wise Brown, *The Sleepy Little Lion,* Harper and Row, Publishers, New York, 1947.

[26] Louise Binder Scott, *Workers In Our Neighborhood,* McGraw-Hill, Inc., New York, 1967.

The little boy is on his way to school. He decides to go a new way. He takes a short-cut because he is late. (*Immediate interest.*)

He hears a mew and sees a kitten. The kitten is caught in the wire fence. If he stops and helps the kitten, he may be late for school. (*Problem.*)

The little boy wants to help the kitten. He pulls, but he can't get her loose. (*Failure.*)

The clouds are getting blacker and blacker. The little boy has no umbrella. He pulls the kitten again. He pulls easily so he won't hurt the kitten. Then he gets her loose. (*Success.*)

The little boy runs fast to school. He gets there on time and then it starts to rain. (*Problem resolved.*)

Since the plot excites and holds the interest of the children, probing a problem can prove a real challenge, become an enjoyable experience for a class, and can help them to learn to think critically. The *Tell-Again Story Cards*[27] are materials which provide an order of events, definite plots, familiar characters, and discussion possibilities.

A picture should meet certain basic qualifications if it is to be considered effective for use with young children. It should be suitable for the occasion for which it is intended. It should be appropriate to the specific subject matter and not burdened with too many details. There should be authenticity in the portrayals; animals should resemble animals and insects should be scientifically depicted. A picture should be large enough to be seen easily from a distance and mounted on durable material, such as tagboard, posterboard, or heavy cardboard.

There are many excellent commercial pictures available, yet some teachers prefer to collect their own by making use of discarded books, calendars, advertising bulletins, and magazines. Parents usually are pleased to add to the collection.

### THE PICTURE WINDOW

Draw a 3 ft. x 5 ft. picture window on a background of newsprint and tack the drawing to a bulletin board. The window frame around the drawing should be about 4 inches in width and might be made from

[27] Louise Binder Scott, *Tell-Again Story Cards*, McGraw-Hill, Inc., New York, 1967.

brown and white corrugated paper, colored construction paper, or tagboard. The picture window will look very realistic if it has ruffled curtains held up by a strip of elastic, pulled tautly.

The view within the area of the window space should portray daily experiences and interests of the children in the center. For instance, the first few days it might show a boy and girl walking to school, then a duck in a pool, a fish in a pond, or new puppies. By the end of two weeks, the picture in the window will need to be changed to a different scene, perhaps one of the city streets with a milkman or postman.

Each morning, the window should be covered with a shade that is made from brown wrapping paper and cut with pinking shears to form a design. This shade can be fastened along the top of the window with thumb tacks.

When the children are all assembled they may chant with the teacher:

>Come to the window.
>Come, everyone.
>What do we see
>As we let in the sun?

Then raise or remove the shade so that the children can see the surprise picture.

The picture window is an excellent springboard for conversation as it lends itself to almost any topic chosen. A variety of textures may be used and background colors changed to depict weather or time of day.

At the end of the language period, this chant may be said or sung:

>When we came to the window,
>We came everyone.
>We saw many things
>As we let in the sun.
>—O.M.A.

## STORY PLATES

Select paper plates with dark backgrounds or cover them with brown contact paper. Glue a small bit of cellulose sponge to the back of an animal picture or to a miniature toy. Glue the other side of the sponge to the center of the plate so that the picture or toy stands out. Suggest that the children help find small bits of food for the animals and glue them to the appropriate plates.

Some story plates to begin with might include:

| | |
|---|---|
| Hen—grains of corn | Rabbit—carrot or rabbit pellets |
| Squirrel—nut | |
| Horse—wisps of hay | Cow—grass clippings |
| Bear—honey tied in plastic wrap | Bird—seeds |
| | Dog—bone |

If real "food" cannot be obtained easily, pictures will do. Display the plates on the bulletin board and use them for storytelling.

## WHAT WILL THE PICTURE BE?

After you have read a picture-storybook to the class, turn back to the first picture and ask, "What will the next picture be?" Continue this questioning until all pictures have been shown. If the children have difficulty in recalling the sequence after a first reading, postpone the activity until they have heard the story again. For this second telling, turn to each picture and ask individuals to "read" the pictures.

## ARRANGING PICTURES FOR STORYTELLING

Most education centers for young children have felt cutouts of animals, toys, and people. Before the storytelling session, ask a volunteer or an aid to arrange a scene on the flannelboard using some of the felt cutouts. Place the flannelboard at the front of the room; the children may take turns "reading" the picture.

## A PICTURE FILE

An uncovered box decorated with attractive contact paper makes a good filing box if it will hold oaktag filing folders comfortably and in upright positions. Tape the sides of each folder and label each so that a picture can be found expediently when needed. File the pictures by categories or alphabetically.

Following are suggestions of the types of pictures every teacher of young children finds useful and easy to locate in magazines:

| | |
|---|---|
| Circus, zoo, or farm | City and country life |
| Animals | Holidays |

| | |
|---|---|
| Insects | Land vehicles |
| Toys | People |
| Scenery | Shapes |
| Colors | Foods |
| Furniture | Buildings |
| Clothing | Machine |

## PLAYING A STORY

Playing a story is adapting a story to play form. The child recalls a series of story events in sequence and embellishes them with his own dialog as he plays the role of a character.

*In dramatic play,* a child often operates alone and interprets real-life situations, moving from fantasy to reality. *In playing the story,* he now depends upon already-prepared materials from which to build additional fantasy. He also cooperates with others, listens to them, and adjusts himself, his actions, and dialog to the group.

The child can choose a story, be anyone or anything, and travel to any part of the world as he plays a story. What he does through projection into a character is very real to him. *He uses divergent thinking* in recreating or branching off from a story already plotted. *He uses convergent thinking* by molding his ideas of dramatization with those of the group in order to obtain a common result.

In this kind of dramatization, a child is not concerned with form and memorized words or speeches. Scenery or costumes are unnecessary for him to believe in his role. However, many young children like to select from the "dress-up" box pieces of clothing which they believe will make more satisfying characters.

*What materials can be used?* Anything which tells a story and lends itself to dramatization of the play activity is acceptable. *Nursery rhymes* are easiest to dramatize since they have a minimum of characters and succinct, easy-to-recall story lines. Each rhyme has a beginning, a middle, and an end; most of the lines are familiar and adaptable to the level of four and five year olds.

The old fairy tales are excellent starters, too. "The Little Red Hen," for example, has story-play values for these reasons:

It is a favorite and is familiar to the child and teacher.
It has a vivid chain of events easily recalled.
It contains few characters and exciting action.
It presents a problem to be solved and offers a message.

The ingredient for playing need not be a story; a situation growing out of any subject in the curriculum can be played. What a group needs is an idea, a chance to develop a plan and to present a play.

*How should this activity begin?* Pantomime, with or without music, is the simplest and surest way to initiate creative dramatics, for pantomime frees the body and allows a child to perform without need for verbalization. When it is time to introduce oral language into the activity, decide which story can be used. Will it be a modern selection or an old fairy tale, a poem, a story picture, or a real-life situation? Will the group play the entire story, or will the narrator stop the story at a strategic place and ask different groups to end it in different ways?

The open-end story which children must finish, using their own insight and ideas of right and wrong, is difficult for very young children, but it can be used on a very simple scale. For example, let children end "The Gingerbread Man" or "Chicken Little" as the characters meet the fox. There is a great affinity between children and animals; often, children will create an ending in which the characters out-maneuver the evil old fox.

Usually, when young children have had little or no experience with creative dramatics, the whole sequence of events is discussed step by step. In this case, a simple format would be followed:

Tell the story and talk about the characters.
Encourage the children to volunteer for parts.
Suggest that they dramatize their characters by creating their own dialogs as they go along.
Give the group a chance to dramatize a second time, if they wish.
Try to allow all groups an opportunity to play the same story.

Since the teacher knows the children and the story they will play, she can prepare for the activity by guiding each child toward a group where he can best create and perform this work. The members of the group he joins should be chosen carefully so that his self-image will have positive reinforcement. Self-concepts are determinants of behavior and they can be modified or even changed when a child has someone to listen to him and when he is provided with opportunities to build adequacy and success. Favorable group action can help him feel important and safe.

Some shy or withdrawn children may fear assuming a role, although they may be intensely interested. The play opportunity should be so appealing that they will want to join. As a contrast, a child who lacks self-control and an ability to play with others can be helped to express himself freely and to cope more firmly with his emotions.

Imaginative play sometimes tends to become chaotic or dominated by certain individuals, and in such a distracting atmosphere, the effectiveness diminishes. There is need, then, for quiet play after the creative dramatic period to achieve proper balance in activity.

If the children are to have uninhibited and unstructured participation, the teacher should not stress perfection on her terms. Children who feel that their efforts are accepted by an authority figure will want to engage in the activity again and again. Therefore, praise and encouragement of both the individual and group contributions must be given freely and enthusiastically. Emphasis on "we" instead of "I" can help foster concerted group effort. Though one of the goals of playing a story is to build social concepts, an immediate purpose is to satisfy personal, basic needs of children; the social concepts will grow out of this.

The teacher can help the children evaluate their performances by asking, "What did you like about the way this story was played? What would you have done if you had been Goldilocks? Was there anything else that the pig and the cat might have done?" Always direct evaluative remarks to the story character itself, rather than to the child. Throughout the experience of story-play, the teacher should be in the background, sensitive and relaxed.

*The values gained from playing a story are many*:

Language, speech fluency, and self-expression are improved.
Listening is improved.
Creative power is developed.
Individuality as an accepted member of the group is attained.
Confidence in abilities is built.
Attitudes and behavior are modified.

As stated in previous chapters, play is an important part of the child's growth and development. Through communication and working with other children, a child discovers that there are other points of view to be considered, and as a result, may better understand the inner forces operating within himself. These inner forces are so closely united with language development and growth of intelligence that it is impossible to speak of them separately.

The child who takes part in playing a story moves one more step toward appreciating good literature and attains a richer philosophy of living.

## QUIET TIMES

A relaxed classroom where children are working happily, where movements are quiet, where voices are pleasant and well modulated, and where there are silences for contemplation is an ideal to be desired. However, children are not born with the same nervous structures, and they bring to the center varieties of listening and speaking habits acquired in the home. All children, therefore, cannot fit into a behavior pattern such as we have described, nor would we wish them to do so.

As listening is a matter of personal involvement, so are the needs for quiet and calm. Some children seem to be able to create under somewhat chaotic conditions, while others need quiet surroundings. If a child is not easily distracted and is engaged in play which he enjoys, he may need fewer planned quiet times. However, all children need rest and feelings of serenity at times during the day to satisfy their growing needs. Security lies in order and some routine. Therefore, all children need a stable, well-planned program so that chaos and disorganization can be prevented. Children like to know that after block play, they will sing, then have a snack, listen to a story, have outdoor activities and then a rest period.

Relaxation cannot be forced. The ability to feel calm must come from within. Thus, the teacher should evaluate her own speech and movements, remembering that children are sensitive to an adult's actions and personality. As a first step, she can minimize her movements, slow down her speech, and talk softy. She then can set a mood of calm for the techniques which are described in this chapter and are designed for pleasurable relaxation at times when the children need them most. However, even very young children should realize and understand that it is best for the teacher who feels irritable and tired to sit as she talks to the children, and admit that she is tired or not feeling well.

Relaxation usually occurs when pressures are removed so that ideas can flow freely. When materials are interesting and thoughts challenging, work itself can be ideal relaxation. If the child experiences success at a task he has efficiently performed alone or in relation to people, he can then proceed to another task with renewed vigor, calm, and interest. Through relaxed working conditions, the child discovers what he can do and a self-image emerges which gives him a sense of well-being and peace.

Although work can be relaxing, it is important for a child to experience some *planned relaxation periods* through many of the ideas which follow.

## IDEAS FOR RELAXATION

*Rag doll*: Bring in a limp toy and ask the children to feel its floppy legs, arms, and body. Ask them to *be* rag dolls (Raggedy Ann or Andy) in order to experience the feeling of relaxed bodies and minds.

*Catching yawns*: Show pictures of people or animals yawning.

*Melting candles*: Ask the class to stand straight and tall like candles and then to melt into a puddle of wax as the sun shines and warms them.

## RESTING TIME

Parents can be asked to send small rugs or mats to the center for resting time. The children may then recline on their own "beds." Play soft music or tell a quiet story. Children also enjoy music box tunes and soothing poems which induce calm and creative thoughts.

## REST AND LISTEN

I like to rest and listen.
Let me listen as I rest.
I'll close my eyes so I can't see,
And let the music play for me.
Shhhhhhhh! Listen while I count to ten,
Then we'll let the music play again.

—L.B.S.

Play a music box as you say the poem softly. The children respond by closing their eyes.

## I'M A TREE

I'm a tree out in the woods.
   (*Hands above heads.*)
I stand so still all day.
But when the wind begins to blow,
My trunk begins to sway.
   (*Move body slowly back and forth.*)

Back and forth—back and forth—
My hands are leaves, you see.
   (*Wiggle fingers.*)

Back and forth—back and forth—
I am a big, tall tree.
  (*Stand still.*)
                          —L.B.S.


## RESTING

Quiet—quiet—the sun is going down.
Night is coming quietly.
The sun is going down.
Make believe you're sleeping;
Make believe it's night.
Make believe you're sleeping;
Close your eyes tight.
Quiet—quiet—night is coming.
The sun has gone down.
                          —L.B.S.


Read very slowly as the children are resting.

## BABY BIRDIES

We are baby birdies in a nest.
We are yawning—nodding—stretching.
  (*Children act out.*)
We have all been fed,
And now we're in bed.
We are yawning—nodding—stretching.
                          —Unknown

## SLEEPY TIME

The little gray mouse has gone to sleep;
The frog rests down in the pond so deep.

The little squirrel hurries to her nest;
The skunk finds a hollow stump to rest.

The little brown bunny in weeds so still
Will look for his burrow on top of the hill.

The swallow in nest with her babies three,
Is perched in the leaves of a sycamore tree.
—L.B.S.

After reading the poem, ask the children to tell how other animals sleep. Show pictures of animals resting. Discuss the differences and similarities in the way they rest.

### I'M A SUNFLOWER TALL

I'm a sunflower tall growing by a wall.
  (*Stand.*)
I nod to the left, I nod to the right.
  (*Bend back and forth.*)
I bend to the left, I bend to the right.
I'm a sunflower tall growing by a wall.
—L.B.S.

The children act out the rhyme.

Pretend to be a fairy with a magic wand. Say: "When I wave my magic wand, the flowers will sleep. When I say 'The sun is up,' the flowers will all wake up."

This poem can be used also for teaching the concepts of left and right.

### RAGGEDY ANN[28]

Raggedy Ann is my best friend.
She is so relaxed; just see her bend,
First at the waist, and then at the knee.
Her arms are swinging, oh, so free!
Her head rolls around like a rubber ball.
She hasn't any bones at all.
Raggedy Ann is stuffed with rags.
That's why her body wigs and wags.
—L.B.S.

---

[28] Louise Binder Scott and J. J. Thompson, *Talking Time* (Second Edition), McGraw-Hill, Inc., New York, 1966, p. 58.

As you say the poem softly, the children act it out, letting their arms, legs, and body go limp.

## KITTY CAT

Kitty Cat purry, Kitty Cat furry,
Stretching in the sun. (*Stretch.*)
Kitty Cat purry, Kitty Cat furry,
Yawning in the sun. (*Yawn.*)
Kitty Cat purry, Kitty Cat furry,
Sleeping in the sun. (*Close eyes and curl up.*)
—L.B.S.

## ALEXANDER'S SLEEPY TIME

Puppy said, "I cannot go to sleep until I have said goodnight to Alexander. He gives me bones to chew and he pats my head with his gentle hands. It is bedtime for dogs and children, but I cannot go to sleep until I have said goodnight to Alexander."

So Puppy went to see if Alexander was asleep, but he wasn't—not quite—but almost.

One puppy went into the room,
 (*Children repeat this refrain.*)
Creep, creep, creep,
To see if Alexander was asleep,
 sleep, sleep.

"I cannot go to bed," said Kitten Cat, "until I have said goodnight to Alexander. He lets me play with a ball of string and he cuddles me in his arms. It is bedtime for cats and children, but I cannot go to bed until I have said goodnight to Alexander."

So Kitten Cat went to see if Alexander was asleep, but he wasn't yet—not quite.

One kitten went into the room,
 (*Children repeat.*)
Creep, creep, creep,
To see if Alexander was asleep,
 sleep, sleep.

"I cannot go to bed," said Baby Bunny, "until I have said goodnight to Alexander. He picks me up so carefully and he never pulls my long ears. Sometimes Alexander gives me a sweet carrot. It is bedtime for bunnies and children, but I cannot go to bed until I have said goodnight to Alexander."

>One bunny went into the room,
>    (*Children repeat.*)
>Creep, creep, creep,
>To see if Alexander was asleep,
>    sleep, sleep.

And he WAS! *Sound asleep!* (*Children whisper.*)

Adapted and rewritten by L.B.S. from<br>*Baby Ray* by EUDORA BUMSTEAD, 1890.

## THE SLEEPY, SLEEPY PLACE

Once there was a sleepy, sleepy place under a shadowy, shade tree. In that sleepy, sleepy place lay a small, brown puppy. The puppy stood up and yawned; he yawned and he stretched and he stretched.

Then he went to look for something to nibble and gnaw. (*Children yawn.*) He found a juicy bone and took it into his doghouse. He gnawed it for awhile, but he couldn't keep his eyes open. So he went back to the sleepy, sleepy place and soon he was fast asleep. (*Children lay clasped hands beside head.*)

Once there was a furry, purry, little, gray ball of a kitten.

She said in a wee voice and such a sleepy voice, "Oh, my! I am so sleepy."

So she yawned and yawned and yawned. (*Children yawn.*) She found a basket on the back porch and climbed inside, but she couldn't sleep. So she went to the sleepy, sleepy place under the shadowy, shade tree and soon *she* was fast asleep. What a furry, purry kitten. (*Whisper.*)

>There was a baby chick all yellow and sweet.
>And he looked all around for something to eat.

"Peep, peep," peeped the yellow chick.

The mother hen knew that her baby chick was hungry, so she found some yellow meal for him. She knew that her baby chick was tired, so she went to the sleepy, sleepy place under the shadowy, shade tree. She sat down and spread out her feathers so that the little, yellow chick could creep under them. Then what do you think happened? (*Responses.*)

> Oh, it was such a yawning day,
> That nobody wanted to work or play,
> And EVERYBODY felt the very same way.
>
> There was a duckling who quacked and quacked.
> He had soft down upon his back.
> He was tired of swimming and everything,
> So he put his head down under his wing.
> And there under the shadowy, shady tree
> He slept until it was half past three!
>    (*Children place clasped hands beside head.*)
>
> A little, old pig gave a big, loud squeal,
> As he ate every scrap of his noonday meal.
> And under the shadowy, shady tree
> He slept as quietly as could be.
>    (*Children act out.*)
>
> A butterfly, blue, green, and red,
> Sat with her wings above her head
>    (*Fold arms over head and close eyes.*)
> Up on a branch of the shadowy tree.
> Oh, what a sleepy place to be!

A little boy saw all of these marvelous sleepy things and just looking at them made him feel so—sleepy. He lay on his back under the shadowy, shade tree just as you are lying now in your very own quiet, sleepy, sleepy place.

—L.B.S.

## THE FOG ELF

Have you ever seen fog? Have you ever felt it? Fog is gentle and very soft. It feels wet on your face if you are walking on the street. It smells of seaweed and salty ocean waves.

Now a little fog elf lives by the ocean. He wraps a blanket of fog around buildings and trees and he will not let the moonbeam elves be seen.

One night the quiet, little fog elf came and sat on Teddy's window sill when he was in bed, and Teddy said, "Who *are* you?"

The fog elf whispered, "I am the fog elf. How do you do, Teddy?"

Teddy answered, "I'm fine, thank you. But you are so quiet, Fog Elf. I can smell and feel the fog around you, but I cannot see you."

"It doesn't matter," said the fog elf in a very still voice. "The moonbeam elves are trying to peek through the fog now and soon I shall have to leave."

"Oh, please don't go, Fog Elf," begged Teddy.

But the fog elf whispered, "Good-by, good-by, good-by. Another foggy night I'll come to see you, Teddy. Good-by."

By that time, Teddy's eyelids were so heavy with sleep that he didn't even know that the moonbeam elves had come and the fog elf had disappeared to be part of the big, wide ocean.

—L.B.S.

The story should be told very slowly, almost in a whispered tone. Discuss fog before reading it.

SUPPLEMENTARY REFERENCES

Arbuthnot, May Hill: *Children's Books Too Good to Miss*, Western Reserve University Press, Cleveland, 1966.

Briggs, Raymond: *Fee-Fi-Fo-Fum*, Coward-McCann, Inc., New York, 1964.

———: *The Mother Goose Treasury*, Coward-McCann, Inc., New York, 1966.

Cremonini: *Golden Treasury of Wonderful Fairy Tales*, Golden Press, Inc., New York, 1960.

De Angeli, Marguerite: *Book of Nursery and Mother Goose Rhymes*, Doubleday and Company, Inc., Garden City, New York, 1954.

Huber, Miriam, ed.: *Story and Verse for Children*, The Macmillan Company, New York, 1965.

Ohanian, Phyllis Brown: *Favorite Nursery Songs*, Random House, Inc., New York, 1956.

Radlauer, Ruth Shaw: *Of Course, You're a Horse*, Abelard-Schuman, Ltd., New York, 1959.

Siks, Geraldine B.: *Children's Literature for Dramatization: An Anthology*, Harper and Row, Publishers, New York, 1964.

Smith, James S.: *A Critical Approach to Children's Literature*, McGraw-Hill, Inc., New York, 1967.

Wagner, Joseph, and R. W. Smith: *A Teacher's Guide to Storytelling*, William C. Brown Company, Publishers, Dubuque, Iowa, 1958.

CHAPTER 4

# Where We Live, Work, and Play

The education of young children begins in the home and in the immediate community. The center extends and enriches these previous learning experiences and helps to lay the groundwork for the child's physical, emotional, intellectual, and social life. The school is a new environment where the child must make adjustments to the teacher, other adults, and classmates, and meet new challenges of learning.

To enable him to meet the necessary challenges of change, the school provides appropriate surroundings and understanding. It helps him relate to his family and neighborhood by creating attitudes toward and concern for the individuals who work constructively to make a good, functioning community. The center helps the child to accept and enjoy learning by beginning at his level of maturity, motivating him, and making successes for him possible.

The question of what to teach children at the preschool level is answered by Betty Willsher: "I give them a chance to learn, to be independent, to mix, adjust, make friends, concentrate, have fun and work, and play together. I don't *teach* them, but *I let it happen.*"[1] Setting the stage for all learning means beginning with the *present*. The child's interest in what is happening is interest in immediacy.

The present is the education center which can bewilder the child and cause stress and anxiety. In this new environment, where he must learn both self-sustained and cooperative play, the sudden impact of adjustment can be disturbing. This change is intensified by the fact that he is one among many, and cannot have the sole attention of the teacher.

The child's center of operation up to now has been the home where his behavior and concepts were formed through interaction with the people in that home. The transition from the narrow confines of the

---

[1] Betty Willsher. *School Before Five,* Faber and Faber, Ltd., London, 1959, p. 40.

home to the wider area of the school now takes place. Thus, the child's community life extends to a larger group where he must begin to relate to new adults and to children his own age. This adaptation to the community is an inevitable part of education. The teachers and administrators of the education center arrange the circumstances so that this adaptation is as smooth and comfortable as possible.

Human beings begin with few ready made patterns of adaptation to the environment as contrasted with creatures who live by instinct. Though the child has powerful urges and a sensory system that directs his learning, that system must be controlled and modified by favorable, environmental conditions and experiences.

From the family, the child has learned his behavior and his way of feeling. He now comes to the education center equipped with varieties of these patterns. The home has provided love and safety for him or it has created a negative self-image and feelings of insecurity. Through careful observation, the teacher discovers and determines the child's individual needs so that she can become more perceptive in opening avenues of learning to him and in giving him freedom to grow.

The teacher can stimulate conversation about the home and thus learn much about it.

> What does a mother do for you?
> What does a father do for you?
> What do you do for your parents?
> Who lives in your home?

The children's responses will help give the teacher insight into each child's attitudes and problems, and she may learn something about the needs of the family as well. Shared conversation can create a better relationship with the environment as the child learns how his home is similar to or different from that of his classmates. The teacher should be careful, however, not to imply that any single home composition or grouping is the acceptable one.

Suggestions for further questions are:

> Who is a neighbor?
> What is a neighborhood?
> Who serves us?
> Who helps to make our neighborhood safe?
> What can we do to make our neighborhood
> a nicer place to live?

If the education center is intelligently organized with adequate play equipment suitable for young children, it can help them to grow in understanding of how members of the family work and how their work can be pleasurable and rich in real personal compensation for effort expended. The capacity of a child to learn from experience and the potent, urgent need to adapt to a very complex and often chaotic society involve understanding. Proper equipment and materials with learning possibilities are a necessity.

Within this chapter are stories, poems, devices, and ideas which the teacher can use to help the children understand the work which people perform and the contributions these people make to society. These activities will also help foster an appreciation of the home, family, and school.

## WORKERS IN OUR NEIGHBORHOOD

There's the man who feeds the lions in the zoo,
And the man who drives an engine to a fire.
There's the man who sells an ice cream cone to you,
And the man who mends a high electric wire.

There's the man who drives a sweeper
    through the streets,
And the baker with a cookie or a bun.
There's the butcher man who sells my mother meats,
And I'm very glad we've got them, every one!

—V.S.P.

If possible, show a picture of each worker mentioned in the poem; discuss his work, and relate it to the neighborhood in which the child lives. Ask: "Why are we glad to have the zoo keeper? The butcher? The fireman? The baker? What does a mailman do? A dentist? What is your doctor's name? Your grocer's name?"

## DADDIES

There are daddies and daddies, all kinds of daddies;
Daddies do kind things for me and for you.
There are daddies and daddies, all kinds of daddies,
There are all kinds of work for daddies to do.

Some daddies are funny circus clowns;
They turn somersaults and stand upside down.
Some daddies are barbers that cut our hair
As we sit up straight in the barber chair.

Some daddies are milkmen that come to the door
Each morning early at half past four.
Some daddies are policemen who stand on a beat
And help little children to cross the street.

Some daddies are mailmen who bring the mail
Through snow and sleet and rain and hail.
Some daddies are bakers who cook and bake
Doughnuts and pie and birthday cake.

Some daddies are cowboys who like to ride
Over the trails and prairies so wide.
Some daddies are farmers who work on a farm.
They have silos and tractors and horses and barns.

Some daddies are firemen with ladder and hose;
They save our homes, our toys, and our clothes.
Some daddies are doctors who like to tell
Boys and girls how to try to keep well.

Some daddies are soldiers who stand up tall.
They always travel where duty calls.
Some daddies are teachers who teach us well,
How to read and write and spell.

Some daddies are grocers who sell potatoes,
And peas and cabbage and ripe red tomatoes.
Some daddies are artists who paint baby faces,
And beautiful scenery in far away places.

There are daddies and daddies, all kinds of daddies;
Daddies do kind things for me and for you.
There are daddies and daddies, all kinds of daddies,
There are all kinds of work for daddies to do.

—L.B.S.

Read the poem in parts and show pictures of the workers if available. Ask: "What other kinds of work are there? Do you know anyone who is a custodian or truck driver? Tell what he does. What work would you like to do when you grow up?" Encourage the children to play the worker they like best. Use different ethnic puppet dolls for dramatizing the activity.

### WHO USES IT?

Bring in the suggested tools or objects which are associated with these jobs:

| | |
|---|---|
| menu—waiter (waitress) | scissors—barber |
| letter—postman | book—librarian |
| cookies—baker | broom—custodian |
| telephone—installer | hatchet—fireman |
| carton—milkman | hammer—carpenter |
| whistle—policeman | thermometer—nurse |
| stethoscope—doctor | curlers—beauty operator |
| flowers—gardener | toothbrush—dentist |
| typewriter—secretary | compass—pilot |
| window spray—service station man | shopping bag—supermarket clerk |
| tool box—mechanic | microscope—scientist |

Display the tool or object. Ask the children to describe it and tell which community helper or worker uses it. More than one worker may be named for some items.

### OUR BABY SITTER

When my folks must go away.
And grandma or my aunts can't come,
The baby sitter comes. And say!
We always have the best of fun!

My mother tells her where to call
In case that anything goes wrong.
We've never had to phone at all.
We help each other get along.

She reads us stories and we sing,
Or play some quiet games instead;
Or else we do some coloring
Until it's time to go to bed.

—V.S.P.

Before reading the poem, ask: "Has a baby sitter ever stayed with you while your mother was away? Tell how the baby sitter helped you. What did you do to make things easier for her so that you could have a good time? What are some quiet and interesting things to do before going to bed? Why does a baby sitter have to be responsible? What does the word *responsible* mean?"

The girls will enjoy playing baby sitter with their dolls in the playhouse.

## TRAFFIC LIGHT

Red on top and green below.
Red means STOP, and green means GO.
Yellow means SLOW.

—Anonymous

Cut three holes, one under the other, in two rectangular pieces of black tagboard. Glue red, yellow, and green tissue or crepe paper behind the holes of one; then glue the rectangles securely together. The children take turns holding a lighted flashlight behind each color as the rhyme is said by the class.

### THE METER READER

The meter reader comes around.
He has a pencil and a book.
He walks up to our meter box;
He squints and takes a careful look.

He writes the numbers that he sees;
They show how much we have to pay
For water and electric lights.
He writes it down and goes away.
—V.S.P.

Before reading the poem, ask: "Have you seen a meter box? Where? Does the meter man come to your house?" If there is a meter at school in an accessible place, take the class on a tour to see it.

Suggest that the children play the worker.

### AIRPLANES

In the sky the airplanes sail
With the people and the mail.
As they fly along the way,
Folks eat dinner from a tray.
—L.B.S.

Ask: "Have you ever ridden in an airplane? Do you know of someone who has? Do you know anyone who is a pilot? A stewardess? What does a pilot do? A stewardess? Who helps pilot a plane?" If a child has taken a ride in an airplane, ask him to tell about his experience.

If possible, take the class to the airport and get permission for someone to conduct the group through the cabin and cockpit of a plane. At snack time pretend to be eating dinner on a plane.

### BIG SCHOOL BUS

Don't you want to come with us
And ride inside a big school bus?
Our driver guides the bus with skill
Around a curve or down a hill.

He watches traffic carefully,
And he's as jolly as can be.
Don't you want to come with us
And ride inside a big school bus?
—L.B.S.

If the children travel in a school bus, ask: "Why do you like the ride on the school bus? Why do you feel safe? How can we help the bus driver?" If some children walk to school, discuss why others must ride a bus. Ask: "Would you like to ride a bus to school? Why?"

Ask the class to join in saying the first and last two lines of the poem.

## FIRST AID

This little froggie hurt his toe.
This little froggie cried, "Oh, oh!"
This little froggie said, "That's bad."
This little froggie said, "How sad."
This little froggie, helpful and good,
Ran for the nurse as fast as he could.
—Old rhyme

Use this rhyme as a finger play or with flannelboard characters, or stick puppets. Discuss how the school nurse helps children. Ask her to visit the class and talk about her duties.

## PLAYING COWBOY

One is for the mountain, (1)
Two is for the sea. (2)
Now I have a cowboy hat.
I hope it will fit ME!
—O.M.A.

As you say the poem, draw the two configurations on the chalkboard. The numerals at the end of the first two lines correspond to the numbered parts of the picture.

Discuss cowboys and the work they do. Ask: "Have you ever seen a cowboy? Where? Would you like to be a cowboy? Why?"

Galloping music and stick horses for the children may be provided. Stuff a large sock with discarded nylon stockings or other filling. Add felt ears, eyes, nostrils, and reins. Fit the stuffed sock over a broomstick and tie securely.

## A PLAY ELEVATOR

A child pretends to be an elevator operator and opens the door that leads to the hall or to the outside as several playmates enter. He closes the door and calls out the floors, letting each child out (back into the room) as he reaches a desired "floor."

## THE TRAIN RIDE

In the amusement park, there was a little train.
The bell went, "Ding, ding!" (*Children repeat.*)
The engine went, "Choo-choo-choo!"
  (*Children repeat.*)
The little train went, "Ch, ch, ch, ch, ch."
Then it slowed down—and stopped,
"Ch, ch, ch, ch—SHHHHHHHH." (*Children repeat.*)

A boy with a blue shirt got on. His name was ―――――. (*Use the name of a child in the class who is wearing a blue shirt.*)

The bell went, "Ding, ding!"
The engine went, "Choo-choo-choo!"
The little train went, "Ch, ch, ch, ch, ch."
Then it slowed down and stopped,
"Ch, ch, ch, ch—SHHHHHHHH."

A girl with a green dress got on. Her name was ―――――. (*Use the name of a child in the class.*)

The little train picked up many passengers as it ran around the track in the amusement park. The children had a jolly time. But of course, they all had to get off and go home to supper.

So the bell went, "Ding, ding!"
The engine went, "Choo-choo-choo!"
The little train went, "Ch, ch, ch, ch, ch."
It slowed down, "Ch, ch, ch — SHHHHHHHH."

And it stopped to let _____ off. (*Supply the names of all the children who were riding on the train.*)

—L.B.S.

Continue each part of the story until every child in the group has had a chance to ride and get off. Each child can recognize himself from the clothing or personal description the teacher supplies.

### VISIT A HOME BEING BUILT

When you take the children to see a home being built, they will observe the vast amount of materials and equipment being used, and the number of workers in action. To visit on successive days will give the group a chance to see that one day's work follows another in order to give the desired results. This excursion will lead to all kinds of follow-up and play activities and will include each child.

Different kinds of buildings may be discussed. Ask: "What building would you like to make here in the classroom? What materials would you use?"

Toy wagons can be used for carrying away materials at the end of the play session. However, most children are ingenious at improvising and using their own ideas for cleaning up.

### RIDDLES IN RHYME

I am part of your house,
And you open me wide;
Then you shut me
As soon as you come inside.
Who am I? (Door.)

I am slanted up high,
And I point toward the sky.
Sometimes I am wet;
Sometimes I am dry.
Who am I? (Roof.)

I am made of glass,
And I let in the light.
I have two curtains
So clean and white.
Who am I? (Window.)
—O.M.A.

Use hand and finger movements to pantomime the answers.

### DOS PATITOS (Two Little Ducks)

Dos patitos se encontraron.
  (Two ducks met.)
  (*Move two fingers toward each other.*)
El patito graznó:—¿Adónde vas, amigo?
  (Little duck quacked,"Where are you going, my friend?")
  (*Wiggle right thumb.*)
El patito graznó: Voy a la escuela.
  (Little duck quacked, "I am going to school.)
  (*Wiggle left thumb.*)
—¿Adónde vas, amigo?
  ("Where are you going, my friend?")
  (*Wiggle left thumb.*)
—Voy a mi casa.
  ("I am going home.)
  (*Wiggle right thumb.*)
—Adiós.
  ("Good-by.")
  (*Put right thumb behind back.*)
—Adiós.
  ("Good-by.")
  (*Put left thumb behind back.*)

—L.B.S.

Cut two duck shapes from felt; add features with felt tip pen and a felt sombrero to each one. Be sure that the ducks face each other. The children may move them on the flannelboard as puppets.

## THE PLAYHOUSE

Playing in a miniature house is not expected to serve as a pastime to keep children busy. This activity is an integral part of the education program of the center. Care and planning are given to the creation of the playhouse area in order that learning and enriching experiences can occur. Yet, the children's play in the area is spontaneous, satisfying, and delightful, and is without adult pressures.

Many children find that trying to fit into adult standards is bewildering and sometimes exacting. If a young child can play adult work in a simulated adult setting, this substitution can hasten his adaptation to society. The girl may eventually become a mother; the boy may become a pilot or drive a truck. Dolls and blocks, therefore, can help the child to move more easily toward adjustment to real-life situations.

The playhouse is a place where the child can cope with the strains of everyday life and act out his desires, hostilities, angers, and inner conflicts. Here is a safe, work-play center where he can travel at his own speed while feeling, touching, observing, exploring, moving, pushing, talking, listening, and questioning. The only limitation he encounters is that it is someone else's turn at the playhouse or it is time to play in the yard or to go home.

The playhouse has tremendous appeal for young children at all times of the year. It provides an opportunity for both individual and small group activity. As children play and work together, their linguistic and reasoning powers are developed in an atmosphere of mutually valuable interaction. This social interplay increases a child's chances to enrich and extend his vocabulary, to exchange ideas and thoughts, and to formulate sentences. Language experiences within the playhouse serve as a setting for acceptable social behavior, problem solving, and decision making. Number concepts, health, safety, art, music, and dramatic play are also among the learning experiences enjoyed in the playhouse setting.

Aside from practice in oral communication skills, aesthetic experiences, and cognitive values, children gain many social benefits as well. They learn the duties performed within the home; they gain insight into how individuals cooperate and work together; they begin to appreciate those workers in the neighborhood with whom they come into direct contact; and they gain practice in caring for the home itself.

The child finds stability through the support of another child as he works and plays. He can contribute at his own level of ability and he can guide and be guided by another. He works beside someone who perhaps has mastered certain skills better then he, and who can serve as a model for him. Each child, then, shares his own talents and experiences.

The flexibility in working with a playhouse and the freedom to choose partners enable a child to learn in a leisurely fashion as he explores, listens, observes, imitates, absorbs, and communicates.

## PLAYHOUSE IDEAS

If the playhouse is a large carton, the children may gain the experience of papering it, using the school's recommended paste. If movable screens are used in and around the playhouse area, the children may attach wallpaper to the screens with thumb tacks. Suggest that they paint their own wallpaper designs on large easel paper.

Make use of materials from the scrap box for table cloths, napkins, and curtains. (Check with the custodian on any fire laws which may prohibit the use of cloth curtains.)

Provide a schedule for occupancy so that the children will know when they can take turns playing in the playhouse.

Suggested articles and equipment for dramatic play are:

| | |
|---|---|
| two dolls | ironing board and iron |
| two carriages | a full length mirror |
| chest for doll clothes | dress-up clothes |
| doll bed and bed clothing | wastebasket |
| furniture | a doctor's bag |
| kitchenware | play money |
| broom and mop | a stethoscope |
| telephones | hats |

## KEEPING THE HOUSE CLEAN

Set the table,
Sweep the stairs,
Pick up papers,
Dust the chairs.

Ask the class to tell other ways to keep a house clean. After saying the rhyme a few times, children may begin to chant their own rhymes.

## ON WASHING DAY

On washing day, on washing day,
The washer scrubs the clothes this way.
   (*Children pantomime actions.*)
On washing day, on washing day,
Mother hangs the clothes this way.
On washing day, on washing day,
Mother irons the clothes this way.
On washing day, on washing day,
We do our work and then we play.
          —Author unknown

Say: "Tell how your mother washes the clothes. How do you help her on washing day?"

## READY FOR SCHOOL

Here is a circle which is my head.
   (*Hands at side of head.*)
Here is my mouth where food is fed.
   (*Pointer fingers at each side of mouth.*)
Here are my eyes that help me see.
   (*Point to eyes.*)
Here is my nose that is part of *me*.
   (*Point to nose.*)
Here is the hair that grows on my head.
   (*Hand on head.*)
Here are my lips that are pink or red.
   (*Point to lips.*)
Here I am ready for work and play!
   (*Spread hands apart.*)
Here I am ready for school today!
   (*Fold hands.*)
          —L.B.S.

## HELPING MOTHER

Danny and Susie wanted to know how they could help Mother. They had a long talk about it because they knew helping Mother would please her very much. Here are some of the things Danny and Susie did. You can do these things, too.

They picked up papers off the floor.
They wiped finger marks off the door with a sponge.
They held the clothespin bag for Mother as she hung clothes upon the line.
They dusted chairs.
They helped pick weeds in the yard.
They swept the sidewalk with a small broom.
They helped Mother fill the grocery cart at the supermarket.
They brought in the newspaper.
They picked some flowers for the table.

—V.S.P. and L.B.S.

Ask: "What are some ways you can help *your* mother?" Make a book of children's illustrations which depict ways in which they help their mothers. At the bottom of each page, record the child's dictated sentence about his picture. Place the book on the browsing table for the children to enjoy.

## OFF TO SCHOOL

TEACHER: Hippety-hop, we are off to school!
CHILDREN: Hippety-hippety-hop.

TEACHER: Hippety-hop, November is cool.
CHILDREN: Hippety-hippety-hop.

TEACHER: Hippety-hop and down the street.
CHILDREN: Hippety-hippety-hop.

TEACHER: Hippety-hop with nimble feet.
CHILDREN: Hippety-hippety-hop.

TEACHER: Hippety-hop and down the block.
CHILDREN: Hippety-hippety-hop.

TEACHER: Hippety-hop, it's eight o'clock.
CHILDREN: Hippety-hippety-hop.

—L.B.S.

The group sings or says the refrain as two or three children take turns skipping lightly around the room.

## A SURPRISE FOR THE TEACHER

One bright September morning, Nathan hummed a happy tune because he was on his way to school and he was five years old. But Nathan had another reason to be happy. There was a surprise in his pocket—a surprise for his teacher.

Nathan skipped along and sang:

>"I have surprise!
>I have a surprise!
>   *(Children say the refrain.)*
>A-ticket-a-tocket,
>Right here in my pocket."

Nathan met a kind policeman at the cross walk.

"Hi," said Nathan.

And the policeman smiled and said, "Hi! My, you look awfully happy, Nathan."

And Nathan sang:

>"I have a surprise!
>I have a surprise!
>A-ticket-a-tocket,
>Right here in my pocket!"

Nathan skipped on his way.

Soon he came to the school and the teacher asked, "Don't you want to take off your jacket, Nathan? You may hang it on any hanger that you like best."

Nathan shook his head for no and said:

>"I have a surprise!
>I have a surprise!
>A-ticket-a-tocket,
>Right here in my pocket."

The teacher smiled and pinned a name card on Nathan's shirt. The name on the card was NATHAN.

The surprise in Nathan's pocket looked like this. (*Show an apple bulge in your pocket or that of a child's.*) Can you guess what was in Nathan's pocket? (*Responses.*)

Nathan tried to take the surprise out of his pocket. He pulled and he pulled, but he couldn't get the surprise out. The teacher pulled and pulled, but she couldn't get it out either.

Finally, the principal came into the room. He pulled and he pulled, but he couldn't get the surprise out of Nathan's pocket.

Then the custodian came in to empty the wastebasket.

"What's this?" asked the custodian. "Could I help?"

Nathan said:

> "I have a surprise!
> I have a surprise!
> Right here in my pocket,
> A-ticket-a-tocket,
> And it WON'T COME OUT."

"Hmmmmm," said the custodian. "Let me have a try.

> "Hocus-pocus, turn about,
> Turn this pocket inside out."

And what do you think?

The surprise was an APPLE—an APPLE for Nathan's teacher.

—L.B.S.

Ask: "What do you think the teacher did with the apple? Can you think of something else the surprise might have been—something that was round like an apple?"

## SARAH FINDS SOMEBODY TO PLAY WITH

Sarah was tired of playing with her dolly.

"I want a real live person to play with," said Sarah. "I want somebody who has real hair and eyes and nose and mouth—somebody who can talk to me."

Sarah met a cow.

"Come and play with my baby calf," said the cow.

"How old is your baby calf?" asked Sarah.

"One week old," replied the cow proudly.

"Oh, dear," sighed Sarah. "Your baby calf is too young. I am five. I want to play with somebody who is my age."

Sarah saw a squirrel eating a nut.

"Please, Mrs. Squirrel," said Sarah. "Do you know of somebody I can play with?"

Mrs. Squirrel said, "You are welcome to play with my baby squirrels if you are gentle with them."

"How old are your baby squirrels?" asked Sarah.

"Three days old," replied the mother squirrel.

Sarah said, "Thank you just the same, but I must find somebody my own age to play with. You see I am FIVE."

"Well," said Mrs. Squirrel, "that's a great many years to be alive."

Sarah walked on and finally she came to a building. Inside the building were fifteen boys and girls. Can you guess what that building was? (*Responses.*)

Of course, it was a school. And inside one wonderful and interesting room, Sarah found somebody to play with—fifteen friends her own age.

—L.B.S.

Add other animals to extend the story for dramatization.

Ask: "Have you ever wanted somebody your own age to play with? Have you ever felt lonesome? How do you go about making friends? Do you like friendly people? What is a friend? Name a special friend whom you like? Can grown-ups be friends, too? What games do you like to play with your friends?"

## A STORY TO FINISH

One day, Penny walked down a garden path all alone.

"Mew," said Tiny Kitten. "Where are you going?"

"I'm going for a walk," replied Penny. "Come with me."

Tiny Kitten mewed, "I'm sorry. I haven't time. I must catch mice. But thank you anyway."

Penny walked on and met Pudgy Puppy.

"Bow-wow," barked Pudgy Puppy. "Where are you going?"

"I'm going for a walk," replied Penny, patting the puppy's head. "Come with me."

"I can't," said round, fat Pudgy Puppy. "I haven't time. I must guard the house to see that my master is safe."

"Well," said Penny, "Tiny Kitten is busy. Pudgy Puppy is busy. I want to be busy, too."

And Penny went right home to find something to keep herself busy. What did she find to do? (*Responses.*)

—L.B.S.

The children will share a variety of responses.

Add other animals for dramatization or use cutouts for the flannelboard. Encourage the children to tell the story in relays. Discuss the difference between "keeping busy" and doing work that is worthwhile. Ask the class to repeat what Penny did to help her mother. Write their responses and read them aloud.

## THE NICEST PLACE IN THE WORLD

A little boy once said, "I want to see the nicest place in the world."
So he started out and he walked and he walked and he walked.
The little boy saw a bird.
"Where is the nicest place in the world?" he asked.

"Right here in this oak tree," replied the bird. "My nest is made of soft grasses and twigs and it is such a comfortable place to be. Oh, yes, this nest in the tree is the most wonderful place in the whole world."

Well, the little boy was too polite to disagree, but he really didn't feel a nest would be the nicest place in the world for him.

"I'm glad you like your nest, little bird," he said as he walked on his way.

He walked and he walked and he walked. Soon he found a pond where a silvery fish was swimming.

"Where is the nicest place in the world?" the little boy asked the silvery fish.

The silvery fish blew three bubbles and replied, "A pond of fresh bubble water is the nicest bubble place in the bubble world. Anyone knows that!"

Of course, the little boy liked water very much for swimming and taking a bath, but he didn't want to live in it forever and ever, so he said good-by to the silvery fish and walked on. He walked and he walked and he walked. And then he came to a neat, white house in a green yard sprinkled with flowers. He walked up the steps to the front door. Right inside the open door stood a beautiful lady with a kind, smiling face.

The little boy asked, "Where is the nicest place in the world?"

"A warm, safe house," said the beautiful lady, who was the little boy's mother.

Then the little boy knew that a *house* was really and truly the nicest place in the world, especially when it was his very own house.

—L.B.S.

Ask: "Did you like the way the story ended? Why? What is the nicest thing you can think of about a house? Which room in the house do you like best? Why?"

The children may dramatize the story using additional animal characters.

Make a room border of the children's drawings of their homes. Put each child's address on his house.

### WAKE-UP STORY

The sun was up. Five chicks, four ducks, three bunnies, two kittens, and one, little bitty dog were waiting for Alexander to appear at his window, but Alexander was fast asleep. He didn't even hear his mother go into the bathroom to turn on the water for his bath.

> The water swished into the tub
> *(Children join in.)*
> For Alexander to have a scrub.

Mother then went to the kitchen and turned on the stove burner so that she could cook Alexander's cereal.

> The water swished into the tub
> *(Children join in.)*
> For Alexander to have a scrub.
> How hot and red the fire looked
> So that his cereal could be cooked.

Next, Mother went to the porch to get a carton of milk which the milkman had left for Alexander.

> The water swished into the tub
> *(Children join in.)*
> For Alexander to have a scrub.
> How hot and red the fire looked
> So that his cereal could be cooked.
> The milk was fresh and it was cool
> To drink before he went to school.

Mother then squeezed oranges for juice and she boiled an egg for Alexander.

> The water swished into the tub
>   (*Children join in.*)
> For Alexander to have a scrub.
> How hot and red the fire looked
> So that his cereal could be cooked.
> The milk was fresh and it was cool
> To drink before he went to school.
> The orange juice was good and sweet;
> An egg was boiled for him to eat.

The five chicks, four ducks, three bunnies, two kittens, and one, little bitty puppy waited for Alexander. Alexander got out of bed and went to the window to wave at them.

He skipped into the bathroom to brush his teeth. He took off his pajamas and got into the tub of warm water. Then he dressed and went hippety-hop downstairs to the kitchen to eat his breakfast before he went to school.

> The water swished into the tub
>   (*Children join in.*)
> For Alexander to have a scrub.
> How hot and red the fire looked
> So that his cereal could be cooked.
> The milk was fresh and it was cool
> To drink before he went to school.
> The orange juice was good and sweet;
> An egg was boiled for him to eat.

And this is the way Alexander's day began!

—Adapted by L.B.S. from an old tale

## MOTHERS VISIT THE CENTER

Effective education calls for continuous cooperation between parents and school. The young child matures socially, emotionally, and educationally much more if the home and the school are not two separate worlds. Since these two environments make up the child's entire existence, sympathetic understanding must be engendered by an exchange of information between teacher and mother. This interaction will result in better support and treatment of the child.

Personal invitations to an open house, tea, or meeting may be sent to the mothers at the beginning of the school session or shortly before it. This contact should be informal because mothers may be reluctant for various reasons to participate in school activities. Sometimes language barriers obstruct the formation of positive relationships, and often parents have had little or no contact with the school. Because they often stand in awe of what they do not comprehend, such a get-together session must be planned thoughtfully with the culture of the people and the neighborhood in mind.

The teacher may secure snapshots of the child, if possible, or take pictures with her own camera. One of these snapshots may be clipped to the mother's name card so that she may be identified by other mothers and by the teacher, who must associate mother and child and recall each name. After greetings and introductions, the mother will enjoy seeing the snapshots shown with an opaque projector.

Each mother should be welcomed individually and asked to visit the child's class so that she can thus observe her own child in relation to the other children of similar age. Consequently, she may take a more objective view of him.

If baby sitting is a problem, perhaps mothers can take turns caring for the very young children so that visitation and assistance by individuals will be possible. A mother "chairman" who is well liked can work wonders at planning activities and delegating responsibilities.

Through careful questioning, the teacher can learn much about the child; this knowledge may help her in understanding and guiding him at the center. The teacher should show genuine interest in the mother's suggestions and refrain from "talking down to her." If a mother feels that her ideas are given consideration, she will be more likely to cooperate with the school. When parents are made to feel relaxed and confident, they tend to share personal information about the home and child. The following questions may be used to obtain this information:

Does he depend upon himself, yet seek comfort when it is needed?
Does he exercise self-control in waiting his turn or in not having his way?
Does he work with others and enjoy being with them?
Does he wash his own hands and face?
Does he show interest in books?
Does he ask questions?
Does he get along with his brothers and sisters?
Does he hear another language spoken at home? If so, which one?

Does he wet the bed, suck his thumb, or have unusual fears?
Does he have temper tantrums?
Does he eat and sleep well?
Does he have a pet?

Plan another informal session for the purpose of explaining the general goals of the center and the learning experiences each child will encounter. Encourage the mothers to ask questions freely and contribute to the discussions.

An important purpose of these relationships with parents is to discover more about the child's:

Perceptiveness
History of childhood diseases
Sleeping habits
Use of toilet facilities
Physical well-being

Sensitivity
Shyness or aggressiveness
Ability to both lead and follow
Acceptance of responsibility
Interests and experiences

This kind of information enables the teacher to work more effectively with the child.

## SCRAPBOOKS

Here are ideas which may be included in a child's personal scrapbook:

Baby photographs
His first words
His drawings or poems
Happenings on his first birthday
Anecdotes about him
His favorite magazine pictures
His hand and foot prints

Inexpensive scrapbooks can be made or purchased at a variety store. Mothers may supply photographs and information to be included. The book may be added to as the child develops and encounters new experiences. He may take his scrapbook home occasionally so his mother can add other information to it. This book will give the child a personal possession to enjoy, discuss, and share with others.

## IDENTIFYING NAME

Ask the mothers for snapshots of the children which can be mounted on tagboard. Write the child's first name under his picture. This picture will help him to identify his name. When he learns to recognize his name without a model in other activities, remove the picture and return it to the mother.

## BABY AND GROUP PHOTOGRAPHS

As a baby picture is viewed with an opaque projector, the group is given an opportunity to guess who the child is. The picture then is returned to the rightful owner.

Show pictures of activities at school: children eating snacks, playing on the playground, or listening to a story. The children will enjoy identifying themselves in these magnified pictures.

## OUR ABC BOOK

Staple large sheets of wrapping paper together to form a book. Make an oilcloth cover for it. Ask the mothers to look for magazine pictures which can be pasted inside the book. Select the best ones and arrange them alphabetically according to the beginning sound of the name of each picture.

## WHAT MOTHERS CAN DO

There are many opportunities for mothers to assume responsibilities in helping with the upkeep of the room, supervising activities in the room and on the playground, and constructing materials.

Mothers may take turns laundering aprons, doll clothes, and dress-up materials for creative play.

They may oversee a group work period while the teacher gives individual attention to one child who may need help in handling scissors, holding crayons, or discriminating colors.

They may help collect and mount seasonal room decorations.

They may make doll clothes and bedding, stuff gingham shapes for toys, construct puppets, and provide textures for the "feel" book.

They may straighten shelves and help children put things away at the end of an activity.

They may provide discarded muffin tins and strainers for the sandbox.

They may take cookies home to bake after the children have cut them and have arranged them on a baking sheet.

Mothers may make paper hats and costumes for parades, rhythm bands, and holiday activities.

They may serve on a telephone committee and call other mothers regarding projects and meetings. This service will cut down on the number of notes that must be sent home. Mothers are more likely to respond to invitations from their neighbors than from printed notes sent from school.

After the teacher has written each child's name on a 4" x 9" piece of tagboard, mothers may cover the boards with acetate. Each child may take this name model home and practice tracing his name with his finger or with crayon. Covering the tagboard with acetate enables the child to erase his marks with a tissue or a damp sponge.

Mothers may paint wooden coat hangers to match the children's coats, so that they can find them more easily.

The experiences that mothers gain through cooperation in school projects are very rewarding, both to them and to the education center.

SUPPLEMENTARY REFERENCES

Barr, Jene, and Cynthia Chapin: *Dairyman Don*, Albert Whitman and Company, Chicago, 1964.
Beim, Jerrold: *Andy and the School Bus*, William Morrow and Company, Inc., New York, 1947.
Buckley, Helen: *Grandmother and I*, Lothrop, Lee and Shepard Company, New York, 1961.
Clymer, Eleanor: *The Tiny Little House*, Atheneum Publishers, New York, 1964.
Curren, Polly: *This is a Town*, Follett Publishing Company, Chicago, 1957.
Harris, Isobel: *Little Boy Brown*, J. B. Lippincott Company, Philadelphia, 1949.
Horvath, Betty: *Hooray for Jasper*, Franklin Watts, Inc., New York, 1966.
Keats, Ezra Jack: *Jennie's Hat*, Harper and Row, Publishers, New York, 1966.

CHAPTER 5

# Special Days

Holidays touch the culture of home, nation, and world. They transmit social values that enrich and unify the lives of individuals and give greater cohesiveness to society. When people of different cultures understand one another's purposes for festivities and beliefs, they realize that many customs overlap. An exchange of information on folkways and special days is of interest and delight to any child.

The holidays, which we cherish and which have become a part of tradition in the United States, will more likely be preserved if they are given proper emphasis in the schools. Programs in early childhood education centers offer early opportunities for fostering appreciation of the various cultures that have helped to make America a great country and a good place to live. Not only can esteem for special occasions and holidays be built, but also foundations for patriotism and love of country.

Observance of holidays and other special days provides variety in the school program and enables a teacher to correlate these occasions with all subjects:

*Science* combines holiday activities with nature study.
*Mathematics* helps the children realize a sense of time in the occurrence of events.
*Social Studies* teaches the children about great men and events that made the history of our country.
*Art* encourages creative expression.
*Music* unifies people who sing together, even when they have no language in common. It is a universal language since thoughts, which often cannot be expressed in words, can be felt in music. It is generally a distillation of the social values of a community that produced it. Great songs of every nation are based on values that society thought were important.

*Language* communicates ideas and makes social contacts pleasant. Language also stimulates the mental processes of evaluating and weighing experiences. Without such considerations, learning can be retarded.

The holiday and special occasion ideas included in this chapter lend particular appeal through stories, poems, and suggested devices and activities.

*Columbus Day* is celebrated not only in the United States, but even more so in Spanish-speaking countries of South and Central America. *Dia de la Raza,* or "the time that the Spaniards came to the new world," is widely celebrated. This day refers to Columbus coming to America. It is possible that, had he not landed on these shores, the course of history might have been changed.

*Halloween,* or "All Hallows' Eve," the day before All Saints' Day, November 1, is observed by both Latin-Americans and people in the United States. This day is associated with pumpkins, corn husking, skeletons, ghosts, shocks of wheat in the fields, and with amusement. Children eagerly look forward to dressing up as witches and goblins, and making the rounds for trick or treat.

*Thanksgiving* is a season for happiness and an opportunity to tie in a celebration with social studies. The founding of America and a study of Indian life are of interest to all children. The basic reason, however, for observance of this occasion should be stressed in expressing thanks for families, friends, possessions, talents, and country.

*Christmas* is richer for all when people learn about the fine, old traditions of each nation in the world. Italy has its manger and star, and Sweden, its horses made either of wood or of cookies. Germany originated the Christmas tree, and Holland contributed Santa Claus (or St. Nicholas) and ice skates. England and France composed most of our carols, while Mexico is known for its colorful piñatas.

Jews celebrate Hanukkah during the season of winter with their traditional Menorah and religious ceremonies. Puerto Ricans enjoy twelve days of Christmas. Children everywhere listen to recordings and sing the enchanting words of "The Twelve Days of Christmas." Though Puerto Rican children believe in Santa Claus, they do not hang their stockings, but wait for Epiphany when the Three Wise Men bearing gifts ride their camels out of the East. The young Puerto Rican child fills cups with grass and water for the thirsty and hungry camels just as another child may leave a sandwich for Santa.

In the United States, there are varieties of state customs. Pageants are performed, town squares are lighted, and yards and homes are decorated with North Pole or religious themes. Alaska, near the Arctic Circle where the sun shines only a few hours, necessarily observes Christmas at night. In Arkansas, a favored Christmas dinner is 'possum and sweet potatoes. In the Ozarks, children are told that cows kneel at midnight to worship the Christ Child. Swedish-Americans serve the traditional lutfisk (fish) dinner which requires three weeks to prepare. Children who live in Hawaii sometimes depict Santa riding a surfboard and coming in on a wave. Every year, a freighter arrives at Pearl Harbor bearing a load of fir trees to enhance the Christmas spirit.

Christmas is celebrated in a host of ways all over the world. Yet underlying all observances, regardless of one's faith, friends are remembered, gifts are exchanged, and there is a spirit of goodwill and a prayer for peace.

*New Year's Day* is one of the oldest known holidays. Civilizations have had many different kinds of calendars so dates of this day may vary. Whichever day is observed, however, there is always feasting and ceremony. The Jewish New Year usually falls in September and is called "The Feast of the Trumpets." The Chinese New Year occurs in February and is celebrated for many days with feasts and dragon parades.

In Scotland, France, and many other countries, gifts are exchanged on New Year's since Christmas is considered a purely religious festival. The Welsh use a twig from a boxtree to flick water in the faces of sleeping people. This act is presumed to bring good luck to a household.

The Pasadena Rose Bowl game and the Tournament of Roses parade are two events highlighted in California and watched from coast to coast on television screens.

New Year's Day is a time to look at the past and plan to improve oneself in the future. Children as well as adults enjoy making New Year's resolutions.

*Lincoln's Birthday,* February 12, is one of the holidays which should be noted in all early childhood education programs. Children should be told of Abraham Lincoln's patience and goodness when the union was torn by war, strife, and dissension. The class will be interested in hearing stories about the qualities that made Lincoln great and beloved. They will learn of his belief in freedom and equal opportunity for all.

*Valentine's Day,* February 14, may have its origin with a man named Saint Valentine, although opinions vary. The day is considered by some church groups to be authentically conceived by this saint who went about doing good deeds for others. Regardless of its beginnings or significance, all children delight in creating and receiving valentines containing hearts which represent "goodness" and "unselfishness," and cupids, which personify love.

*Washington's Birthday*, February 22, is another important holiday to celebrate since George Washington was the father of our country. As a father, he took care of our country when it was new just as fathers care for their children. George Washington, along with many other strong, idealistic, and knowledgeable men like Jefferson and Madison, worked hard to build the strong, stable government that has existed over many decades.

*St. Patrick's Day* is celebrated on March 17. Each year, the Irish population in and around New York City parade down Fifth Avenue, past St. Patrick's Cathedral. The Irish are proud of their native land and wear green to show gratitude and to keep the memory of Ireland fresh and verdant. The shamrock leaf is their native symbol.

*Easter* is older than Christianity itself. All over the world, people of every nation and religion have looked forward to the end of winter and the awakening of nature with its joyous hope of new life and spring. Easter represents the unselfish service which makes hopes come true.

At this time, children enjoy coloring Easter eggs. Baby chicks, ducklings, and large white rabbits may be brought to the education center for observation, petting, feeding, and discussion.

*Birthdays* are always occasions to celebrate. The teacher must be sure that each child who has a birthday during the school year is given recognition. Often, mothers will bake cookies or cake and prepare lemonade so that each celebration may be shared with others.

Though *Mother's Day* is given no special treatment in this chapter, most teachers help the children to observe it by suggesting that they make gifts for their mothers. These tokens of love can be expressed by pressing the hand in clay to make a handprint, putting together a scrapbook of drawings or paintings, or creating a Mother's Day card. The teacher sometimes cuts out silhouettes of the children to send home. Craft books that suggest Mother's Day gifts can be purchased at most school supply stores.

There are endless opportunities for use of language skills while observing all holidays and special occasions. A variety of poems, stories, finger plays, songs, activities and devices are suggested within this chapter so that language may be made vital, interesting, and enjoyable. A bibliography of children's books for holidays and special occasions is suggested on page 250.

## THROUGH THE YEAR

*January* starts the year
When snowmen, skates, and sleds appear.

*February* days are fine
To send a pretty valentine.

*March* brings winds to fly a kite
Up among the clouds so white.

*April* brings the pattering rain
So that seeds will grow again.

*May* is time to dance and sing
Around the Maypole in a ring.

*June* brings flowers, fragrant, sweet;
Skates go skimming down the street.

*July* days are made for play;
We learn of Independence Day.

*August* days bring camp for me
In mountains or beside the sea.

*September,* school begins and then
We can see our friends again.

*October* brings us Halloween
When many spooky sights are seen.

*November* days bring cloudy skies,
Cranberry sauce, and pumpkin pies.

*December* brings the Christmas tree
With friendly thoughts for you and me.
—V.S.P. and L.B.S.

Read the poem aloud pausing after each couplet to discuss other activities occurring during the month.

After a child has become familiar with the poem, encourage him to join in saying the lines about the month in which he was born. Circle his birthday date on the calendar with his favorite color.

Ask: "Why is March a good month for flying a kite? On what day in October do we see children dressed in costumes and funny clothes?

## COLUMBUS

There were three little ships, one, two, and three:
The Niña, the Pinta, the Santa Marie.
*(Hold up one finger for each ship.)*
Over the ocean, over the sea,
*(Move hands to represent ocean waves.)*
The Niña, the Pinta, the Santa Marie.
Sailing to west so far and free,
*(Spread hands wide apart.)*
The Niña, the Pinta, the Santa Marie.
Columbus discovered a land so new,
And this was in 1492.
There was many a mile, and the ships were three,
*(Hold up three fingers.)*
The Niña, the Pinta, the Santa Marie.
—O.M.A.

Children may say the refrain. Suggest that they paint the ships.

## THREE SHIPS

(A Chalk Talk)

First, I'll draw a triangle, (1)
And then another one. (2)
One, two, and three triangles, (3)
But still I am not done.

I'll make a bowl beneath each one (4)
For Columbus and his crew,
In the Niña, the Pinta, and Santa Marie
That crossed the ocean blue.
—L.B.S.

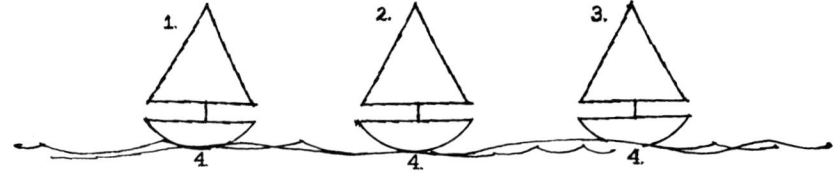

Numerals in the poem indicate the accompanying numbered illustrations. Draw the figures slowly on the chalkboard. After the drawings have been completed, repeat the poem and suggest that the class help you say it. Ask them to follow you in drawing the configurations in the air with their pointer fingers.

Many children will practice these drawings independently at the easel or with finger paint.

### KNOWING HOW TO HAVE HALLOWEEN FUN

Halloween is a time for fun, but it has its serious side, too. Guidance on behavior and safety should be offered. The following suggestions may be included in discussions:

Remembering to show gratitude for treats.
Thanking people even though they have no treats.
Going from house to house quietly.
Wearing masks that do not obscure vision.
Choosing costumes which can be seen by drivers.
Ringing a doorbell or knocking just once.
Asking Mother, Daddy, or an older brother or sister to go along.
Crossing streets on a green light and always looking left and right.
Helping small brothers and sisters to keep Halloween rules.
Savings treats not eaten, and brushing teeth after eating.

### HERE IS A WITCH'S TALL BLACK HAT

Here is a witch's tall black hat.
*(Point index fingers together.)*
Here are the whiskers on my cat.
*(Index fingers and thumbs together pulled back and forth under nose.)*

Here is an owl sitting in a tree.
*(Circle eyes with fingers.)*
Here is a goblin! Hee, hee, hee!
*(Place hand on stomach.)*
—L.B.S.

Cut whiskers, hat, owl, and goblin shapes from felt and place on the flannelboard as you say the poem. Children may take turns pointing to the correct shapes as they join in saying the rhyme.

### A LITTLE JACK-O'-LANTERN

A little jack-o'-lantern
Went walking through the town.
The night was in October,
And a big round moon smiled down.

The jack-o'-lantern's eyes shone;
His nose was very bright.
His mouth was wide and smiling,
And he stayed that way all night.
—L.B.S.

Say: "Have you seen a jack-o'-lantern? When? Where? Have you helped make a jack-o'-lantern? Show how large the pumpkin was? What shape did you make its eyes? Nose? Mouth? How did you make the eyes shine?"

Bring in a small pumpkin and demonstrate how a jack-o'-lantern is made. Place a flashlight inside to light its features. Dry the seeds for stringing.

### HALLOWEEN FUN

Jack-o'-lanterns have crooked teeth,
 *(Point to features.)*
With a nose above and a chin beneath.
 Oo - oo - oo!
 *(Children make sound.)*
On Halloween when hoot owls stare,
 *(Circle eyes with fingers.)*
Such funny sounds are in the air!
 Oo - oo - oo!
Oh, many scary things are seen
 *(Point fingers above head to form hat.)*
When we dress up for Halloween!
 Oo - oo - oo!
—L.B.S.

A tune can be composed for this poem. Prolong or sing the "oo" sound.

To make a room decoration, blow up a balloon and wrap folds of foil around it. Cover the foil with orange crepe paper. Add black construction paper features. Let out the air and attach string to the protruding end of the balloon.

## A FUNNY OLD WITCH

A funny old witch in a pointed cap,
*(Point fingers together.)*
Came to my door with a rap, rap, rap!
*(Rap on floor or table.)*
I went out to see, and a witch was there.
She jumped on her broomstick and flew through the air.
*(Pretend to hold onto broomstick.)*

—V.S.P.

## HALLOWEEN RIDDLES

He is all black with a fluffy tail.
*(Cat)*
He is dressed in a sheet and makes
a loud wail. *(Ghost)*
She wears a big tall, pointed hat.
*(Witch)*
It flaps its wings. It is not a cat.
*(Bat)*
It says, "Hoo - hoo," as it sits
in a tree. *(Owl)*
It rattles as scary as can be.
*(Skeleton)*
It has a smile with a yellow light.
*(Jack-o'-lantern)*
It shines in the sky on Halloween night.
*(Moon)*

—L.B.S.

Children supply the answers to each riddle. For variation, suggest that they draw or paint a picture to answer their choice. Many children will enjoy trying to make up their own Halloween riddles, based upon trick or treat experiences.

## A WITCH CHALK TALK

Here is a triangle; (1)
Here is a hat. (2)
Somebody wears it;
Imagine that!
Here is a witch with
    an ugly face, (3)
And on her broom, (4)
She flies through space.
      —L.B.S.

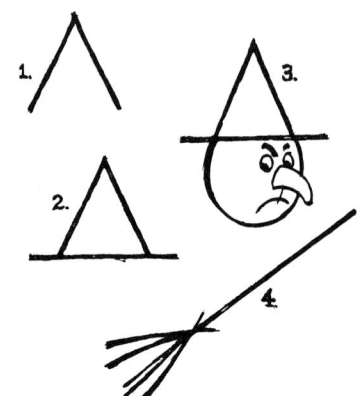

Numerals in the poem correspond to those in the drawings. Sketch each configuration slowly on the chalkboard as you say the poem. During a second or third presentation, ask the children to participate in saying the rhyme as they follow you in drawing the configurations in the air with their pointer fingers. Call attention to the triangle. Ask the class to think of other things that are triangular in shape.

## JACK-O'-LANTERN

Here is a big round pumpkin
    *(Make circle with arms.)*
To use for Halloween.
I'll make the finest jack-o'-lantern
That you have ever seen!

First, I'll cut the top off,
    *(Make circular motion with hand.)*
And scoop out all the seeds.
    *(Motion of scooping.)*
I'll cut a little pointed nose.
    *(Form triangle with pointer*
    *fingers and thumbs.)*
Two eyes my pumpkin needs.
    *(Fingers encircle eyes.)*

And now I'll carve a laughing mouth,
  *(Draw upward curve in air with finger.)*
And use a candle bright
  *(Hold up one forefinger.)*
To light my jack-o'-lantern.
  *(Move thumb and forefinger together.)*
Then it will burn all night!

—L.B.S.

The children may use the ideas suggested in this finger play to cut jack-o'-lanterns from orange construction paper.

## FIVE LITTLE CHILDREN

Five little children dressed like ghosts,
Stood beside some tall fence posts.
The first one hid behind a door.
And when he left, there were just four.

The second one hid behind a tree,
And when he left, there were just three.
The third one jumped and shouted, "BOO!"
And when he left, there were just two.

The fourth one laughed and thought it fun,
But when he left, there was just one.
The last child ran and lost his sheet,
And so he had no trick or treat.

—L.B.S.

The children may assemble in groups of fives to act out this rhyme. Say: "How do you feel about the last child having no trick or treat? How would you end the poem?"

The concepts: *five, one, first, second, third, fourth,* and *last* are emphasized.

## MAKING GHOSTS

Encourage mothers to donate clean, worn sheets and pillow-cases so that the children may use them for Halloween costumes or for making ghost puppets.

Lay a cardboard ghost configuration on the sheeting and ask a child to trace around it with a crayon. Cut out two forms and sew them together, leaving the bottom open to form a hand puppet. Black crayon dots for eyes, nose, and mouth may be added. Insert a pointer finger into the neck, and a middle finger and thumb into the arm areas.

Cut a larger circle from the sheeting. Roll a tight ball of newspaper and fit the circle over it. A maraca may be used also, as it produces an excellent Halloween sound. Tie under the ball, leaving space to insert the pointer finger. Add features described previously.

## THE GOBLIN AND THE COOKIES

A goblin wanted to play trick or treat, so he tippy-toed up to a house and rang the doorbell. A lady came to the door and gave him a cookie.

"Thank you," said the goblin.

"You're welcome," said the lady.

The goblin tippy-toed up to another house and rang the bell. A lady came to the door and gave him a cookie. (*Repeat the action until the goblin has ten cookies. Place a cookie made from brown construction paper and backed with outing flannel on the flannelboard each time the goblin is given one.)*

Now the goblin had a whole sack full of cookies and he was so happy that he turned goblin somersaults all over the place. But as he was skipping along singing a goblin song, he met a witch who was crying as if her heart would break. *(Place witch figure on flannelboard.)*

"Oh, lackaday," cried the witch. "I have no treats for Halloween. People are afraid of me and they shut the door when they take a look at me."

What do you think that dear little goblin did? *(Responses.)* Well, he gave the witch one cookie. Then, how many cookies did he have left? *(Remove one cookie and place it beside the witch as the children respond.)*

—L.B.S.

Continue the story as the goblin meets a black cat, an owl, a ghost, a bat, and a jack-o'-lantern, and gives each one a cookie. Ask: "What do you think the goblin did with the rest of his cookies?"

This story may be used to teach mathematical concepts based upon the maturity and needs of the group. The children will be able to count the cookies, which should remain on the flannelboard so that each cookie may be moved around as needed. It would be helpful to place the cookies directly under or beside the character who receives them.

Encourage children to add episodes and dramatize them.

### A PRAYER FOR HELP

> Help us do the things we should;
> Help us to be kind and good;
> Help us in our work and play
> To grow more loving every day.

Use this rhyme as a prayer before snack time or when dramatizing Pilgrims at Thanksgiving dinner.

The preparation for the celebration of Thanksgiving in the education center affords excellent opportunities for correlating social studies with language experiences. Children of all ages are interested in the founding of America and the life of the Indians. However, when dramatizing these related experiences, the child should be told reasons for giving thanks. Thankfulness is an appreciation of others, an enjoyment of something good which has happened. Appreciating others and feeling grateful for good things are essential to a happy life.

## THANKSGIVING

Every day when we sit down to dinner,
Our table is very small.
There is room for Daddy, *(Let the fingers
    of one hand represent people in the
    family and point to the persons
    named with the other hand.)*
Mother, Brother, and *Me* . . .
That is all.
But when Thanksgiving comes,
   and there's company,
Why you cannot believe your eyes!
   *(Show ten fingers.)*
The table at which we eat dinner
Stretches till it's about this size!
   *(Spread arms.)*

—Adapted from a poem
by MAUD BURNHAM

## TEN LITTLE SQUIRRELS

Ten little squirrels I counted one day
   *(Hold up ten fingers.)*
When we had a Thanksgiving holiday.
One little squirrel scampered away,
   *(Bend down one finger.)*
So how many squirrels were left to play?

No little squirrels were left to play,
But they will all come back to stay.
   *(Hold up ten fingers.)*

—L.B.S.

The number of squirrels is decreased when repeating the third and fourth lines. Continue to bend fingers until the line, "No little squirrels were left to play," is said and all the fingers are down.

Vary the activity by using squirrel shapes on the flannelboard; substitute chipmunks, rabbits, or skunks.

## INDIANS AND TREES[1]

This is the forest of long, long ago.
Here are the trees standing in a row.
   *(Hold up fingers of left hand.)*
Look very closely! What do you see?
Indians peeking out — one, two, three!
   *(Peek three Indian finger puppets on right hand between fingers on left hand.)*
Now they are hiding. The forest is still.
   *(Right hand behind back.)*
Now they are hurrying over the hill.
   *(Show puppets.)*
Ever so quietly, now they are nearing
   *(Whisper.)*
The tepee that stands at the edge of the clearing.
   *(Form triangle with two hands.)*
This is the forest of long ago.
   *(Hold up fingers of left hand.)*
Here are three Indians standing in a row.
   *(Hold up puppets.)*

—SALLY WERNER

Cut small Indian face shapes from brown construction paper and attach a red paper feather to the top of each. Glue the shapes onto strips of paper about a half-inch wide to form three rings which can be placed upon the child's fingers.

## MAKING A THANKFUL BOOK

Staple several sheets of colored newsprint to form a book. Each child may contribute a picture of something for which he is thankful and paste it into the "Thankful Book." Write his name with his dictated comments

[1] From *Child Life,* copyright 1955.

under the picture. Share the book with other children in the class and place it on the browsing table. Each child may talk about his picture.

## INDIANS

One little, two little, three little Indians,
Four little, five little, six little Indians,
Seven little, eight little, nine little Indians,
Ten little Indian boys.

—Old rhyme

Ten children stand in a row and stoop down one at a time as the rhyme is repeated. As the numbers are said backward (ten little, nine little, and so forth), each child rises again. Sometimes it is effective for the children to hide behind a table as they stoop and rise.

## SIX LITTLE PILGRIMS

There were six little Pilgrims on Thanksgiving Day.
And this is exactly what I heard them say.
The first one said, "I'll have a turkey leg."
The second one said, "I'll have a boiled egg."
The third one said, "I will have some green peas."
The fourth one said, "I'll have cranberries, please."
The fifth one said, "I will have pumpkin pie."
The sixth one said, "I'll have cake by and by."
There were six little Pilgrims on Thanksgiving Day.
And that is exactly what I heard them say!

—L.B.S.

This rhyme may be used as a finger play, with Pilgrim cutouts placed upon the flannelboard, or for creative dramatics. It helps teach concepts: *first, second, third,* etc.

## TEN FAT PUMPKINS

Ten fat pumpkins were growing on a vine.
A brown cow ate one; then there were ___.
Nine fat pumpkins were in a row so straight.
One rolled far away; then there were ___.
Eight fat pumpkins growing round and even,

A wagon took one away; then there were _____.
Seven fat pumpkins doing arithmetic.
A little girl picked one; then there were _____.
Six fat pumpkins said, "We'll all survive."
Along came the gardener's hoe; then there were _____.
Five fat pumpkins where ten grew before;
A tall horse smashed one; then there were _____.
Four fat pumpkins, orange as could be;
Tommy made a jack-o'-lantern, then there were _____.
Three fat pumpkins were feeling sad and blue;
Billy's mother took one, then there were _____.
Two fat pumpkins where once there were many;
Grandma made two pumpkin pies; now there aren't ANY!
—L.B.S.

Wait for the children to supply the number before you remove a pumpkin shape from the flannelboard. Use orange felt for pumpkins and draw features with a black felt tip pen.

The rhyme provides practice on *there were* and *aren't*.

### THANKSGIVING DINNER

Food cutouts assembled on paper plates can serve as make-believe dinners. The child asks for a "food" and puts it on his plate. This activity provides practice in constructing sentences, using table manners, and identifying foods. For the child whose experiences with foods and eating have been unhappy, the activity will be enjoyable.

### THREE TEPEES

I'll draw some triangles to start, (1)
And I will draw them far apart.
So here a line for earth will be. (2)
How many tepees do you see?
Count each tepee now with me.
One, two, three! Do you agree?
—L.B.S.

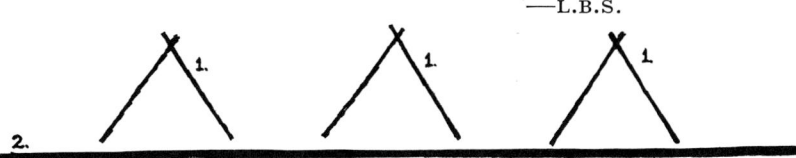

Numerals in the poem indicate the accompanying numbered illustrations. Sketch the figures as the lines are said so that drawing and speaking coordinate. Do not hurry the activity. Repeat it so that the class may make triangles in the air with pointer fingers.

### LITTLE INDIAN'S ADVENTURE

Little Indian went out to look for a buffalo. He took his bow and arrow. *(When the word "Indian" is mentioned, place fingers behind head for feathers.)* Little Indian walked down a path. *(Slap thighs.)* Suddenly he thought he heard something. *(Hand behind ear.)* He stopped and looked all around. *(Shade eyes.)* He saw a squirrel. He walked on. *(Slap thighs.)* He saw a hawk flying. *(Shade eyes.)* He walked on. *(Slap thighs.)* He heard a rustle in the bushes. *(Hand behind ear.)* Rustle, rustle, rustle. *(Rub palms together.)* Little Indian didn't wait a second. He began to run. *(Slap thighs quickly.)* He didn't stop until he reached his tepee.

—Adapted by L.B.S. from an old pantomime

Ask: "What do you think Little Indian heard in the bushes? Could it have been a squirrel? A buffalo? A snake?"

### SHINE, CHRISTMAS CANDLE

Shine, Christmas candle, shine across the snow.
Shine across the meadow where the shepherds go.
Shine, Christmas candle, with your yellow light.
Shine to guide the Wise Men on a Christmas night.
—L.B.S.

Children may wear white construction paper headbands with red paper candles on them and can carry red crepe paper streamers about 1″ x 12″ in one hand as lines are sung or said in unison.

### HANUKKAH CANDLES

Eight pretty candles all in a line.
Eight pretty candles twinkle and shine.
Eight pretty candles in sticks of gold.
Tell us of people and heroes of old.
—Old rhyme

Many books trace the Christmas customs of countries. It is interesting to learn about the background of each child in this respect. Be sure that each custom is given an appreciative welcome and acknowledgment.

## CHRISTMAS SECRETS

I know so many secrets —
  *(Softly.)*
Such secrets full of fun;
But if you know my secret,
Please don't tell anyone!

Here are some twinkly, twinkly lights,
  *(Move fingers rapidly.)*
Here is an ornament.
  *(Make circle with fingers.)*
Here is a box all wrapped in red
  *(Measure size with hands.)*
That Uncle William sent.

And on the very tip, tip-top
An angel you can see!
  *(Arms out for wings.)*
What is the secret? Can you tell?
Why, it's a CHRISTMAS TREE!
  *(Raise arms high.)*
—L.B.S.

## RING FIVE BELLS

Ring the bells, ring the bells,
This is Christmas Day. *(Children repeat.)*

One is for the manger,
Two is for the hay,
Three is for the shining star
That pointed out the way.

Ring the bells, ring the bells,
This is Christmas Day. *(Children repeat.)*

Four is for the shepherds
Who saw the angel light.
Five is for the little Boy
Born that happy night.

Ring the bells, ring the bells,
This is Christmas Day. *(Children repeat.)*
—O.M.A.

Children like to ring tiny sleigh bells as they say or sing the refrain. Vary the activity by encouraging each child to create his own Christmas finger plays.

### FIVE LITTLE BELLS

Five little bells ring with a chime
*(Hold up five fingers.)*
To tell of happy Christmas time.

Four little bells ring sweet and clear
*(Hold up four fingers.)*
To tell that Christmas Day is here.

Three little bells ring soft and low
*(Hold up three fingers.)*
To tell of stockings in a row.

Two little bells ring merrily
*(Hold up two fingers.)*
To tell of toys beneath the tree.

One little bell rings silver bright
*(Hold up one finger.)*
To welcome Santa Claus tonight!
—L.B.S.

Suggest that the children ring song or sleigh bells as the poem is said.

## CHRISTMAS DEVICES

*Puzzles:* Find magazine pictures of candles, large Santas, trees, and other symbols of Christmas. Cut out and glue the pictures firmly to tablet backs or pasteboard. Let them dry under heavy weights so that the edges will not curl. Cut each picture into three or four pieces with a razor blade, making sure that there are no points that will break off.

*Christmas stocking:* Obtain a large commercial Christmas stocking or make one from red or green felt. Place small objects inside for feeling and identifying.

*Santa sack puppet:* From colored construction paper, cut facial features and paste on top and under the flap of a number 3 or 4 paper sack. Add cotton whiskers and a felt tongue. Fingers will fit over the closed flap. To make the puppet talk, the child moves his fingers up and down, and speaks simultaneously.

## LITTLE HANDS

| | |
|---|---|
| TEACHER: | Little hands trim the branches |
| CHILDREN: | On the Christmas tree. |
| TEACHER: | Little hands string the popcorn |
| CHILDREN: | On the Christmas tree. |
| TEACHER: | Little hands put the light bulbs |
| CHILDREN: | On the Christmas tree. |
| TEACHER: | Little hands tie the ribbons |
| CHILDREN: | On the Christmas tree. |
| TEACHER: | Little hands put the presents |
| CHILDREN: | On the Christmas tree. |

—L.B.S.

Ask the class to show what their little hands would do as the lines are read.

## DRAWING A CHRISTMAS TREE

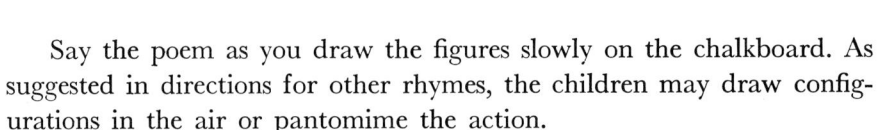

Here is a Christmas tree
On the floor.
   *(Draw triangle and trunk.)*
Here are ornaments
One, two, three, four.
   *(Draw four circles
   on the tree.)*
Here is a star on the top, you see.
   *(Draw star.)*
And here are five candles
Bright as can be!
   *(Draw five straight lines.)*

—L.B.S.

Say the poem as you draw the figures slowly on the chalkboard. As suggested in directions for other rhymes, the children may draw configurations in the air or pantomime the action.

Cut candle, tree, star and ornament shapes from colored construction paper, or from large scraps of solid colored felt or other substantial fabric. Give each child the appropriate number of each (as indicated in the poem) to decorate his own Christmas tree. Suggest that the children paste their ornaments on their tree shapes.

## A JOLLY SANTA CLAUS[2]

Once upon a time, there was a boy named Charles and a girl named Susan who wanted to stay up and watch for Santa Claus.

"But," said their mother, "Santa does not come when children are awake."

"Please, pretty please!" they begged.

"All right," said their mother. "Since this is Christmas Eve and a very special time, you may wait for Santa."

So Charles and Susan curled up in a big arm chair and waited and waited *(hands clasped)* for Santa to come. As they were waiting, their eyes began to droop and soon they were fast asleep.

WHOOSH! Down the chimney came two black, black boots and they sat right down on the warm, warm floor. And still Charles and Susan slept and slept *(hands clasped beside head)* and waited and waited for Santa to come.

WHOOSH! Down the chimney came two short, short legs and they sat right down on the black, black boots on the warm, warm floor. And still Charles and Susan slept and slept and waited and waited for Santa to come.

WHOOSH! Down the chimney came a long, long jacket and it sat right down on the short, short legs on the black, black boots on the warm, warm floor. And *still* Charles and Susan slept and slept and waited and waited for Santa to come.

WHOOSH! Down the chimney came two long, long sleeves and they sat right down on the long, long jacket on the short, short legs on the black, black boots on the warm, warm floor.

WHOOSH! Down the chimney came two fat, fat mittens and they sat right down on the long, long sleeves on the long, long jacket on the short, short legs on the black, black boots on the warm, warm floor. And still Charles and Susan slept and slept and waited and waited for Santa to come.

WHOOSH! Down the chimney came a jolly, jolly face and it sat right down on the long, long jacket with the long, long sleeves with the fat, fat mittens on the short, short legs on the black, black boots on the warm, warm floor. And *still* Charles and Susan slept and slept and waited and waited for Santa to come.

But Santa had already come! He filled all of the stockings and socks with goodies, and put presents under the Christmas tree for the family.

[2] Arlene Caster, "A Jolly Santa Claus," *Speech in the Elementary School,* Publication #479, Los Angeles City Schools, 1951.

Then WHOOSH! Away went the jolly, jolly face. WHOOSH! Away went the long, long jacket with the long, long sleeves with the fat, fat mittens. WHOOSH! Away went the short, short legs. WHOOSH! Away went the black, black boots.

Just then Charles and Susan woke up and as they did so, they heard a prancing and pawing on the roof top, and somebody called, "Happy Christmas to all and to all a good-night!"

And that is the story of the jolly, jolly Santa Claus and his visit to Charles and Susan's house one Christmas Eve.

—Adapted by L.B.S.

Make felt or pellon cutouts. The children may take turns placing these figures on the flannelboard as the story is told. Santa pieces may be used also as a puzzle.

The repetition will enable the class to join in with the narration almost immediately.

### CHRISTMAS IN MOTHER GOOSE LAND

Mother Goose dusted off her tall, pointed hat and tied the ribbon under her chin.

"Where is my Christmas list?" she asked herself, peering over her glasses and looking everywhere in the room.

She found the Christmas list in her pocketbook where it was all the time!

"I must do my Christmas shopping today," she said.

Who in Mother Goose Land might receive presents from Mother Goose, boys and girls? *(Responses)*

Mother Goose wrapped her long cloak around her shoulders, took her purse and a big shopping bag, and climbed on the back of an old gray gander. Away they flew over hills and housetops to Nursery Town.

The old gander landed right in front of a department store and gave a loud honk.

"You wait right here for me," said Mother Goose, climbing off his back. "They don't allow ganders in department stores. And please don't honk while I am gone or you might start a commotion."

Mother Goose walked into the department store and began looking around for presents. She went over her Christmas list carefully, peering through her glasses.

"I must not forget anyone," she said thoughtfully.

Humpty Dumpty was first on the Christmas list.

"Hmmmmm," said Mother Goose. "Humpty Dumpty is always taking tumbles off walls where he seems to like to sit, so I'll buy him a tube of glue. Then he can stick himself back together again if he falls off another wall."

Second on the Christmas list was Little Miss Muffet. Now what would Mother Goose buy for Miss Muffet? *(Responses.)*

What do you think she would buy for Little Boy Blue? *(Responses.)* And for Old Mother Hubbard who went to the cupboard? *(Responses.)* And for Jack Horner? Why, a Christmas pie, of course! What about Jack-Be-Nimble? *(Responses.)* And Wee Willie Winkie? *(Responses.)* And Bo-Peep? Now what do you suppose? A pair of glasses for her nose so that she could look for her lost sheep. What did Mother Goose buy for Old King Cole? *(Responses.)* Those were good guesses. Let's see if you were right.

Christmas morning dawned bright and clear. All of the Mother Goose folks arrived at Mother Goose's house to drink some of her famous hot chocolate with whipped cream and to look at her lovely Christmas tree. Then there was much excitement when Mother Goose passed out presents to one and all! Why, they never *dreamed* they would receive presents and it was such a marvelous surprise!

Boy Blue was so thrilled that he could hardly wait to blow his new horn and call the cows from the corn and the sheep from the meadow. He thanked Mother Goose, gave her a big, warm hug, and went out to the meadow where he could blow his new horn as long and as hard as he pleased.

Mother Hubbard opened a mysterious package and took out a big, juicy bone. Her little dog laughed and danced when he saw that bone!

Jack Horner had learned not to put his thumb into a pie again. He cut his plum pie and passed it around so that everybody could have a piece. Jack-Be-Nimble let everyone jump over his candlestick and Humpty Dumpty almost had a great fall because he was so excited about his tube of glue.

"I'll try to be more careful," he said. "But it will be so nice to have this tube of glue in case I have an accident."

Wee Willie Winkie appreciated his new nightgown for his old one was worn thin. Bo-Peep tried on her glasses and they fit perfectly. Old King Cole sang a song about his new pipe and bowl.

Oh, it was such a jolly Christmas! But the Mother Goose people felt sad for they had brought no presents for Mother Goose. Can you think of something they might say to her or do for her? *(Responses.)*

—L.B.S.

Ask: "Did Mother Goose expect to receive presents? What might be a good way to end this story? Tell how you might thank Mother Goose for a present."

Before reading or telling the story, show pictures of characters from Mother Goose listed in the bibliography at the end of Chapter 3. If possible, bring in real objects they might have received: a tube of glue, stool, bone, or candlestick.

Add other Mother Goose characters to the story when it is dramatized.

### SNOW IS PART OF CHRISTMAS

CHILDREN: Snow is part of Christmas,
TEACHER: Soft, feathery, and white.
CHILDREN: Snow is part of Christmas,
TEACHER: Falling in the night.
CHILDREN: Santa is part of Christmas,
TEACHER: Bringing gifts and toys.
CHILDREN: Santa is part of Christmas,
TEACHER: A friend of girls and boys.
—L.B.S.

Ask: "What else is part of Christmas?" Record each child's answer inside a folded piece of colored construction paper (7" x 14"). The children may decorate the outside of the paper using scraps of materials to make their own Christmas cards.

### THE CHILDREN WHO WANTED TO THANK SANTA CLAUS

Once there were three children who said, "Santa has been so good to us every year. Let's find him and thank him."

So on Christmas Eve the three children dressed warmly because they knew Santa lived at the North Pole where it was cold. They started out while everyone else was sleeping soundly. The North Star shone down brightly and guided them as they walked along over the frozen ground.

After a long time the children came to the house of a white polar bear.

"Can you show us the way to the North Pole?" they asked. "We want to find Santa Claus."

"Why," said the polar bear, "Santa was here just an hour ago. But wait, I think I hear his sleigh bells now!"

Just then, eight reindeer whizzed into sight, and Santa shouted, "Whoa!"

He climbed out of the sleigh and asked, "Where are you going, children?"

The children replied, "We came to see you. We wanted to thank you for being so good to us each year, Santa."

Old Santa put on his glasses and peered at each child, his eyes twinkling merrily.

"We wanted to bring you some gifts, Santa," said the three children, "but we had no money to buy them."

Santa gave each child a big, warm hug and said softly, "You have brought YOURSELVES, and that is the best gift of all. Now, I'll take you home to your mothers and fathers."

So they all jumped into the sleigh and wrapped themselves snugly in blankets. The eight reindeer galloped over the housetops and away!

The next morning, what do you think? The three children woke up *in their own beds!* They rubbed their eyes and looked all around.

"We had such a wonderful dream," they said.

—L.B.S.

Ask: "Would you like to have such a dream? Tell about one nice dream you have had. Can you name the reindeer?" The class will enjoy hearing "A Visit from St. Nicholas" by Clement Clark Moore.

## ON NEW YEAR'S DAY

On New Year's Day, on New Year's Day,
This is what I always say:
Happy New Year, Daddy.
 *(Point to middle finger.)*
Happy New Year, Mother.
 *(Point to ring finger.)*
Happy New Year, Sister.
 *(Point to thumb.)*
Happy New Year, Brother.
 *(Point to small finger.)*
On New Year's Day, on New Year's Day,
This is what I always say:
HAPPY NEW YEAR!

—Old rhyme

## HAPPY NEW YEAR

(An Old Folk Tune)　　　　　　　　　　　　　　　V.S.P.

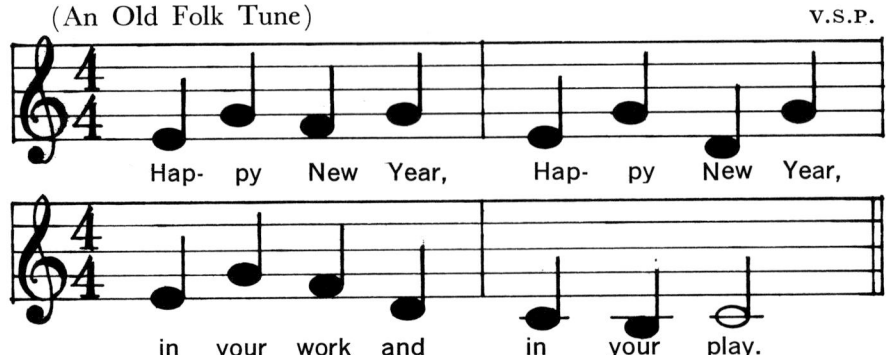

Repeat tune: Happy New Year, Happy New Year, every day a Happy Day.

Tune a jar or water glass (by adding or decreasing the water) so that a clear "G" is produced when it is tapped. As the children sing the song, tap the glass whenever they sing "G."

## NEW YEAR'S BELLS

Manufactured song bells are excellent, yet sometimes children enjoy making their own. Peanut-butter jars or old tumblers make lovely bells when you put water into them to raise or lower the tones. The children can enjoy a simple science experience and a home-made musical instrument at the same time. To play a tune, strike each jar gently with a pencil or fork.

—V.S.P.

## VALENTINE'S DAY AND DEVICES TO USE

Many areas of the curriculum may be integrated with the holiday, Valentine's Day. In social studies, services of the postman can be dramatized as a child delivers valentine mail to each member of his class. Children can enjoy creative art expression as they make and decorate valentines for their mothers or friends. Social skills can be emphasized in experiences which require sharing and cooperating with others.

*Valentine store.* The class uses blocks to "build" a store where valentines can be "sold." Ask the mothers to save valentines from year to year and donate them for such activities. The children can create their own valentines from materials such as ribbons, paper doilies, buttons, and wallpaper scraps from the odds-and-ends box.

*Mail time.* All children like the experience of pretending to mail valentines they have bought for their classmates. A number 8 brown paper sack is decorated by each child to use as an individual mail bag. The teacher needs to label each one plainly with the child's name.

The simplest way to display these sacks is to staple them at mailing height on as many bulletin boards around the room as are necessary. A special time may be selected for mailing valentines. During the party, the teacher may distribute these mail pouches to the children.

—O.M.A.

## FIVE PRETTY VALENTINES

Five pretty valentines waiting at the store.
\_\_\_\_\_ bought one and then there were \_\_\_\_\_.
Four pretty valentines shaped just like a "V."
\_\_\_\_\_ bought one and then there were \_\_\_\_\_.
Three pretty valentines said, "I love you."
\_\_\_\_\_ bought one and then there were \_\_\_\_\_.
Two pretty valentines—this was so much fun!
\_\_\_\_\_ bought one and then there was \_\_\_\_\_.
One pretty valentine sitting on the shelf.
I felt sorry for it, so I bought it for myself!

—L.B.S.

Ask the children to name the number of remaining valentines after each couplet is said. Be sure that all children have a turn at hearing their names mentioned.

Cut out white hearts and write the name of a child on each one as the class watches. Attach two paper clips to each heart before dropping it into a box. Children may use a magnet attached to a string to fish for their own names.

## MY COUNTRY'S FLAG

L.B.S.  V.S.P.

I am proud of my coun- try's flag. It's

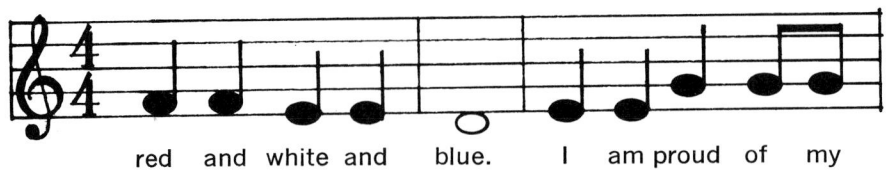
red and white and blue. I am proud of my

coun-try's flag. I know that you are, too.

## MY FLAG, I SALUTE YOU

—O.M.A.

My flag, my flag, I sa-
Red, white, and blue, I sa-

lute you.
lute you.

## SALUTING THE FLAG

Five young children come to school.
   *(Hold up five fingers.)*
They sometimes work and sometimes play.
At nine o'clock, they stand up tall,
   *(Stand.)*
And say the flag salute each day.
   *(Hand over heart.)*

—L.B.S.

The first line may be changed to read: "All of the children come to school." Teach the song, "An American,"³ by Virginia Sydnor Pavelko.

## ABRAHAM LINCOLN

### (A Discussion)

Abraham Lincoln was one of our great Presidents. When he was a little boy, he lived in a cabin made of logs. The cabin was very small and it had big cracks in the walls that let in the cold wind. Sometimes rain swished through the cracks, and in summer, small mosquitoes, crickets, and even birds found their way into the log cabin.

Abraham Lincoln's family was poor. Sometimes they hardly had enough to eat, but they all worked hard and loved one another.

Would you like to be a grown-up person as fine as Abraham Lincoln? What else do you know about this great President? Do you think somebody poor could be President of the United States one day?

—V.S.P.

Show a picture of Abraham Lincoln. Suggest that a fireplace be built from blocks. Miniature building logs are easily obtained from most school supply houses.

## LINCOLN PENNIES

Bring in a penny containing a picture of Abraham Lincoln. Ask each child to look at it under a magnifying glass to observe the picture and the design clearly.

Give each child a circle of cardboard, about six inches in diameter, on which to paste a silhouette of Abraham Lincoln. Silhouettes can be purchased at almost any stationery or school supply store. Over the silhouette, paste thin, plain brown wrapping paper. Press hard until the picture design can be seen coming through in relief. Turn the edges under and paste a plain piece of brown wrapping paper over the back. Write ONE CENT on the front with a felt tip pen. These "pennies" can be used for table mats at snack time, for counting activities, and for play money.

The same procedure can be used to make "quarters" for a George Washington activity.

—O.M.A.

[3] Virginia Sydnor Pavelko, "An American" in *More Singing Fun* by Wood and Scott, McGraw-Hill, Inc., New York, 1961, p. 77.

## FIVE LITTLE PENNIES

Five little pennies went to the store.
   *(Hold up five fingers.)*
One bought a peppermint; then there were \_\_\_\_\_.
Four little pennies belong just to *me*.
   *(Hold up four fingers.)*
One bought a pencil; then there were \_\_\_\_\_.
Three little pennies I'll share them with you.
   *(Hold up three fingers.)*
One bought a lemondrop; then there were \_\_\_\_\_.
Two little pennies as bright as the sun.
   *(Hold up two fingers.)*
One bought a marble; then there was \_\_\_\_\_.
One little penny was all I had to pay.
   *(Hold up one finger.)*
I put it in my piggy bank for a rainy day!

—L.B.S.

Children say the number of pennies remaining.

## ABRAHAM LINCOLN HELPS A BABY PIG

Abraham Lincoln was a tall, thin, and strong man. He loved little children and they loved him. He would swing them in his long arms.

When any of the neighbors had a party, they always invited Abraham Lincoln because everyone had more fun when he was there. One day, Abraham Lincoln was all dressed up to go to a party. As he walked along singing "Yankee Doodle," he saw a baby pig that was lost from its mother. The baby pig was in a muddy ditch and was trying hard to get out, but the mud was so slippery that the little pig kept falling back.

"Poor little pig," said Abraham Lincoln. "Don't be scared. I'll help you."

Then kind Abraham Lincoln took off his coat, shoes, and socks, and climbed down into the muddy ditch to pull out the baby pig. The pig was so happy that it wiggled around and slushed mud all over Abraham Lincoln's suit. Of course, his clothes were so dirty that he couldn't go to the party, but he didn't mind. He took the baby pig to its mother on a farm nearby. Then he went home to wash and change his clothes.

He missed the party, but people never forgot the man who was so kind that he didn't want an animal to be unhappy if he could help it.

—V.S.P.

Ask: "Did you like the way the story ended? Why? How would you have ended it? Why do you think people liked Abraham Lincoln so much? Why would you want to have someone like him for a friend?"

### GEORGE WASHINGTON

Another holiday has come!
Let's wave a flag and beat a drum.
A holiday has just begun —
The birthday of George Washington.

—MAUD BURNHAM

The rhyme can be learned easily by rote and set to music. Discuss George Washington as a great general and the first President. A book which the children may enjoy is *George and the Cherry Tree*.[4]

### CHERRIES RIPE

Cherries ripe, cherries ripe,
Hanging on a tree.
Cherries ripe, cherries ripe,
Pick them for me.

Cut out red felt cherry shapes and add stems and leaves of green. Place them in a row, left to right, on the flannelboard. The children may take turns "picking" the cherries and chanting the refrain. Ask them to count the cherries.

### MRS. BUNNY

One day, Mrs. Bunny looked at the calendar.
"Oh, dear," she sighed, "Easter is just around the corner. I must hurry or the boys and girls will be disappointed."
So Mrs. Bunny hippety-hopped to the meadow to find some soft clover to line her egg basket. Then she tied a bright blue ribbon to the handle, and off she went to look for some eggs to color.
As she hippety-hopped along, she said, "If I don't find some eggs in a hurry, the children will miss an important part of Easter."
"Where are you going?" asked Mrs. Hummingbird, who was buzzing around like a tiny helicopter.

[4] Aliki, *George and the Cherry Tree*, Dial Press, Inc., New York, 1964.

"I'm looking for some eggs to dye," said Mrs. Bunny. "And I must hurry and find some or the children will be disappointed."

Mrs. Hummingbird said, "I would gladly let you have my eggs, but I fear they are too small. A hummingbird's egg is the smallest egg in the world, you know."

"I know," replied Mrs. Bunny. "Thank you for your kindness and I'll be on my way. There isn't much time."

So off she hippety-hopped.

"Where are you going?" asked Mr. Owl, who was sitting on the branch of an oak tree.

Mrs. Bunny didn't know if Mr. Owl was speaking to her since he wasn't looking in her direction. Owls stare straight ahead. They do not move their eyes as we do.

"Where are you going?" repeated Mr. Owl.

"Oh, I beg your pardon," apologized Mrs. Bunny. "I'm looking for some eggs to dye for Easter. If I do not find some in a hurry, the boys and girls will be disappointed."

Mr. Owl winked and blinked his large, round eyes.

"Well," he said slowly, "my mate has three round eggs in her nest. I am sure she would share one of them with you, Mrs. Bunny."

"Oh, no thank you," said Mrs. Bunny. "Mrs. Owl surely wants to hatch some baby owls and she will need her eggs. So I'll be on my way."

Hippety-hop went Mrs. Bunny.

Mr. Robin was bobbing his head and looking for worms. He turned his head from side to side listening as he hopped along the ground.

"Where are you going?" asked Mr. Robin.

"I'm looking for some eggs to dye. If I do not find some in a hurry, the children will be disappointed," replied Mrs. Bunny.

"You *do* have a problem," said Mr. Robin. "The eggs of my mate are blue and pretty to see, but they are not right for Easter eggs.

"Excuse me, please, I think I hear a worm crawling under the ground."

And Mr. Robin hopped away, bobbing his head from side to side and listening for the sound of worms crawling under the ground.

Hippety-hop went Mrs. Bunny. Now, she hippety-hopped very slowly for she was getting tired.

All at once she heard some fierce-sounding noises: "Grrrrrrrr! Row! Ow-ump! Eek, eek! Snarl! ROAR!"

What do you think might be making those noises? *(Responses.)*

Yes, Mrs. Bunny had reached the zoo. The animals were in their cages and couldn't get out, so Mrs. Bunny was not afraid of the fierce animal sounds. She hippety-hopped fast now to get out of the zoo, but near the gate, there was Mrs. Ostrich! Since Mrs. Bunny had never seen an ostrich, she didn't know what it was. She sat and stared at Mrs. Ostrich who is the biggest bird in the whole world.

And Mrs. Ostrich stared at Mrs. Bunny. Then Mrs. Ostrich saw the Easter basket and she knew what Mrs. Bunny was looking for because somewhere she had heard all about bunnies gathering eggs around Easter time. Now Mrs. Ostrich had a HUGE egg, but she didn't want to part with it for she wanted to sit on it and hatch a baby ostrich. But she didn't have to worry a bit for her egg was much too big to fit into Mrs. Bunny's basket.

Then hippety-hop out of the zoo went Mrs. Bunny. Hippety-hop through the town! Hippety-hop back to the meadow! Hippety-hop to the farm!

"Where are you going?" asked Mrs. Hen.

"I'm looking for some eggs to dye. If I do not find them in a hurry, the children will be disappointed," replied Mrs. Bunny.

"Why, it's very simple," said Mrs. Hen. "Just come to the hen house and take all the eggs you want."

Mrs. Hen showed the way to a hen house filled with nests. In the nests were freshly laid eggs. All of the hens were singing happily for they were so glad they had laid such fine eggs and could share them with Mrs. Bunny. They even helped her fill her basket.

"Thank you, thank you," said Mrs. Bunny gratefully. "Now the children will not be disappointed."

—L.B.S.

Ask individual children to suggest different endings for the story.

Discuss colors and sizes of eggs. Bring a hen's egg and a bird's egg for the children to compare. Boil an egg in preparation for dyeing.

### MRS. BUNNY GETS READY FOR EASTER

After Mrs. Bunny had found enough eggs to share with the children, she was ready to dye them. But first, she must boil the eggs. She wanted them to be just right so she used an egg timer. *(Show and explain a timer.)* As the eggs boiled slowly, she turned the timer over twice and soon each egg was ready for coloring. She took the kettle off the flame. While the eggs were cooling, she went to the cupboard to get her dyes, but there was only a drop of each color left. *(Ask the class to name the colors.)*

Quick as a flash, Mrs. Bunny had an idea. She hippety-hopped to the garden to find her colors. She borrowed orange from carrots and pumpkins. She borrowed red from tomatoes.

What else is red and good to eat? *(Responses.)*

She borrowed green from peas.

What else is green, grows in a garden, and is good to eat? *(Responses.)*

She borrowed blue from some pretty cornflowers which grew near the fence. She borrowed yellow from a long squash.

What else is yellow and good to eat? *(Responses.)*

She borrowed the brown she needed from some potatoes and she borrowed purple from eggplants and grapes. Happily, Mrs. Bunny had all of the colors she needed and home she went, hippety-hop.

She mixed the colors together so she could have many light and dark shades. After all of the eggs were dyed and delivered, she went to bed because she was very sleepy, and tired from all of that hard work.

Easter morning, the children found beautiful eggs of every color imaginable on their doorsteps.

—L.B.S.

Each child should use an egg timer and have the experience of boiling his own egg.

Pour a variety of food colorings into cups of very warm water and set them inside a cardboard box lid to steady them. Add a few drops of vinegar to the water. (Vinegar helps to set the dye.) Each child may place his egg on a spoon and dip it into the mixture. In this way, his hands will be protected from dye.

Each child may dispose of his egg in the way he wishes:

He may decorate it with gummed paper features.

He may take the egg home for a snack.

He may use the shell to make a mosaic.

He may fill two half shells with soil and plant nasturtium or radish seeds, tie a piece of wool around each one, and hang both little baskets in the window.

## EASTER EGG SURPRISES

Colorful plastic eggs (the kind that open) can be found in many variety stores. Collect miniature objects: a ring, jacks, thimble, coin, or button. Show and name the objects. Place one object inside each egg.

Ask the children to tell the color of a particular egg and its contents as you shake it. Do not use more than four or five objects at a time. Gradually, add more eggs and objects.

## MARY IS ABSENT

Each child may have a cardboard egg shape with his name on it. Punch a hole in each end of the egg. Thumb tack the egg to the attendance bulletin board. When a child is absent, turn the egg so that his name is shown upside down. When he returns to school, let him turn his egg right side up.

A Humpty-Dumpty face may be drawn on the upper part of the egg.

## FIVE LITTLE CHICKS

There were five little chicks and not a feather more;
One went to nibble grass; then there were _____.

Four little chicks began to disagree.
One went into the coop; then there were _____.

Three little chicks grew and grew and grew.
One became a rooster; then there were _____.

Two little chicks fluffed their feathers in the sun.
One went to find a bug; then there was _____.

One little chick was left all alone.
He went to find the Mother Hen; then there were none.

—L.B.S.

Pause at the end of each couplet so that children may supply the number. Make stick puppets or use chicken cutouts for the flannelboard.

## HIPPETY-HOP

Hippety-Hop came hopping by,
Hippety-hippety-hop.

He wiggled an ear and he winked his eye,
Hippety-hippety-hop.

He hopped in the meadow; he hopped on the hill,
Hippety-hippety-hop.

And as far as I know he is hopping still,
Hippety-hippety-hop.

—L.B.S.

Several children may pretend to be rabbits and give three hops to accompany the refrain.

## A ST. PATRICK'S ELF

(Make felt cutouts of the elf and his clothing.)

I met a little elfman once.
He wore a stovepipe hat.
   *(Place elf's green hat on flannelboard.)*
His face was round and mischievous.
   *(Place head under hat.)*
He stopped awhile to chat.

I asked, "Why are your trousers green,
   *(Place trousers on board.)*
Instead of red or blue?
Your coat is green, and there I see
   *(Place coat on board.)*
A buckle on each shoe."
   *(Place legs and shoes on board.)*

I asked, "What are you doing here?"
And this I heard him say:
"Why, I have come to visit you
This fine St. Patrick's Day!

"I'm dressed in green from head to toe,
For I'm an Irish elf.
I wear a buckle on each shoe
Which I made by myself."

He said, "I've come to visit you
This fine St. Patrick's Day."
He sang a song and danced a jig,
And skipped far, far away!

—L.B.S.

Say: "Think of a song the St. Patrick's Elf might have sung. Let's paint a picture of him? Show how he would dance a jig."

Children may put the felt pieces together on the flannelboard.

## DISCOVERING ME ON MY BIRTHDAY

On top of the mountain is a bunch of grass.
*(Point to hair.)*
Under the grass are two bright lights.
*(Point to eyes.)*
Under the lights is a little hill.
*(Point to nose.)*
Under the hill is a little pond.
*(Point to mouth.)*
Inside the pond are ten white stones.
*(Point to teeth.)*
And a little red fish jumps in and out.
*(Tongue tip moves in and out.)*

## BIRTHDAY FINGER PLAY

The first year I could only crawl.
The second year I stood up tall.
The third year I could ride a "trike."
The fourth year I could fly a kite.
The fifth year I grew very tall.
I marked the place upon the wall.
I swam and waded in the pool,
And then I started off to school!

—Adapted from an old rhyme

Use for teaching concepts of first, second, etc. Mark the height of each child on a chalkboard or a long strip of wrapping paper attached to the bulletin board.

## BIRTHDAY PRESENTS

Make an apron from unbleached muslin. To the lower part of the apron, sew eight colored percale pockets: red, yellow, blue, orange, green, purple, pink, and brown. Be sure that colors are arranged so that orange and yellow, blue and green, or blue and purple do not appear side by side.

Little objects can be hidden in the pockets and taken out as surprises when telling this story:

Libby had a birthday. Aunt Sue sent her a present. Was it something for Libby's neck? Guess what it was. *(Pull out necklace or scarf.)* Was it something for Libby's finger? Guess what it was. *(Show a ring.)* Was it something for Libby's feet? Can you guess? *(Take out the socks.)* Was it something for Libby's hair? Guess. *(Display ribbon or barrette.)* Was it something for Libby to smell? Guess. *(Show perfume or flower.)* Was it something for Libby to feel? *(Pull out small stuffed toy.)* Did you guess right? No? Was it something for Libby to taste? What do you think it was? *(Take out the candy.)*

—L.B.S.

Put into the pockets anything else which may have sensory appeal. Use this story for a "feel and identify" activity.

## BALLOONS FOR A PARTY

Here are balloons for a party
For this is my birthday today.
I have some balloons for all of my friends
Who are coming to my house to play.

Here is a pretty, round, blue balloon
As blue as my kitten's eyes.
Here is a flaming, round, red balloon
That is just about this size.
   *(Form circle with arms.)*

Here is a happy, round, yellow balloon
As yellow as bright sunshine.
Here is a lovely, round, purple balloon
Like purple grapes on a vine.

Here is a little, round, orange balloon
Like oranges from the store.
Here is a round, grassy green balloon,
And now there are no more.
 (*Put arms behind back.*)

—L.B.S.

Cut round, felt balloon shapes and attach a strip of yarn to each one. Ask for volunteers to place the right colors on the flannelboard or remove them as the rhyme is chanted.

## TWO BIRTHDAYS

Mary came to school but she didn't feel happy. Mary cried because she missed her mother and baby brother. Although there were fifteen other boys and girls at school, Mary still felt lonesome.

Then Janet came along. Janet did not have dark hair and eyes like Mary. Her hair was gold and her eyes were blue. But Janet was a little girl just like Mary, and she said, "Hello," in a friendly voice.

Mary played with Janet. She talked to Janet. She sang with Janet. Janet pushed Mary in the swing and she helped Mary put a puzzle together.

Soon Mary smiled. She was not unhappy anymore. She had found a friend. Also, she had discovered something very interesting! She found that she and Janet had birthdays on the very same day. So when the boys and girls sang "Happy Birthday," they sang to both Janet and Mary at the same time.

—L.B.S.

Use this story for a discussion on how homesickness can be overcome. The young child at school is often away from home for the first time and needs the support of an adult with whom he can identify. Ask: "Have you ever felt lonesome? How did it feel? Can pets feel lonesome? What makes people lonesome? Do you have a birthday on the same day as someone else?"

## BIRTHDAY CAKE

Nancy was just five (or four) years old.

How old are you? *(Responses.)*

Mother made Nancy a big, round cake with beautiful, pink candles set in five (four) pink rosebuds.

Nancy wore a pink crepe-paper cap on top of her head.

Mother lit the candles which burned brightly. Oh, it was a pretty sight!

"Blow out the candles, Nancy," said Mother.

"Whoosh, whoosh," went Nancy's breath as she blew out the candles and made a wish.

Nancy thought that the cake was too pretty to eat, but Mother said, "I will cut around the parts where the candles are."

So Mother cut four pieces which looked like triangles: one for Daddy, one for Mother, one for Grandma, and one for Nancy.

Then Mother said, "I'll have a piece later so give this piece to Mrs. Brown who lives next door."

And do you know, that cake lasted *five whole days?*

—L.B.S.

Ask: "What do you think Nancy wished for when she blew out the candles?"

A pink felt, square-shaped cake with removable felt candles can be placed on the flannelboard each time a child has a birthday.

A lovely birthday cake can be made from a square piece of cardboard. Cover it with pink crepe paper, glue five cardboard candles to it, and decorate the cake with small candies. Clip a child's name to the cake when he has a birthday. A small, round, covered hatbox will make a realistically looking cake.

### Supplementary References

Anglund, Joan Walsh: *Christmas is a Time of Giving*, Harcourt, Brace and World, Inc., New York, 1961.

Bannon, Laura: *The Scary Thing*, Houghton Mifflin Company, Boston, 1956.

Brown, Margaret Wise: *The Golden Egg Book*, Golden Press, Inc., New York, 1965.

Liang, Yen: *Happy New Year*, J. B. Lippincott Company, Philadelphia, 1961.

McNeill, Janet: *The Giant's Birthday*, Henry Z. Walck, Inc., New York, 1964.

Milhous, Katherine: *Appalonia's Valentine*, Charles Scribner's Sons, New York, 1954.

Waber, Bernard: *Just Like Abraham Lincoln*, Houghton Mifflin Company, Boston, 1964.

CHAPTER 6

# All The Year Round

In the early childhood education center, it is important to foster a love for nature. The teacher, who helps a child to understand and develop sympathy for nature, molds values which might not be learned in other ways, and opens new vistas. Each season is a magical time of the year for providing these experiences.

*Economic values* are encountered and explored as the children begin to understand how the seasons affect our supply of food. A trip to the supermarket contributes to an appreciation for the farmer's services and provides firsthand knowledge about fruits and vegetables.

Pure air and water, sheltering trees, singing birds, amphibians, and insect life are all parts of seasonal study which help to create positive attitudes toward and reverence for living things. There can be excursions to parks, hills, and woods which will call attention to hundreds of plants and creatures that are part of our everyday existence.

*Social and ethical values* are developed as the child learns to assume responsibility for keeping the home, school grounds, and classroom attractive, neat, and clean. Even though a child may live in the heart of a desolate and economically impoverished neighborhood, he can learn respect for another's property and possessions. Research indicates that where there is sympathy with nature, there is less tendency to vandalize by destroying property, trees, and plants, or to kill birds, toads, and insects which are beneficial to the growth of crops. Communion with nature helps to ameliorate the most squalid conditions and brings new hope to an individual.

*Aesthetic and spiritual* values are inculcated when children are brought into contact with nature. An appreciation of harmony and symmetry is developed when nature is studied and its beauty reaches the recesses of a child's mind and soul.

As children observe, experiment, manipulate, and study, they learn how things feel, live, and grow. Gardening affords firsthand experiences for children to dig in the soil, plant seeds, and watch roots sprout almost magically. Lack of space in most city schools prohibits this experimentation on a wide scale, yet many varieties of flowers and plants grow well indoors and in windowboxes. The dish garden, described on page 253, presents a simple gardening experience which enables children to observe changes in growth. A sweet potato produces a beautiful indoor vine. One reward of loving nature is learning how to make one's own environment, however poor, more attractive.

A birdhouse provides another kind of observation. Birds become willing tenants when a few bread crumbs from lunch are shared with them. In winter, some European children fasten sheaves of grain together and tie them to posts, buildings, and trees to serve as birds' feasts.

There is a tremendous need for the child from economically and socially deprived city areas to come into visual and tactile contact with nature by visiting the zoo; by petting, feeding, and caring for classroom creatures; and by observing flowers and plants growing in a botanical garden. *Sadness and despair diminish where nature smiles.*

This chapter contains a variety of seasonal suggestions that use many language approaches:

> *Finger play:* "Busy Squirrel"
> *Action rhyme:* "Little Brown Seeds"
> *Chalk talk:* "Half an Apple"
> *Pantomime:* "Making a Snowman"
> *Discussion:* "Autumn"
> *Choral speaking:* "Warm Clothes"
> *Aesthetic appreciation:* "Dear Little Tree"
> *Flannelboard story:* "Sleepy Snowflakes"

A bibliography of children's publications on nature is located on page 267.

—L.B.S.

## LITTLE BROWN SPARROW

Little Brown Sparrow is flying around
  *(Motion of flying upward.)*
Up to the treetops, and down to the ground.
  *(Lower fingers.)*

Come to my window, dear sparrow, come.
    *(Hands spread apart.)*
See! I will give you a tasty bread crumb.
    *(Hold out hand.)*

If you are tired, here is a nest.
    *(Cup hands.)*
Wouldn't you like to fly here and rest?
—L.B.S.

## TEN WHITE SEA GULLS

Ten white sea gulls *(Hold up ten fingers.)*
Are ready to fly *(Motion of flying.)*
Over the hill,
And up to the sky. *(Raise arms high.)*

Ten white sea gulls *(Hold up ten fingers.)*
Swift as can be, *(Sweep hands to one side.)*
Spread out their wings, *(Motion of flying.)*
And fly to the sea.

Ten white sea gulls *(Hold hands high.)*
Are up in the sky;
Pretty white sea gulls,
Good-by, good-by!
—L.B.S.

Accompany children to the beach where they may gather shells, smell ocean spray, and hear sea gulls crying. If a beach is not available, bring a variety of shells, books, and pictures for the browsing table.

## THE DISH GARDEN

The children bring empty, foil, TV dinner containers to the education center. Each child places a small portion of granulated charcoal in his plate, then a layer of small stones, and last, some rich soil. He adds bird or vegetable seeds, sprinkling them over the surface of the soil. A little loose soil should be scattered on top.

Encourage each child to water his own dish garden daily, but sparingly.

Lima bean growth is a spectacular thing to watch. A magnifying glass should be kept handy so that a child can use it frequently for examining the sprouting plant. Sometime during the growth process, set aside a special period for discussion of the changes which occur.

If sectional TV dinner plates are used, leave one division empty. It may be filled with water on which to float a walnut half-shell boat.

A cardboard scarecrow or a tiny party favor parasol will add a delightful touch. After the children have observed the plants over a two-weeks' period, they may take their dish gardens home.

—O.M.A.

## A MINIATURE FOREST

Select a gallon-sized, mayonnaise jar. Place it on its side inside a cardboard lid which will absorb moisture. Scatter a layer of good soil and peat moss inside the jar. Sow grass seeds and corn, and moisten the dirt well. Set a ceramic figure in the jar to stimulate added interest.

After the seeds have germinated to a height of one-half inch above the soil, seal the jar lid with masking tape. The grass and corn will continue to grow and will fill the jar like a miniature forest.

The class can observe moisture forming as it waters the soil inside the jar. This miniature forest will last indefinitely.

—O.M.A.

## APPLE BUDS

Here are two apple buds growing on a tree,
   *(Use thumbs and forefingers to make two circles.)*
Curled up tightly as little buds should be.
   *(Make two fists.)*
Along come the raindrops falling from the skies,
   *(Raise arms and lower fingers gradually.)*
And two little apple buds open up their eyes.
   *(Open fists slowly, and extend hands.)*

—L.B.S.

## SEASONS

TEACHER: Autumn is here; autumn is here.
           The little gray squirrels tells us,
CHILDREN: "Autumn is here!"

TEACHER: Winter is here; winter is here.
The soft falling snow tells us,
CHILDREN: "Winter is here!"
TEACHER: Springtime is here, springtime is here.
The patches of green tell us,
CHILDREN: "Springtime is here!"
TEACHER: Summer is here, summer is here.
The flowers in bloom tell us,
CHILDREN: "Summer is here!"

—L.B.S.

Ask: "Which season do you like best? Why? What kind of fun can we have in the fall? What kind of fun can we have when snow falls? In the rain? In warm summer?"

## BUSY SQUIRREL

The little, gray squirrel makes a scampering sound,
  *(Wiggle fingers.)*
As he gathers the nuts which fall to the ground.
  *(Hold fingers high and then let them move down slowly.)*
He buries the nuts in a dark, secret place,
  *(One hand over other.)*
And covers them over with never a trace.
The little, gray squirrel always seems to know
  *(Hands outstretched.)*
That the robins have gone and it's time for snow.
  *(Hold fingers high and then lower them slowly.)*

—L.B.S.

Read this rhyme to motivate the spirit of autumn. Ask: "Why does the busy squirrel hide nuts? Why do birds fly south?"

## AUTUMN

### (A Discussion)

It is autumn. We sometimes call this season fall. Leaves turn different colors and fruits in the orchards ripen. Leaves and fruit fall to the ground when they are ripe.

Trees rustle their boughs and say, "Come pick up our apples, pears, and plums."

What can we do with apples? Pears? Plums? Which fruit do you like best? *(Responses.)*

In autumn, turnips and potatoes that grow under the ground say, "Come dig us up."

Who eats turnips and potatoes? Which vegetable do you like best? *(Responses.)*

In autumn, the trees in the woods call to us, "We are ready to let our acorns and nuts fall. Come gather them!"

Who eats nuts? *(Responses.)*

In autumn, the bushes whisper, "Our berries are ripe. Please come and pick them."

What kind of berries do you like best? *(Responses.)*

Happy squirrels, birds, and people love autumn.

I am thankful for autumn for it brings the harvest. Why are you thankful for autumn? *(Responses.)*

—L.B.S.

This selection may be used during the Thanksgiving holiday.

Magazine cutouts of foods may be placed in a small basket so that children may select their favorite foods and talk about them. Provide vegetables and fruits that children can touch, smell, and observe their colors.

A tongue depressor inserted in one end of a potato, turnip, or large carrot makes a fine puppet. Buttons or other materials from the odds-and-ends box may be pinned or glued on for features.

## HERE IS A TALL TREE

Here is a tall tree *(Stand.)*
With leaves of brown. *(Raise arms and spread fingers.)*
Here are some brown leaves
Fluttering down. *(Lower and move fingers slowly.)*

## WHAT TO DO WITH LEAVES

Provide varieties of leaves. Compare their colors with bits of colored construction paper, cloth, plastic or real flowers. Lay all of the leaves of one color in a pile. Remove one pile of leaves after the children have closed their eyes. Ask what color was taken away.

Dip the leaves in water and use them as little boats, letting them float in a pan of water. Discover how much brighter they become after being dipped in water. Read Robert Louis Stevenson's "Where Go the Boats" to the class.

Press leaves on clay to make leaf designs. Lay a leaf underside up on the table and cover it with lightweight paper. With the side of a crayon, rub the paper. The leaf veins and outline will appear. Compare the shapes and midribs of leaves.

Cut out paper leaves on which each child's name can be written.

—V.S.P.

## WHAT TO DO WITH SEEDS

The children may spread watermelon or cantaloupe seeds on a sheet of wrapping paper to dry. When dry, the seeds may be glued to tablet backs or pieces of cardboard to form interesting mosaics.

The seeds also may be strung while they are pliable and moist.

## PICKING APPLES

Here's a little apple tree.
  *(Hold up left arm, fingers spread.)*
I look way up and I can see
  *(Look through circle made with thumb and forefinger of right hand.)*
Ripe, red apples juicy sweet.
Ripe, red apples I will eat.
I will shake the apple tree,
  *(Shake raised arm.)*
And let the apples fall on me!
  *(Arms raised and lowered slowly.)*
  —Adapted from an old rhyme

## WHERE DO THEY GO?

TEACHER: Where do all the daisies go?
Underneath the snow they creep,
  *(One palm over the other hand.)*
Nod their heads and go to sleep.
  *(Hands clasped beside head.)*
CHILDREN: That's where daisies go.

TEACHER: Where do little robins go?
    Far away from winter snow
      *(Motion of flying.)*
    To the warm, warm South they go.
CHILDREN: That's where robins go.

TEACHER: Where do little babies go?
    Little babies, snug and warm,
    Softly lie in Mothers' arms.
      *(Motion of cradling in arms.)*
CHILDREN: That's where babies go.

—Unknown

## THE WIND

(A Chalk Talk)

The wind blew and blew: "Whoo-oo-oo-oo." (1)

It blew the clouds across the sky. (2)

The little clouds began to cry. (3)

The big round sun began to shine. (4)

Up grew a straight and lovely vine! (5)

—L.B.S.

Numerals at the end of each line correspond to the drawings which are produced simultaneously to narration.

After drawing the figures once, erase them. Many children will want to experiment with these configurations in finger paint or at the easel.

The rhyme may be acted out in the following ways:

    First line:    Turn around.
    Second line:  Run across room.

Third line:   Slump body sadly.
Fourth line:  Make big circle with arms.
Fifth line:   Stand tall, and wiggle fingers for leaves.

## SNOWFLAKES

Snowflakes look like dainty lace.
I felt one soft upon my face.
I felt one on my chin and lip.
I caught one on my finger tip.
—L.B.S.

After reading the poem, ask: "Does it snow in our city? Have you ever played in the snow? Have you ever tasted snow? How does it taste? How does it feel on your face? What can you make from snow?"

## WARM CLOTHES

TEACHER:   I have two red mittens.
              *(Show hands.)*
           My snowsuit is white.
              *(Rub hands over clothes.)*
CHILDREN:  They keep me snug and warm.

TEACHER:   I have a brown jacket
              *(Hands hug body.)*
           That zips me up tight.
              *(Act out.)*
CHILDREN:  It keeps me snug and warm.

TEACHER:   I have a green scarf.
              *(Hands placed on neck.)*
           That comes up to my nose.
              *(Touch nose.)*
CHILDREN:  It keeps me snug and warm.

TEACHER:   And a pair of galoshes
              *(Show feet.)*
           That cover my toes.
CHILDREN:  They keep me snug and warm.
—L.B.S.

Children will receive practice in using the pronouns *it* and *they*. Ask: "How do you dress in winter? In summer?"

### DEAR LITTLE TREE

Dear little tree, what will you do
When winter winds start to blow,
And all of your leaves fall down to the earth,
And your branches are filled with snow?

"I will be a house for a little mouse,
Or a hole for a squirrel to hide.
And my trunk will make a very nice place
For a skunk to sleep inside."

—L.B.S.

After reading the poem, ask: "How do trees help us? How do they help animals? Which animal would you like to be? Why? Let's pretend we are asleep inside a tree trunk as soft music plays for us." Play the piano, music box, or a record as the children relax.

### SLEEPY SNOWFLAKES

The ground was bare;
The trees were gray,
And it looked as if
It would snow all day.

But it didn't. There was not one flake of snow. Now how could Santa make a trip around the world without snow? And especially on Christmas Eve?

One little snowflake on a dark cloud said to his brothers and sisters, "Hurry! It's Christmas Eve. Wake up!"

Four little snowflakes woke up. *(Place pellon or paper snowflake cutouts on the flannelboard.)*

One, two, three, four little snowflakes said, "Hurry! It's Christmas Eve. Wake up!" *(Place all snowflakes on the board.)*

The sleepy little snowflakes rubbed their sleepy eyes, and looked around.

When the snowflakes saw that it was dark, they cried, "We're late! We're late! Santa will not wait!"

Now the little girl snowflakes were wide awake from so much commotion, and they hurried as fast as they could to put on their fluffy white dresses, while the little boy snowflakes put on their best white robes.

They looked up and saw the round, shining moon.

"Oh, thank you for giving us light," they called to the moon.

"I'll light the way for you," called the happy old moon.

Fluttery, fluttery, down, down, down. The little snowflakes covered the gray, bare branches of the trees. They made everything sparkle in the moonlight. Then in the distance, they heard tinkling sleigh bells. *(Ring bells softly.)* The sound of the bells came closer and closer and closer. *(Ring bells more loudly.)*

The little snowflakes called to Santa, "We're here! We're here!"

"Ho, ho, ho!" laughed Santa in a big booming voice. "Ho, ho, ho, you beautiful snowflakes! Thank you for coming! Now the boys and girls all over the world will have a *wonderful* Christmas!"

—L.B.S.

The children may fold squares of white paper several times and cut notches to create snowflakes. Construction paper will stick to the flannelboard if the board is slanted slightly. Santa, trees, and a moon can be found in December issues of magazines. Back these pictures with outing flannel, and display them as the story is told.

## MAKING A SNOWMAN

Nan and Johnny thought it would be fun to make a snowman. So they put on their warm jackets, caps, mittens, and boots and went outdoors.

Johnny took a handful of snow and he patted it and patted it and patted it. *(Children repeat and act out.)* Soon he had made a little ball of snow. He rolled it around and rolled it and rolled it around and around. *(Children act out.)* Nan helped him. Soon he had a big ball of snow. *(Make circle with arms.)*

And the snowball was so HUGE that Johnny and Nan couldn't move it.

Nan made a ball, too. She scooped up a handful of snow and she patted it and patted it and patted it. *(Children repeat and perform actions.)* Then she rolled it and rolled it and rolled it, around and around on the snowy ground. *(Children act out.)* Johnny helped her. Together the two children put Nan's little ball of snow on top of Johnny's big snowball and the snowman was almost ready.

But wait! Not quite! Johnny thought of something. He found a carrot for the snowman's nose and an apple for his mouth. Nan found some potatoes for his eyes. Mother helped, too. She looked in the shed and found an old hat.

My! He was a MAGNIFICENT snowman and so FAT! *(Spread hands.)*

"What shall we do with our snowman?" asked Johnny.

—L.B.S.

Ask: "How would you end the story? What name do you think the children gave their snowman? Have you ever made a snowman? Would you like to make one? Could you make a pretend snowman out of clay? Show how you would melt like a snowman if the sun came out."

### A TIME FOR GROWING

Wake up, little roots
In the earth below.
Wake up, little roots,
It is time to grow.
The rain is so warm,
And the earth so new.
Wake up, little roots,
I am waiting for you.

—L.B.S.

Use this rhyme during a rest period. The children may stretch their arms on the last line.

Sing the verses.

### LITTLE BROWN SEEDS

Little brown seeds so small and round
  *(Pretend to hold seeds in hand.)*
Are sleeping quietly under the ground.
  *(Place palms beside face.)*
Down come the raindrops, sprinkle, sprinkle,
  sprinkle. *(Raise arms and lower them
  slowly moving fingers rapidly.)*
Out comes the rainbow, twinkle, twinkle,
  twinkle. *(Draw a big arc in the air.)*

Little brown seeds way down below,
Up through the earth they grow, grow, grow.
*(Children bend to floor and rise slowly.)*
Little green leaves come one by one.
They hold up their heads and look at the sun.
*(Children look up and extend arms.)*
—L.B.S.

Sing: "Little Seeds."[1]

## LITTLE HONEYBEES

One busy honeybee in the orchard flew.
Along came another! Zzzzzz!
   Then there were two.
Two little honeybees near the apple tree.
Along came another! Zzzzzz!
   Then there were three.
Three busy honeybees liked to explore.
Along came another! Zzzzzz!
   Then there were four.
Four busy honeybees flying to the hive.
Along came another! Zzzzzz!
   Then there were five.
Five busy honeybees buzzed around and then —
Zzzzzz! There was a swarm of bees —
   A hundred and ten!
—L.B.S.

Sketch and cut out large bees from tagboard. Color them orange and black. Mount them on dowel sticks or tongue depressors. Children hold these bee puppets and make the buzzing sound as the rhyme is said.

## PLANTING SEEDS

TEACHER: A farmer once planted some melon seeds.
CHILDREN: Pat, pat, pat, pat, pat! *(Quickly.)*
TEACHER: He gave them some water and pulled up the weeds.
CHILDREN: Pull, pull, pull, pull, pull! *(Slowly.)*

---

[1] Lucille F. Wood and Louise B. Scott, "Little Seeds," *Singing Fun*, McGraw-Hill, Inc., New York, 1954, p. 33.

TEACHER: The melon seeds grew and grew in the sun.
CHILDREN: Up, up, up, up, up! *(Quickly.)*
TEACHER: A pretty green plant came from every one.
CHILDREN: Grow, grow, grow, grow, grow. *(Slowly.)*
TEACHER: And a melon grew on every vine.
CHILDREN: One, two, three, four, five. *(Hold up five fingers.)*
TEACHER: And for breakfast the melons tasted fine.
CHILDREN: Yum, yum, yum, yum, yum! *(Rub stomach.)*

—L.B.S.

Show pictures of different kinds of melons.
Plant or string melon seeds, or use them for collages.

## MY GARDEN

Here is my little garden bed.
   *(Make bowl shape with hand.)*
Now some seeds I'll sow.
   *(Motion of taking seeds from
   bowl and scattering them.)*
Here is my little garden rake.
   *(Scratch with fingers.)*
Here is my little hoe.
   *(Arms outstretched in front of
   body. Bend fingers downward.)*

Here is the big, round, yellow sun
   *(Make circle with arms.)*
Warming everything.
Here are the raindrops falling down.
   *(Raise arms and lower them
   gently, moving fingers.)*
Now we know it's spring.

Little plants will wake up now,
   *(Stoop slowly.)*
And lift their pretty heads.
   *(Raise arms.)*
Little plants will grow and grow
   *(Rise slowly.)*
From their warm earth beds.

—L.B.S.

## HALF AN APPLE

From a little bit of ground (1)
There grows a tiny tree, (2)
With some pretty leaves upon it,
One, two, three. (3)
Now we'll run around it
To see what we can see, (4)
A half an apple just for you,
And maybe one for me.

—O.M.A.

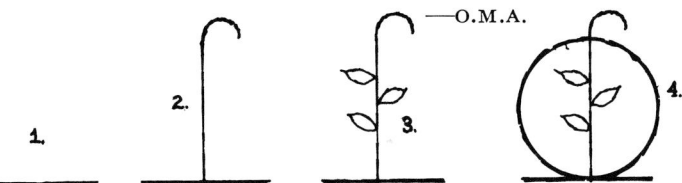

Draw the figures on the chalkboard as the poem is said. Pause after each line to allow time for drawing. Encourage the children to join in saying the words.

## MARCH

I like to fly my paper kite
Up in the clouds and out of sight.
My kite is strong; It has a tail
That helps it soar and helps it sail.
The March winds blow my kite away
If it's a very windy day.
Now Winter's gone and March is here.
I know because the kites appear.
March is the month for kites each year!

—L.B.S.

Read this poem during the first week in March. Show pictures of kites.

Make construction paper kites backed with outing flannel, attach yarn strings, and use on the flannelboard. Sing "Five Kites"[2] as one child removes the kites.

On March bulletin boards, post children's paintings of wind scenes.

[2] Lucille F. Wood, and Louise B. Scott, "Five Kites," *More Singing Fun*, McGraw-Hill, Inc., New York, 1961, pp. 46-47.

## THREE LITTLE ROBINS

Three little robins were fast asleep.
   *(Hands beside head.)*
Three little robins began to peep.
   *(Move pointer finger and thumb together to form beak.)*
Three little robins looked for a worm.
Three little robins began to squirm.
   *(Wiggle fingers.)*

Along came the father with worm number one.
   *(Hold up one finger.)*
The first baby swallowed it, and that was fun.
Along came the father with worm number two.
   *(Two fingers.)*
The second baby swallowed it and he was through.

Along came the father with worm number three.
   *(Three fingers.)*
The third baby swallowed it as fast as could be.
How did the three baby robins feel
After they'd had such a wonderful meal?

—L.B.S.

The children respond to the question.

This rhyme is suitable for creative dramatics. Suggest several groups to play the parts.

Ask: "If you were a robin, where would you build your nest? What would you use to build it? Show with your hands how big you would make your nest."

## FUZZY BUMBLEBEES

TEACHER:  Hear the fuzzy bumblebees
             Buzzing in the apple trees.
CHILDREN:  Bzzzz, bzzzz, bzzzz.

TEACHER:  Listen to their busy hum.
             One sat right here upon my thumb.
CHILDREN:  Bzzzz, bzzzz, bzzzz.

TEACHER: Fuzzy-Wuzzy Bumblebee,
Make some honey now for me.
CHILDREN: Bzzzz, bzzzz, bzzzz.

—L.B.S.

This rhyme provides practice on the "z" sound as in *zoo*. Choose groups of children for dramatizations.

SUPPLEMENTARY REFERENCES

Adelson, Leone: *All Ready for Summer*, David McKay Company, Inc., New York, 1956.
———: *All Ready for Winter*, David McKay Company, Inc., New York, 1952.
Anglund, Joan Walsh: *A Year is Round*, Harcourt, Brace and World, Inc., New York, 1966.
Bannon, Laura: *Little People of the Night*, Houghton Mifflin Company, Boston, 1963.
Brown, Margaret Wise: *The Important Book*, Harper and Row, Publishers, New York, 1949.
Buff, Mary and Conrad: *Hurry, Skurry, and Flurry*, The Viking Press, Inc., New York, 1954.
Conger, Marion: *Who Has Seen the Wind?* Abingdon Press, Nashville, 1959.
Duvoisin, Roger: *The House of Four Seasons*, Lothrop, Lee and Shepard Company, New York, 1956.
Foster, Doris Van Liew: *A Pocketful of Seasons*, Lothrop, Lee and Shepard Company, New York, 1961.
Foster, Willene, and Pearl Queree: *Seeds Are Wonderful*, Melmont Publishers, Inc., Chicago, 1960.
Francoise: *The Big Rain*, Charles Scribner's Sons, New York, 1961.
Gay, Zhenya: *The Nicest Time of the Year*, The Viking Press, Inc., New York, 1960.
Hurd, Edith: *The Day the Sun Danced*, Harper and Row, Publishers, New York, 1966.
Keats, Ezra Jack: *Whistle for Willie*, The Viking Press, Inc., New York, 1964.
Krauss, Ruth: *The Happy Day*, Harper and Row, Publishers, New York, 1949.
Langstaff, John: *Over in the Meadow*, Harcourt, Brace and World, Inc., New York, 1957.
Mizumura, Kazue: *I See the Wind*, Thomas Y. Crowell Company, New York, 1966.
Seidman, M. S.: *Who Woke the Sun?* The Macmillan Company, New York, 1960.
Sewell, Helen: *Blue Barns*, The Macmillan Company, New York, 1964.
Steiner, Charlotte: *Listen to My Seashell*, Alfred A. Knopf, Inc., New York, 1959.
Watson, Jane Werner: *Wonders of Nature*, Simon and Schuster, Inc., New York, 1958.
Yashima, Taro: *Umbrella*, The Viking Press, Inc., New York, 1958.
Zion, Gene: *All Falling Down*, Harper and Row, Publishers, New York, 1951.
Zolotow, Charlotte: *The Storm Book*, Harper and Row, Publishers, New York, 1952.

CHAPTER 7

# Creatures To Love

A child's relationships with animals can be of life-long value to him. Most of the benefits in this association come from interaction between the child and the pet, and from the wholesome fun which play provides. Kindness to animals that respond to love is an enriching and rewarding experience, especially for a child who needs affection. Cuddling, petting, snuggling against, talking to, and gently romping with animals help the child to offer acceptable expressions of affection, for he needs to learn both how to give and to receive love.

In a New York zoo, where the children were allowed to take animals home as they would library books, there was some evidence that the creatures benefited as well as the children themselves. Advice was given on care and feeding; therefore, the children learned about science and humanity from having had direct contact with the animals and some responsibility in caring for them.

A capacity to appreciate creatures can be a lifetime joy. Nearly all famous people have liked animals. Franklin D. Roosevelt cherished his Scottie, Fala. Tad, Abraham Lincoln's son, sometimes brought his pet goat into the White House. Ulysses S. Grant owned a black charger named Cincinnati, and George Washington loved both dogs and horses. When John F. Kennedy was President, young children enjoyed following the adventures of his daughter, Caroline, and her pony, Macaroni.

Many teachers bring pets to the classroom and encourage the children to care for them. There are several advantages to be gained from this practice in the school as well as in the home:

> The child understands the responsibility required in caring for a pet.
> He gains insights into ways in which an adult cares for him.
> He grows in self-confidence as he assumes responsibility.
> He is able to feel needed because of his constructive contributions.

The teacher can discuss and demonstrate proper procedures in caring for small creatures. A veterinarian or pet shop owner will offer good advice and suggestions.

Classroom pets should be chosen prudently. Some can be handled, and some should be watched only. The following suggestions may help the teacher to choose a classroom pet.

*Fish* are fun to watch as they swim around and dart to the top of the tank for food.
*Brightly-feathered canaries* sing now and then and provide entertainment as they hop and swing.
*Red ants* are among the best insects for a classroom. They need a glass box and a drop of honey occasionally. There are easy directions for keeping ants as pets listed in reference books.
*Silk worms* are fed on mulberry leaves which grow in some states. These insects may be raised from the egg to adult stage.
*Caterpillars* are interesting to watch since they pass through a life cycle in a comparatively short period of time.
*Hamsters,* that fill their cheeks like balloons when they eat fruit and vegetables, are fun to observe. Children enjoy watching these little animals use the exercise bars or trapezes in their cages. Hamsters can be picked up gently by the scruff of the neck.
*Guinea pigs and other small mammals* offer opportunities to study nutrition, genetics, physiology, and cleanliness.
*White rabbits* can be petted and handled carefully also. They like bits of lettuce or carrots.
*Turtles* may be bought at most pet stores. They need a terrarium with no top, warm water, and a rock on which to climb. "The Turtle" by Vachel Lindsay is a favorite poem which young children enjoy learning and pantomiming.
*Frogs, toads, salamanders, and lizards* also need to be housed in a terrarium. They eat insects and worms.

Pets arouse interest at once. Since they provide a variety of subjects for discussion, they help to open the door of communication.

"Farm friends" included in this chapter describe some of the well-known creatures which appear in children's books. Added space is allotted to subjects of chickens and ducks since they are associated not only with the farm, but also with Easter and Spring. They make excellent classroom pets, too.

Included within this chapter are some of the common members of the animal family who venture near urban areas and often are seen there. These creatures are common to all parts of the United States and, therefore, are more easily identified when encountered. They are safe friends for a young child, and most of them are adaptable to classroom study.

—L.B.S.

## CHICKS

This little chick was the first to hatch.
   *(Hold up one finger at a time for each chick.)*
This little chick went out to scratch.
This little chick made his two eyes blink.
This little chick took a long, cool drink.
This little chick said, "Peep, peep, peep!"
This little chick fell fast asleep.
Mother Hen called to the tiny things,
And they all crept under her soft, warm wings.
   *(One hand on top of the other.)*
She cuddled them under her wings of brown,
   *(Cup hands.)*
And they all went to sleep as the sun went down.
   *(Palms together beside head.)*

—V.S.P.

Make felt chick cutouts and place them on the flannelboard as the rhyme is said.

## MY KITTEN

I had a baby kitten;
Her name was Fluffy Gray.
My little kitten ran from home,
And traveled far away.

A lady found and fed her
On milk to make her fat;
And now I have her back again.
My kitten is a cat!

—L.B.S.

Ask: "Why did you enjoy the poem? Why do you like people who are kind to animals? What color is nice for a kitten? What would you name a kitten? Show how kittens sleep? What do they say when they are hungry? If you had a pet kitten and, one day, you found that it was gone, what would you do?"

## THE OLD GRAY PUSSYCAT

The old gray pussycat, pussycat, pussycat,
The old gray pussycat sat in the house.
The old gray pussycat, pussycat, pussycat,
The old gray pussycat jumped at a MOUSE!
—Old rhyme

Children's voices become softer and softer until the last line is spoken in a whisper. "MOUSE" is said in a normal voice.

Move only the lips, using no voice as the children imitate you. This selection is excellent to use after a playground period.

## FIVE BLACK KITTENS

Five black kittens stayed up late,
   *(Hold up five fingers.)*
Sitting on top of the barnyard gate.
The stars came out and the moon did, too.
   *(Wiggle fingers for stars and make circle
   with arms for moon.)*
And the five little kittens began to mew.
   *(Hold up five fingers.)*
Along came the mother with a lovely purr,
   *(Move thumb of opposite hand toward "kittens.")*
And she took the kittens back home with her.
   *(Lock thumb with little finger and pull five
   "kittens" toward one side of body.)*
—L.B.S.

## BABY KITTEN

(A Science Lesson)

When the day begins to fade,
Baby Kitten, aren't you afraid?

The night is dark. There is no star.
I hope you are not going far.

You are so little and alone.
Shouldn't you wait till you have grown?

Said Baby Kitten, "Night is nice
For cats and skunks and owls and mice.

Our eyes can see to light the way.
They see as well as in the day.

At night we like to prowl around
And listen for each nighttime sound.

Our eyes are lamps that give us light
When we go prowling in the night."
—L.B.S.

When reading this poem, show a picture or hold a live kitten. The children may say "Mew, mew, mew" after each two lines.

### BUNNIES

"It's time for my bunnies to go to bed,"
The dear little mother rabbit said.
"But I must count them all to see,
If each one has come back to me.
One little bunny, two little bunnies,
Three little bunnies dear.
Four little bunnies, five little bunnies,
Yes, they are all here!
Why, they are the sweetest bunnies alive —
One, two, three, four, five!"
—Adapted from a poem
by MAUD BURNHAM

Make rabbit cutouts from white pellon for the flannelboard. Color features with crayons. Place the bunnies on the board as the rhyme is said. On a second rendition, ask the children to help count the bunnies, left to right.

## A PUPPY AT PUPPYGARTEN

Puppy went to Puppygarten where he learned all sorts of interesting things, especially drawing. From the very first time he began to draw, Puppy's drawings were most *remarkable!*

He drew a bone
For himself alone,
With two straight lines (1)
And a circle at each end. (2)
(A bone is a puppy dog's very best friend.)

He drew a doghouse (1)
With a triangle roof,
Woof (2), woof (3), woof (4).

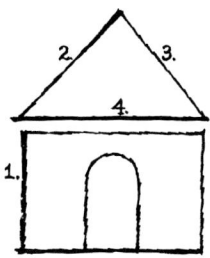

He drew whiskers for his face,
Three in each place,
Right (1) and left (2),
Not just any old place,
But neatly for a face.

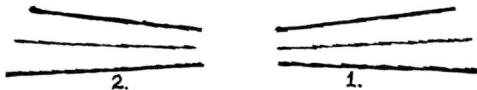

He drew an old shoe.
Can you do that, too?
Not a shoe that is new,
But a very old shoe.

—L.B.S.

This story with rhyme encourages creative drawing and presents four basic configurations: horizontal line, circle, triangle, and square. After the children observe the chalkboard drawings carefully, erase the drawings and repeat the rhyme slowly, giving the class time to draw the configurations in the air. Say: "Let's draw more pictures of Puppy's Puppygarten pictures."

### BABY ANIMALS

Little lamb, little lamb,
Where do you sleep?
In the green meadow
With my mother sheep.

Little bird, little bird,
Where do you rest?
Close to my mother
In the warm nest.

Little calf, little calf,
Where do you lie?
Out in the meadow
With Mother close by.
—Old rhyme

Discuss other mother and baby animals: dog, puppy; sow, pig; hen, chick; goose, gosling; horse, colt; cat, kitten; duck, duckling; deer, fawn; goat, kid. Talk about the legs of animals; their skin coverings and the sounds they make; what they enjoy eating; where and how they sleep.

After several repetitions, the class will be able to answer the questions posed in the rhyme.

### HOW ANIMALS SLEEP

How do different animals sleep?
Rabbits rest in burrows deep;
Horses stand up in a stall;
Kittens curl up in a ball.
Birds tuck heads beneath their wings;
Little snakes roll up in rings.
Sheep will sometimes lie in sheds;

Cows like straw or grassy beds.
Meadow, burrow, stall, or nest —
Each one likes his bed the best!
—L.B.S.

Ask the children to tell how these and other animals sleep.

## THE LITTLE PIGS

Two mother pigs lived in a pen.
*(Hold up thumbs.)*
Each had five babies and that made ten. *(Hold up both hands.)*
These five babies were new and pink, *(Hold up left hand only.)*
And these five babies were black as ink. *(Hold up right hand.)*
But all ten babies liked to play:
*(Wiggle fingers.)*
They rolled and they rolled in the mud all day.
*(Roll hands.)*
At night, with their mothers, they curled in a heap,
And they squealed and they squealed
Till they went to sleep. *(Palms together beside head.)*
—MAUD BURNHAM

This rhyme affords an opportunity to teach number concepts.

## LADYBUG

Ladybug went to Switzerland;
Ladybug went to Spain.
Ladybug went to Germany;
And then came home again.

Ladybug went to Africa;
Ladybug went to Rome.
Ladybug stayed in America,
For, of course, that was her home.
—L.B.S.

If a globe is available, show children the places Ladybug visited. Display pictures of ladybugs. Read *Fast Is Not a Ladybug: A Book About the Meaning of Fast and Slow*.[1]

### ONE LITTLE BUG

One little bug ran out in the yard,
Out in the yard to play.
A fuzzy duckling waddled by,
And the little bug ran away.

Two little bugs ran out in the yard,
Out in the yard to play.
A hungry rooster came along,
And the little bugs ran away.

Three little bugs ran out in the yard,
Out in the yard to play.
A yellow chicken said, "Peep, peep,"
And the little bugs ran away.

Four little bugs ran out in the yard,
Out in the yard to play.
A baby gosling looked at them,
And the little bugs ran away.

Five little bugs ran out in the yard,
Out in the yard to play.
A robin redbreast hopped along,
And the little bugs ran away.
—L.B.S.

Hold up the correct number of fingers to represent bugs. Cut felt bug shapes for the flannelboard to help establish number concepts.

In order to vary the procedure, make stick toad puppets for two children to hold as you read the poem.

Ask: "Why did the first little bug run away? Why did all the little bugs run out in the yard?"

---

[1] Miriam Schlein, *Fast Is Not a Ladybug*, William R. Scott, New York, 1953.

## DRAW A FROG

Draw two round circles (1)
And you will see
Places where
Two eyes will be.

Now make a curve (2)
And another one, (3)
And a round, fat body. (4)
Oh, what fun!

Draw two legs, (5)
And that will do.
Here's a funny
Frog for you!

—V.S.P.

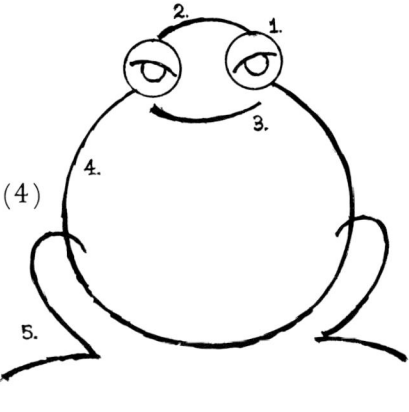

## HERE IS MISTER FROGGIE

Here is Mister Froggie, hop, hop hop!
  *(Extend middle and index fingers and
  make hopping motions.)*
Now he jumps into the pond, KERFLOP!
  *(Motion of diving with both hands.)*

—L.B.S.

## FOUR LITTLE MICE

Four little mice went out to play;
  Squeak, squeak, squeak.
And that is what I heard them say;
  Squeak, squeak, squeak.
Four little mice found a furry cap;
  Squeak, squeak, squeak.
They climbed inside and they took a nap;
  Squeak, squeak, squeak.
Along came Mrs. Pussy Gray;
  Meow, meow, meow.
And the four little mice all scampered away;
  Squeak, squeak, squeak.

—L.B.S.

Children say the refrain. Ask: "Would you say all of the squeaks the same way? How would the mice squeak if they were happy? Sad?"

### FRIENDLY SKUNK

Oh friendly, little animal
With a furry coat of black,
And a lovely snow-white stripe
Along your tail and back —
Could you be a kitten?
And can you say, "Meow?"
You look just like a tiny
Little kitten somehow.

"No, I'm not a kitten,
Though kittens are quite nice;
But I have a fluffy tail,
And I like to feed on mice.
I'm drowsy in the winter;
Into my hole I creep,
And there upon my bed of leaves,
I have a good long sleep."

You friendly, little animal,
You are a SKUNK, I'll bet.
If you didn't have such strange perfume,
I'd like you for a pet.
—L.B.S.

After reading the poem, ask: "Have you ever seen a skunk? Where? Have you smelled a skunk's perfume?"

Read: "What Was It?"[2]

### THIS LITTLE CRICKET

This little cricket played a violin.
This little cricket joined right in.
This little cricket made a crackly song.
This little cricket helped him along.

---

[2] Louise B. Scott, "What Was It," *Talking Time* (Second Edition), McGraw-Hill, Inc., New York, 1966, p. 40.

This little cricket said, "Oh, dear me!
The concert is over, and it's time for tea."

—L.B.S.

Use as a finger play.

Keep a cricket in a glass jar. Punch holes in the lid. Feed the cricket moist bread, bits of lettuce, or pieces of apple.

## THE LITTLE, NEW BUNNY

Timothy found a brand-new baby bunny. The rain had flooded it out of its home under the ground, and the baby bunny was cold and hungry. Poor, shivering little bunny!

Timothy took the soft baby bunny home and fed it with a medicine dropper, just one drop of milk at a time. He wrapped it in a piece of fuzzy blanket to keep it warm. You know that all babies need to feel warm and comfortable when they sleep. And the baby bunny felt so warm and comfortable that it slept and slept.

In nine days its eyes opened; every day from that time on, the baby bunny grew and grew.

Timothy watched the baby bunny hop around and nibble grass in the yard. Now it was no longer a baby, and it didn't need to be fed one drop of milk at a time.

The bunny's ears stood up and it wrinkled its nose right where its whiskers were.

Timothy moved the bunny to a box in the garden. Now if it wanted to hop back to its family and live with the other bunnies in the meadow, it could.

And one day, *IT DID!*

—L.B.S.

Ask: "Where did the baby bunny go?" Suggest that the children end the story.

## DEAR LITTLE PUPPY

Once there was a dear little puppy who could say nothing, but "Bow-wow." He said "Bow-wow" when he was sad or glad. He said "Bow-wow" when he was hungry, tired, cold or comfortable.

Now the dear little puppy had no home. He just didn't seem to belong anywhere. So he wandered here and he wandered there.

He looked at everyone and barked, "Bow-wow."

As he wandered along looking for a home, he saw a butterfly resting on a cornflower.

"Bow-wow," he said.

The butterfly was sorry for the puppy, but she couldn't understand what "Bow-wow" meant, so she couldn't help him.

Then the dear little puppy saw a robin hopping on the grass and nodding its head from side to side, listening for worms under the ground so that he could pull one out to feed one of his baby robins.

"Bow-wow," said the dear little puppy.

But the robin didn't understand puppy talk and he just didn't pay any attention to the dear little puppy.

So the dear little puppy wandered here and there, looking for a home. One day, there stood a little girl right in front of him!

"Oh, you soft, furry little puppy," she said happily, picking up the dear little puppy and cuddling him in her arms. "I'm going to take you right home to live with me."

And that is exactly how the story ended.

—L.B.S.

Ask: "Would you have ended the story a different way? Did you like the ending? Why? Tell how you would take care of a puppy if you had one. What would you feed him? Why do puppies make good pets?"

## LOUIS

Louis said, "I wish I were a kitten. All kittens do is lap milk, chase mice, and curl up when they want to sleep."

"Very well," said Louis's mother. "You may be a kitten. But if you are a kitten, you should act like one, and you should live like one."

So Louis drank some milk from a saucer. He tried to curl upon the floor, but the floor was too hard. Then he thought about chasing a mouse and suddenly he knew that he did not want to do that!

Louis said, "I don't think I want to be a kitten. I'd rather be a bird."

His mother said, "Very well. You may be a bird. But if you are a bird, you should act like one and live like one."

So Louis went into the yard and climbed a tree. He pretended he was sitting on a nest, but soon he became hungry. So he climbed down and went into the kitchen where his mother was baking chocolate cookies.

"Did you have fun being a bird?" she asked as she gave him a delicious cookie.

Louis said, "I guess I'd rather be a chicken after all."

"Very well," said his mother. "But if you are a chicken, you should act like one and live like one."

Louis pretended his arms were wings. He flapped them and cackled. He tucked his head under one arm and tried to take a nap just as he had seen Biddy Hen do. But it was very uncomfortable.

Louis said, "I don't really want to be a chicken at all. I'd rather be a mouse."

"Very well," said Louis's mother. "But if you are a mouse, you should live like one and act like one."

So Louis crept into a dark closet and pretended it was a hole. He snooped for cheese in the kitchen and found a whole package. Louis ate and ate cheese. But that was all he had to eat, and pretty soon Louis's tummy felt very full and it growled from so much cheese.

Louis said, "I guess I don't want to be a mouse after all."

He went into his room and played with some blocks. Then he had a nap on his own bed, and when he woke up, he went to find his mother.

"I'm hungry," said Louis.

"Who are you?" asked his mother. "Are you a mouse, a chicken, a bird, or a kitten?"

"I'm LOUIS," said Louis.

"Then," said his mother smiling and handing him a glass of milk, "you can live like a little boy again, can't you?"

"Yes," replied Louis, between swallows of milk. "It's a lot more fun being a little boy."

—L.B.S.

Ask: "Have you ever wanted to be somebody or something else? What did you want to be?"

Dramatize the story, using different groups of children.

## BABY CHICKS

Mother Hen sat on her nest. Underneath her feathers were six, warm, smooth eggs. Half of the eggs were white and half were brown. Mother Hen sat on both the white and the brown eggs.

After three weeks of patient sitting, Mother Hen heard "snick-snack," and out of the shell stepped one, wet little chick. After he was dry, he was all fluffy and yellow. He had bright eyes and tiny little feet. Mother Hen was so glad to see him.

"Welcome to this big, wide, wonderful world," she said. "I'm going to call you Sunny."

"Peep, peep," said the yellow chick. "I have some brothers and sisters. Wait awhile and they will come out of their shells, too."

And sure enough they did. There was a black chick, and Mother Hen called him Inky Black. There was a brown chick and Mother Hen called him Brownie. Then there was a white chick, and he was called Snowball. Another white chick with a spot on his little head was named Spottie. The very last little chick looked just like Sunny. Mother Hen called him Peep. There they were—six baby chicks as cute as buttons, chirping for food.

"Come, babies," invited Mother Hen. "Eat some cornmeal."

The babies were hungry. They ate and ate, and Mother Hen was so glad to see them eat.

Then the whole family went to the brook to get cool drinks. They stood in a row and let their heads go back, and they drank and drank and drank of the cool water.

Sunny, the yellow chick, saw himself in the water.

"Oh, Mother," he said, "I see a chicken that looks like ME."

Then all of the little chicks saw their reflections in the water. They bent down, took sips of water, and let their heads go back so that the cool water could run down their throats. Mother Hen was SO glad to see them drink.

"Cluck, cluck," she said as she led them back to the nest.

Then she sat down and ruffled out her feathers. Every single one of those new baby chicks crept under her soft feathers and soon all six baby chicks were fast asleep.

—L.B.S.

Bring in a newly hatched chick. Let the children touch its soft feathers. Discuss ways that chicks, puppies, kittens, and other animals eat and drink.

## PERCY

Percy was a squiggly, wiggly tadpole who lived in a still pool near the woods. The bottom of the pool was dark and soft with mosses, and there Percy lived with his many brothers and sisters.

All day long, Percy swam. He had a very long tail, and tiny gills that let air pass through to him so that he could breathe. He had a very tiny mouth to help him take in bites of delicious water plants.

One day Percy was very tired so he had a long sleep. As he slept, he hung onto the edge of a lily pad.

When Percy woke up, he found that he wasn't as round or fat as he had been, and he discovered that he had two, little bitsy hind legs. He swam off to show them to his tadpole brothers and sisters. Kick, kick, kick! Fun, fun, fun! Percy loved his new hind legs.

One night he slept again. When he awakened this time, he had two wonderful flippers for front legs. Percy swam to the top of the water and took a deep breath. Then he paddled away to show his new legs to his brothers and sisters. Now that he had two little hand-like legs, he felt very important.

Percy's tail grew shorter and his legs grew longer.

One day Percy jumped out of the water onto a lily pad, where he sat and looked at his reflection in the water. Percy saw that his mouth was very large, and his skin was green with beautiful black stripes. Yes, he was a handsome frog!

Then what a perfectly marvelous time Percy had hopping from lily pad to lily pad, catching little bottle flies, and swimming in the still pool as he sang, "Glug, glug, glug!"

—L.B.S.

Put a tadpole and a frog in the terrarium for the class to observe.

### Supplementary References

Anderson, Hans Christian: *The Ugly Duckling*, Charles Scribner's Sons, New York, 1965.
Brown, Margaret Wise: *The Dead Bird*, William R. Scott, Inc., New York, 1958.
Carroll, Ruth: *Where's the Kitty?* Henry Z. Walck, Inc., New York, 1962.
Duvoisin, Roger: *Petunia*, Alfred A. Knopf, Inc., New York, 1950.
Ets, Marie Hall: *Play with Me*, The Viking Press, Inc., New York, 1955.
Freeman, Don: *Cyrano, the Crow*, The Viking Press, Inc., New York, 1960.
———: *Fly High, Fly Low*, The Viking Press, Inc., New York, 1957.
———: *The Turtle and The Dove*, The Viking Press, Inc., New York, 1964.
Gay, Zhenya: *Small One*, The Viking Press, Inc., New York, 1958.
Kopczynski, Anna: *Jerry and Ami*, Charles Scribner's Sons, New York, 1963.
Littledale, Harold: *Alexander*, Parent's Magazine Press, New York, 1964.
Newberry, Clare: *Marshmallow*, Harper and Row, Publishers, New York, 1942.
Peterson, Hans: *Brownie*, Lothrop, Lee and Shepard Company, New York, 1965.
Rand, Ann: *So Small*, Harcourt, Brace and World, Inc., New York, 1962.
Zolotow, Charlotte: *Mr. Rabbit and the Lovely Present*, Harper and Row, Publishers, New York, 1966.

CHAPTER 8

# Good Times At The Circus And Zoo

Homes of any economic level may fail to provide the child with enjoyable experiences which are acceptable to the neighborhood and rewarding to the child himself. Children who do not know a true, happy childhood of play and wholesome family fun often become lonely adults, incapable of making the most of their abilities and opportunities.

It is the child from a disadvantaged or unhappy environment who must be helped to learn enjoyment for its own sake. Genuine fun is a spur to creativity, to learning, and to the development of a healthy personality. Fun is based upon honest reality and an increased understanding of oneself and one's associates. This honest reality and a chance to know oneself and others may be difficult to find in crowded, sprawling cities.

Teachers should be particularly alert for chances to plan rewarding amusement for young children. The circus and the zoo can provide the setting for recreational excursions. There can be good times, learning and thrills of combined sights, sounds, and smells. No audiovisual device can replace real experiences.

At the circus there are daring feats of acrobatic skill. The discipline of circus performers and the risks they take will stir the child's imagination and show what can be accomplished through long, daily practice. Children can understand the purposes and values of cooperation as they learn something about the work of ticket sellers, roustabouts (men who put up tents), drivers of circus wagons, wardrobe keepers, water boys, animal feeders, cooks, and veterinarians. Though only performers are afforded the spotlight, many workers are needed behind the scenes.

The zoo is especially valuable and enjoyable if the initial visit is made at an early and impressionable age. Young children will notice the differences in the sizes of animals and observe their eating, sleeping, and playing habits. Exact colorings and textures, which cannot be indicated accurately through animal picture-books, may be noted. Tactile experiences are provided if the children are allowed to pet some animals (such as rabbits, llamas, or sheep) and take rides on giant turtles.

After a visit to the zoo or circus, a flood of communication will be encouraged and increased learning will take place. There will be more perceptive awareness in the child's life. These trips will provide endless situations for children to sing about, to dramatize, and to discuss. It is small wonder that adults often refer to such excursions as the happiest of their childhood memories!

## A CIRCUS PARADE

Children will enjoy selecting scarves, neckties, or hats from the dress-up box to make costumes for a circus parade.

Decorated paper sacks which fit over the children's heads will add realistic touches to the event. Draw features on each sack and cut out eyes, noses and mouth; appendages, like an elephant trunk, horns, or large ears, can be added.

## THIS LITTLE CLOWN

This little clown likes to laugh and play.
This little clown does tricks all day.
This little clown makes a great, big frown.
This little clown turns upside down.
This little clown rolls around like a ball,
And this little clown stands proud and tall.

—L.B.S.

Children point to or bend down one finger at a time. Stick puppets may be used also.

## FINGER RING CLOWNS

Cut clown head shapes from construction paper and draw the features with a felt tip pen. Glue the head parts together, but leave a small opening so that the pointer finger can be inserted.

Suggest that children make up a tune for "This Little Clown," and move the clown's head in time to the music.

—O.M.A.

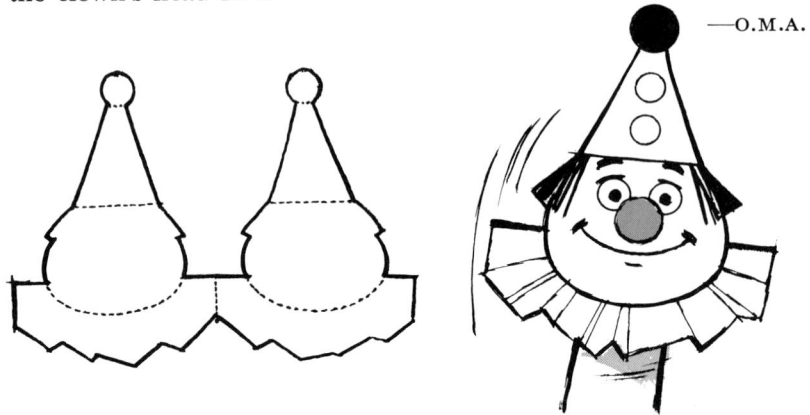

## A CLOWN WALKING PUPPET

Cut a clown pattern similar to the one shown here. Use tagboard. Cut circles for inserting two fingers which will serve as legs. Children will enjoy coloring their clowns and making them walk. The exercise is beneficial to finger dexterity.

## DRAWING A CIRCUS CLOWN

(A Chalk Talk)

First I'll draw a circle, (1)
And then a pointed hat. (2)
Could this be a puppy,
A mouse, or a cat?
I'll draw two little circles, (3)
And a big one here will do. (4)
Now I'll draw a funny ear, (5)
And another one makes two. (6)
Have you guessed it? Have you?
He lives in circus town.
Now, I'll draw a happy mouth; (7)
Now here is *Mister Clown!*

—L.B.S.

Numerals at the end of the lines indicate the figures to be drawn as the rhyme is narrated. Call attention to the triangular, circular, and half circular parts.

## BIG CLOWN AND LITTLE CLOWN

Gary's daddy is a clown in a big circus.

One day, when Gary was five years old, his daddy said, "Here's a birthday present for you, son."

Gary was so excited! When he opened the box, there was a clown suit just exactly like his daddy's big, baggy suit. It was a very fine clown suit wth a funny little hat and some HUGE rubber feet. What colors were in the clown suit? *(Responses.)*

Gary dressed up in his new clown suit, his funny little hat, and his HUGE rubber feet with toes like a giant's so that he could do tricks with his daddy. Gary was now Little Clown!

Crowds of people were waiting to see the tricks. They clapped and they cheered when Gary and his daddy walked into the ring. Big Clown made faces. Little Clown made faces. Big Clown danced and Little Clown danced. What else did they do? *(Responses.)*

Big Clown ran around the ring. Little Clown ran after him. Around and around the ring they ran. Big Clown and Little Clown held hands and bowed low. They turned somersaults all the way out of the circus tent.

Gary *knew* that when he grew up, he was going to be a circus clown just like his daddy!

—L.B.S.

Pantomime the actions of Big Clown and Little Clown. The dress-up box will provide costume materials. To enable more children to participate, suggest that some children be circus animals.

### THE PIGGY-BACK-MERRY-GO-ROUND[1]

Toot! Toot!
The merry-go-round
   is going to go round!
Who wants to ride
   on the merry-go-round?
The jumping blue horse
   is stamping the ground!
Hurry and climb
   on the merry-go-round! Toot! Toot!
The jumping blue horse
   is leaving the ground,
The little pink horse
   is leaving the ground,
The music is making
   a galloping sound,
And the merry-go-round
   is starting around! Toot! Toot!
The jumping blue horse
   goes racing around,
The little pink horse
   goes chasing around,
The lions and tigers
   go pacing around,
And the jumping blue horse
   goes racing around!
Toot! Toot! The merry-go-round
   is whirling around,

---

[1] Daniel Safier, "The Piggy-Back-Merry-Go-Round," *The Listening Book*, Caxton Printers, Ltd., Caldwell, Idaho, 1952. Copyright by special permission of Caxton Printers.

The animals all
    are swirling around,
The mirrors and lights
    are twirling around,
The ticket man comes
    a-curling around,
Toot! Toot! The merry-go-round
    goes around and around,
And around and around
    and around and around
And around and around
    and around and around!
Toot! Toot! Till the jumping blue horse
    . . . . . . slows down.
Now the little pink horse
    puts her feet on the ground.
Now the lions and tigers
    are just standing around.
And the jumping blue horse
    . . . . . . sits down!

—DANIEL SAFIER

The merry-go-round rhythm makes it easy for the children to participate orally.

## KANGAROO

TEACHER: Old hoppity, loppity kangaroo
    Can jump much higher than me or you.
CHILDREN: Hoppity, loppity, jump one—two.
TEACHER: His tail is bent like a kitchen chair
    So he can sit down while he combs his hair.
CHILDREN: Hoppity, loppity, jump one—two.
TEACHER: But when he jumps, he uses his tail
    So he can jump high and almost sail.
CHILDREN: Hoppity, loppity, jump one—two.

—V.S.P.

Several individuals can be kangaroos and give two jumps as the children say the refrain slowly.

## RHINOCEROS

TEACHER: Who has a big horn on his nose?
CHILDREN: A rhinoceros.
TEACHER: Who snorts and rumbles as he goes?
CHILDREN: A rhinoceros.
TEACHER: Who has deep wrinkles in his hide?
CHILDREN: A rhinoceros.
TEACHER: Who is it that you cannot ride?
CHILDREN: A rhinoceros.
TEACHER: Who has big hoofs on all his feet?
CHILDREN: A rhinoceros.
TEACHER: Who likes sweet grass and hay to eat?
CHILDREN: A rhinoceros.

—L.B.S. and V.S.P.

These question and answer rhymes are excellent for speech development because of the refrains.

## MONKEY SEE AND DO

*(Children repeat and dramatize lines 4, 6, 8, 10, 12, 14, 16 and 18.)*

I saw a monkey in the zoo.
His name was Monkey See and Do.
I stood on my toes.
    He stood on his toes.
I wiggled my nose.
    He wiggled his nose.
I touched my feet.
    He touched his feet.
I pretended to eat.
    He pretended to eat.
I winked my eye.
    He winked his eye.
I started to cry.
    He started to cry.
I scratched my head.
    He scratched his head.
I went to bed.
    He went to bed. *(Close eyes.)*

—L.B.S.

The class may add their own words and actions.
Use the rhyme to emphasize pronouns *I, he,* and *his.*

## DRAW A HIPPOPOTAMUS

(A Chalk Talk)

Look! I made a big round ball! (1)
But, of course, that isn't all.
Now, I'll use a light bulb here, (2)
And on each side
I'll draw an ear, (3)
Two teeny eyes, (4)
And hoofs for feet, (5)
And my fat hippopotamus
Is now complete!

—O.M.A.

Draw the figures and narrate the lines slowly.
Bring in zoo or circus books for the browsing table.

## HIPPOPOTAMUS

CHILDREN: Hippopotamus lives in the zoo.
He hasn't very much to do.
I like the hippopotamus;
He hardly ever makes a fuss.

TEACHER: The lazy hippopotamus is cousin
to a pig.
Except that he is fatter, and he's
many times as big.

CHILDREN: Hippopotamus lives in the zoo.
He hasn't very much to do.
I like the hippopotamus;
He hardly ever makes a fuss.

TEACHER: The lazy hippopotamus lies in water
all the day,
But he is always hungry when the
keeper gives him hay.

CHILDREN: Hippopotamus lives in the zoo.
He hasn't very much to do.
I like the hippopotamus;
He hardly ever makes a fuss.
—L.B.S.

Show the class a picture of a pig and a hippopotamus so that sizes may be contrasted and shapes compared.

### TIGER WALK

Walk, walk, softly—slow—
This is the way the tigers go!
Walk, walk; get out of the way!
Tigers are coming to school today.
Creep, creep—softly—slow—
This is the way the tigers go!
Creep, creep; come and play.
Tigers are coming to school today.
—L.B.S.

Children pretend to be tigers and move to a slow, creeping rhythm as the lines are said. Paper sack head puppets with black stripes may be made by the class.

### TIGER[2]

There's a tiger in the zoo, in the zoo;
And his stripes run up and down and
    sort of round and round,
And his stripes are black and orange
In the zoo!

The tiger's in a cage in the zoo,
And the cage is big and stout, so he never
    does come out,
And he has a dish of water
In the zoo!

[2] From the book *Stories To Begin On* by Rhoda W. Bacmeister. Copyright, 1940, by E. P. Dutton & Co., Inc., New York. Reprinted by permission of the publishers.

When the tiger wants his dinner in the zoo,
The keeper hears him roar, and he opens
   up the door,
And he gives him meat to eat
In the zoo!

Then the tiger has a grin on his chin in the zoo,
And he whiffles with his nose, and he washes
   off his toes,
And he jumps upon a shelf and goes to sleep
In the zoo!

      —RHODA W. BACMEISTER

Children join in saying the refrain, "In the zoo!"

## DRAWING A FISH AT THE ZOO

I draw an egg. (1)
And here we see
Something round as it can be. (2)
Here is an eye. (3)
Here's a fin to swim. (4)
And here is a mouth (5)
That is part of him.
Here is a funny tail to swish! (6)
There! I've drawn a big, fat fish!

      —L.B.S.

Young children enjoy these "chalk talks" and will learn the words very quickly.

After the fish is drawn, the children may use a chalkboard pointer to indicate the parts as the poem is repeated.

## THE GIRAFFE

Jerry had never been to the zoo; so Jerry's mother decided to take him to visit one. They traveled to the zoo on a bus. When they arrived, they bought two tickets and went through the turnstile.

There was a large, furry bear down in a pit walking around on his hind legs.

"Imagine that!" said Jerry.

Jerry and his mother heard a monkey chattering. It was holding tightly to the bars of its cage. It looked at Jerry a long time. Then it swung by its tail on a branch.

"Imagine that!" said Jerry.

Jerry and his mother saw something HUGE. It was gray, and its long flapping ears hung down like two fans. It swung its trunk back and forth, and the trunk curled up and it stretched. But it couldn't reach Jerry because Jerry was on the other side of the fence.

"Imagine that!" said Jerry.

What was this animal? *(Responses.)*

As Jerry and his mother continued their walk, they saw a tall, yellow animal with brown spots. It had four, long legs with sharp hoofs at the end of them. The animal was not fat like the bear and it had no trunk like the elephant. It could not swing by its tail like the monkey. It had a THIN neck, and it was the tallest animal in the zoo.

Jerry saw a neck, but he didn't see a head. He looked up, up, up up, up, up, up. But the neck was so long that Jerry had to bend his head way back to see the animal's head on top of its long neck.

"Imagine that!" whispered Jerry.

What was the animal? *(Responses.)*

—L.B.S.

This story may precede or follow an excursion to the zoo.

### FIVE BIG ELEPHANTS

Five big elephants — oh, what a sight!
Swinging their trunks from left to right.
Four are followers; one is the king,
And they all walk around in the circus ring!

—L.B.S.

Choose five children at a time to dramatize this poem. Each child swings one or both arms to imitate an elephant's swinging trunk.

### ANIMAL PUPPETS

Discarded coloring or children's books and magazines can furnish many pictures of zoo and circus animals. Cut out the pictures, back them with tagboard for stability, and glue them to tongue depressors.

After a trip to the circus or zoo, the child chooses an elephant, tiger, or monkey puppet, holds it up, and tells his story in first person. When he fully projects himself into the character, he speaks more freely and is better able to relate incidents of the excursion in a personal way. Examples of what a child might say are:

| I am a monkey. | I am a lion. | I am an elephant. |
| I swing by my tail. | I roar. | I have a trunk. |
| I eat bananas. | I like meat. | I walk quietly. |

## PAPER SACK HEAD-PUPPETS

A large, grocery paper sack may serve as a clown or an animal head which the child wears to dramatize events at a circus or zoo. Cut eyes and mouth spaces so that the child can see and breathe easily. He may want to decorate his clown face with scraps from the odds-and-ends box, and use crayons to color features so that his clown will have personality. By adding appendages, many kinds of animals can be constructed: a length of curled wrapping paper for an elephant's trunk; construction paper ears and pipe cleaner whiskers can be used for tigers, lions, cats, or mice.

## FOLLOW-UP ANIMAL ACTIVITIES

1. Reproduce sounds of individual animals. Children will enjoy making these sounds and asking their classmates to guess the animals they are representing.

2. Discuss and show pictures of new animals which the class may never have seen. Talk about necks, bodies, and characteristic features.

Use descriptive words that will enrich vocabulary: spotted, shaggy, matted, striped, smooth, wrinkled, tall, fat, thin, fierce, angry, gentle, mischievous, sly, timid, and furry.

3. Make animal cutouts. Cut a double configuration and fold in half so that the animal will stand up. Flap pictures are also effective. Glue the picture of the animal to a folded piece of tagboard so that you can have a long row of different animals depicting a parade.

4. Build zoo enclosures from large blocks. Cut bars in shoeboxes to represent cages and place small plastic animals inside them.

5. Shoeboxes also make good circus trains. Add cardboard wheels and let the children decorate the cars of the train with wallpaper bits. Stand folded pictures of animals inside the cars.

6. Have a circus parade. Use two toy wagons. Make masks and utilize materials from the dress-up box. Play recordings that depict clowns tumbling, elephants walking, etc.[3]

7. Make folded books with pasted on pictures of animals.

8. Display animal books on the browsing table. A list is presented in the bibliography at the end of this chapter.

### THE LITTLE LOST ZEBRA

Clop, clop, clop, clop, clop, clop! The little zebra walked away from his mother. He walked past the zoo keeper, and he walked out of the zoo. For a long time the little zebra walked. Clop, clop, clop, clop, clop, clop! And he kept on walking, walking, walking.

The little zebra was lost. But still he kept walking. Clop, clop, clop, clop, clop, clop!

He was hungry.

---

[3] *Children's Rhythms in Symphony,* Bowmar Records, North Hollywood, California.

He had missed his lunch and his tummy growled, "I want some hay!"

But there was no hay — anywhere, so the little zebra walked on. Clop, clop, clop, clop, clop, clop!

The little zebra reached a pasture where many horses were eating grass.

They all stopped and looked at the baby zebra and one horse said, "What is *that?*"

A second horse replied, "It looks as big as my colt, except that it is white with black stripes. How odd!"

Just as the little zebra was about to nibble a mouthful of fresh, green grass, a third horse whinnied, "Ee - ee - ee - ee - ee!" in a shrill voice. The little baby zebra was scared and he stood stock still in his tracks for a moment; then he galloped away lickety-clip. Clippety-cloppety-clippety-cloppety-clippety-cloppety!

When he was far away from the meadow, he stopped to rest. Then he walked on. Clop, clop, clop, clop, clop, clop!

When he saw a brook, he realized how very thirsty he was. A cow and her calf were having a long, cool drink. They were so busy enjoying the refreshing water, that at first, they didn't see the little baby zebra who was quietly drinking close beside them.

Suddenly, the cow mooed, "How dare you drink water from my brook, you funny looking horse!"

The frightened, little baby zebra hurried away from there quickly. Clippety-cloppety-clippety-cloppety-clippety-cloppety!

"You should be ashamed of yourself," a squirrel said to the cow. "The water in that brook belongs to everyone, even a baby zebra."

"So *that* was a zebra," said the cow. "I've always wondered what a zebra was like. Well, I'm sorry. If the baby zebra comes back here, I'll be kind to him."

But the little baby zebra was far away now. And it was safe to walk again. Clop, clop, clop, clop, clop, clop! How lonesome he was! How hungry he was! How tired he was! He stopped to rest. A robin flew down and sat in front of him.

"Little zebra, you're a long, long way from the zoo," said the robin.

"I'm lost," sighed the little baby zebra sadly. "I don't know the way back."

"I'll help you," said the robin. "Just follow me."

So the baby zebra galloped after the robin. Clippety-cloppety-clippety-cloppety-clippety-cloppety!

—L.B.S.

Ask: "How do you think this story ended?" *(Responses.)*

Use sound effects when telling this story. Coconut shells make lovely clip-clops, but palms of the hands slightly cupped and clapped against each other will provide walking and galloping effects. Children may beat the rhythm of the refrains: "Clop-clop" and "Clippety-cloppety" as they clap and say the words.

Bring in zoo books which contain pictures of zebras. Zebra pictures are enjoyable for the class to paint.

Discuss other striped animals, such as a skunk or a tiger. Show striped cloth materials to the class so that they will understand the concept of "stripe."

## MRS. ROO KANGAROO

Once there was a kangaroo whose name was Mrs. Roo. Mrs. Roo had a pocket in which she carried her baby. It was a nice, roomy pocket into which the baby kangaroo fitted snugly and comfortably as her mother leaped with two, big, strong hind legs.

Soon the baby kangaroo outgrew his mother's pocket. He had big, strong hind legs; a large, strong tail; and he could leap. In fact, he could almost keep up with his mother.

"Well, well," said Mrs. Roo. "Now I can use my pocket for other things."

And Mrs. Roo began filling her pocket with this and that: lunch, umbrellas, galoshes, and all sorts of things which perhaps didn't belong in pockets at all.

Finally, the pocket was so full that it seemed almost ready to burst. You see, when Mrs. Roo's relatives found out that Mrs. Roo was making such good use of her pocket, they asked her to carry things for them. Soon, all of the neighbors asked her to carry things for them, too. Because Mrs. Roo was so kind, she wanted to help everyone. But her pocket stretched and stretched until it was so full that it would no longer hold even one tiny thing more. So she had to make herself an apron with six pockets. That solved the problem and everyone was happy, including Mrs. Roo who loved doing things for others.

—L.B.S.

Cut a kangaroo shape from brown posterboard and draw in features with a felt tip pen. Make a substantial apron with a bib and six or more pockets from felt. Add two ribbons to the bib so that it can be tied around the neck. The children will delight in putting objects into the pockets, taking them out, and naming them.

Read the story "Katy-No-Pocket" listed below in the bibliography.

SUPPLEMENTARY REFERENCES

Bennett, Rainey: *The Secret Hiding Place*, The World Publishing Company, Cleveland, 1960.

Brown, Marcia: *The Little Carousel*, Charles Scribner's Sons, New York, 1946.

Durell, Ann: *The Lost Bear*, Doubleday and Company, Inc., Garden City, New York, 1959.

Ipcar, Dahlov: *I Like Animals*, Alfred A. Knopf, Inc., New York, 1960.

McGovern, Ann: *Zoo, Where Are You?* Harper and Row, Publishers, New York, 1964.

Massie, Diane: *The Baby Beebee Bird*, Harper and Row, Publishers, New York, 1963.

Payne, Emmy: *Katy No-Pocket*, Houghton Mifflin Company, Boston, 1944.

Petersham, Maud and Miska: *The Circus Baby*, The Macmillan Company, New York, 1950.

Purdy, Susan: *If You Have a Yellow Lion*, J. B. Lippincott Company, Philadelphia, 1966.

Ruck-Pauquet, Gina: *Little Hedgehog*, Hastings House, Publishers, Inc., New York, 1959.

Ward, Lynd: *The Biggest Bear*, Houghton Mifflin Company, Boston, 1952.

Warner, Edythe R.: *Siamese Summer*, The Viking Press, Inc., New York, 1964.

Ylla: *Two Little Bears*, Harper and Row, Publishers, New York, 1954.

# Epilogue

The purposes of this book are many for they cover all areas of the language spectrum. The philosophy is concerned with helping a young child to achieve intellectual, social, emotional, physical, and aesthetic growth. Its contents follow essentially the guidelines set forth by the Association for Childhood Education International in the pamphlet, *Basic Propositions for Early Childhood Education*. *Learning Time with Language Experiences for Young Children* includes specified techniques for:

Functional language and listening experiences;
Active and passive interests;
Individual and small groups;
Investigations that invite love of knowledge and create desire for future learning;
Simple numbering, measuring, and quantity activities;
Self-expression and creativity;
Development of sense perceptions;
The building of sensitivity and responsibility toward others;
Stimulating emotions of love, compassion, and sympathy.

This book's emphasis is upon *language development and functional usage* since language is basic to all activities in the child's ever expanding and imaginative world. Language is a continuous process of learning with every step in that process related to and part of the child's thinking and his communications with others.

*Learning Time with Language Experiences for Young Children,* as the title indicates, deals with learning experiences of which language is a significant part: language of warm encouragement that helps a child to build a secure and satisfying self-concept; language that fosters social interaction upon which the development of intellect depends; language that serves to establish constructive feelings and attitudes toward home, school, and community; language that accompanies and follows exploration, investigation, and creativity; and language that furthers emotional strength and personality growth.

Before these language goals can be reached, however, the teacher and child must walk together side by side. The teacher must gain the child's trust so that he may trust himself and feel eager and strong enough to seek new adventures in learning. To gain a child's trust, one must learn how he thinks. In short, to become fully aware of the child, a teacher must remember how it feels to *be* a child; she must be sensitive to his verbal and bodily expressions, and needs; and to the workings of the young mind. To be a child is to believe in love and beauty; to believe in belief; to be so small that the inconspicuous can be seen because the world is so close, so new, so lovely, and so filled with myriads of sights, sounds, smells, tastes, and exciting things to feel. Dew becomes diamonds on the grass. A spider's web turns into a fairy's hammock. A mud pie resembles a feast. A carton is a truck, a jet plane, a pirate's den, or a hideaway. To be a child is to listen to the personal secrets of an elf; to a chorus of crickets that suddenly changes into a concert of night musicians; to the staccato rain talk of slickers, boots, red umbrellas, and growing seeds. To be a child is to turn depression into loftiness and nothing into everything.

There is soul magic in a child that enables him to be king of infinite space and to escape from being insignificant in an exacting, limited, and often hostile world into something big and mighty.

To be a child is to know rhythm. As day follows night, as winter follows autumn, as rest follows work and play, and as one heartbeat follows another, the child experiences rhythm each time he dances, walks, runs, skips, hops, jumps, climbs, sorts, carries, or builds. He expresses rhythm verbally in spontaneous, poetic phrases and uses varieties of pitches and loudnesses in amazing ways for one so young.

Early childhood is a priceless gift. We can help the child to keep that inheritance so that he will maintain indestructible strength and enchantment throughout his life.

My personal gratitude is offered to Virginia Sydnor Pavelko and to Olive M. Amundson for spending many months working closely with me on the preparation of the manuscript, for creating and developing sparkling ideas, and for revising and refining pages of materials used in experimentation with young children. To Dr. Robert L. Douglass, I owe sincere appreciation for sharing his profound knowledge of language development and child psychology with me, for writing the foreword and for lending his support in the preparation of several chapters. My thanks goes to Mrs. Christina R. McDonald for contributing the chapter, "Bringing Children and Good Picture-Storybooks Together."

Frances Clarke Sayers once said that "judgment grows by what it feeds upon." Bibliographies are listed to help the teacher to "feed upon" many rich treasures in books and a love of words that will introduce young children to eventual reading on a very personal level. As the teacher in the early childhood education center plans her daily program, it is hoped that she can use many of the suggestions contained in *Learning Time with Language Experiences for Young Children*. It is also hoped that this publication wll give her even half the satisfaction that it gave an author who researched, organized, and prepared materials with the help of extremely efficient colleagues.

—LOUISE BINDER SCOTT

# INDEX FOR UNIT INTEGRATION

ANIMALS (See Circus and Zoo)
  Baby Animals, *274*
  Baby Chicks (Story), *281*
  Baby Kitten, *271*
  Bunnies, *272*
  Chicks, *270*
  Dear Little Puppy (Story), *279*
  Five Black Kittens, *271*
  Five Little Chicks, *245*
  Four Little Mice, *277*
  Friendly Skunk, *278*
  Here Is Mister Froggie, *277*
  How Animals Sleep, *274*
  Little, New Bunny, The (Story), *279*
  Little Pigs, The, *275*
  Louis (Story), *280*
  My Kitten, *270*
  Old Gray Pussycat, The, *271*
  Percy (Story), *282*
  Puppy at Puppygarten, A, *273*
  This Little Cricket, *278*

BIRTHDAY
  Balloons for a Party, *248*
  Birthday Cake (Story), *250*
  Birthday Finger Play, *247*
  Birthday Presents, *248*
  Discovering Me on My Birthday, *247*
  Two Birthdays (Story), *249*

CHALK TALKS
  Draw a Frog, *277*
  Draw a Hippopotamus, *291*
  Drawing a Christmas Tree, *230*
  Drawing a Circus Clown, *287*
  Drawing a Fish at the Zoo, *293*
  Half an Apple, *265*
  Puppy at Puppygarten, A, *273*
  Three Ships, *214*
  Three Tepees, *225*
  Wind, The, *258*
  Witch Chalk Talk, A, *218*

CHRISTMAS
  Children Who Wanted to Thank Santa Claus, The (Story), *234*
  Christmas Devices, *229*
  Christmas in Mother Goose Land (Story), *232*
  Christmas Rhymes, *25*
  Christmas Secrets, *227*
  Drawing a Christmas Tree, *230*
  Five Little Bells, *228*
  Jolly Santa Claus, A (Story), *231*
  Little Hands, *230*
  Ring Five Bells, *227*
  Shine, Christmas Candle, *226*
  Sleepy Snowflakes (Story), *260*
  Snow Is Part of Christmas, *234*

CIRCUS AND ZOO
  Animal Puppets, *294*
  Big Clown and Little Clown (Story), *287*
  Circus Parade, A, *285*
  Clown Walking Puppet, A, *286*
  Draw a Hippopotamus, *291*
  Drawing a Circus Clown, *287*
  Drawing a Fish at the Zoo, *293*
  Finger Ring Clowns, *286*
  Five Big Elephants, *294*
  Follow-up Animal Activities, *295*
  Giraffe, The (Story), *293*
  Hippopotamus, *291*
  I Went to the Circus, *24*
  Kangaroo, *289*
  Little Lost Zebra, The (Story), *296*
  Mrs. Roo Kangaroo (Story), *298*
  Monkey See and Do, *290*
  Paper Sack Head-Puppets, *295*
  Piggy-Back-Merry-Go-Round, The, *288*
  Rhinoceros, *290*
  This Little Clown, *285*

Tiger, *292*
Tiger Walk, *292*

COLORS
Blue Bead, The (Story), *90*
Brian Paints (Story), *89*
Child Paints, The, *82*
Color Is Blue, A, *86*
Colors of Things, *85*
Finding Colors, *43*
Gray Velvet Rabbit, The (Story), *53*
Ice-Cream Cone Game, An, *88*
Make Collages, *86*
Making a Fishbowl, *84*
Paint and String Prints, *84*
Painting Colors, *87*
Salt and Flour Clay, *86*
Somebody's Wearing, *89*
What Colors Tell Us, *23*
What Is a Lovely Sight? *88*
Yellow, Yellow, *85*

COLUMBUS
Columbus, *214*
Three Ships, *214*

COMMUNITY, HOME, AND SCHOOL
Airplanes, *190*
Around the House, *138*
Be a News Announcer, *45*
Big School Bus, *190*
Daddies, *186*
First Aid, *191*
Helping Mother, *197*
Keeping the House Clean, *196*
Learning with a Globe, *14*
Meter Reader, The, *190*
Nicest Place in the World, The (Story), *202*
Off to School, *198*
On Washing Day, *197*
Our Baby Sitter, *188*
Play Elevator, A, *192*
Playhouse, The (Story), *195*
Playhouse Ideas, *196*
Playing Cowboy, *191*
Ready for School, *197*
Sarah Finds Somebody to Play with (Story), *200*
Story to Finish, A, *201*
Surprise for the Teacher, A (Story), *199*
Traffic Light, *189*
Train Ride, The (Story), *192*
Visit a Home Being Built, *193*
Wake-up Story, *203*
What I Want to Be, *11*
Who Uses It? *188*
Workers in Our Neighborhood, *186*

COORDINATION
Balancing, *112*
Balancing on the Head, *112*
Braiding, *113*
Buttoning, *114*
Carrying without Spilling, *112*
Dropping One by One, *111*
Experimentation with Drops, *112*
Little Mousie Monday, *96*
Magnet Fun, *113*
Mounting, *113*
Packing a Suitcase, *114*
Peeling and Spreading, *112*
Permanent Yarn Pictures, *119*
Playing Jack Frost, *111*
Sorting Basket, A, *118*
Sponge Painting, *111*
Yarn Pictures, *118*
Zipper Purse, *114*

CREATIVE DRAMATICS (See Pantomime)
Playhouse Ideas, *196*
Playing a Story, *173*

DIMENSIONAL CONCEPTS (See Sense Perception)
Observing Roundness, *101*
Observing Tallness and Shortness, *101*

Observing Thickness and Thinness, *100*
Tall and Small, *13*

EASTER
Bunnies, *272*
Easter Egg Surprises, *244*
Five Little Chicks, *245*
Gray Velvet Rabbit, The (Story), *53*
Hippety-Hop, *246*
Hot Cross Buns, *147*
Little, New Bunny, The (Story), *279*
Mary Is Absent, *245*
Mrs. Bunny (Story), *241*
Mrs. Bunny Gets Ready for Easter (Story), *243*

FINGER PLAYS AND ACTION RHYMES
Apple Buds, *254*
Ardilla (Spanish), *156*
Big Hunt, The, *14*
Birthday Finger Play, *247*
Busy Squirrel, *255*
Caballo (Spanish), *156*
Chicks, *270*
Christmas Secrets, *227*
Conejo (Spanish), *157*
Discovering Me on My Birthday, *247*
Dolls, *153*
Dos Patitos (Spanish), *194*
Fee, Fie, Foe, Fum, *152*
Finger Fishes, *151*
Five Black Kittens, *271*
Five Little Boys, *155*
Five Little Fingers, *153*
Five Little Pennies, *240*
Flying South, *154*
Guajolote (Spanish), *157*
Here Is a Witch's Tall Black Hat, *215*
Here Is Mister Froggie, *277*
How Tall Am I? *13*
Indians and Trees, *223*
Jump-Rope Rhyme, A, *153*

Little Honeybees, *263*
Little Pigs, The, *275*
Mariposa (Spanish), *156*
My Garden, *264*
Off to School, *198*
Open, Shut Them, *152*
Parts of Your Body, *12*
Ready for School, *197*
Saluting the Flag, *238*
Six Little Pilgrims, *224*
Soldier Drill, *154*
Ten Fingers, *150*
Ten Little Squirrels, *222*
This Little Cricket, *278*
Three Little Robins, *266*
Torteitas (Spanish), *151*
Touching, *13, 102*
Two Little Fingers, *151*
Two Little Redbirds, *155*
Using Both Hands, *154*
Wiggle Your Fingers, *152*

HALLOWEEN
Five Little Children, *219*
Funny Old Witch, A, *217*
Goblin and the Cookies, The (Story), *220*
Halloween Fun, *216*
Halloween Riddles, *217*
Here Is a Witch's Tall Black Hat, *215*
Jack-O'-Lantern, *218*
Knowing How to Have Halloween Fun, *215*
Little Jack-O'-Lantern, A, *216*
Making Ghosts, *219*
Witch Chalk Talk, A, *218*

HANUKKAH
Hanukkah Candles, *226*

LANGUAGE
Animal Sounds, *32*
As Smooth As ———, *108*

305

Bee Voices, *39*
Bringing Leaves to Share, *43*
Bringing Something, *43*
Buy and Bought, *28*
Completing Sentences, *33*
Contractions, *31*
Describing Things, *31*
Expressing Feelings, *35*
Fishing from the Flannelboard, *33*
Game for Use of Positional Words, A, *29*
Haven't—Hasn't, Hid—Hidden, Find—Found, *28*
Hear and Heard, *27*
Identifying Game, An, *33*
Interest Table, *36*
Is, Isn't, and Aren't, *27*
Letting a Puppet Share, *44*
Making Comparisons, *35, 91*
Mystery Box, *32*
Plurals, *29*
Positional Words, *29*
Pronouns and Verbs, *37*
Pumpkin Faces, *40*
Puppet Who Likes Pretty Things, The, *35*
Roll Call, *32*
See, Saw, and Seen, *28*
Sensory Words, *37*
Sharing Books, *44*
Sharing Facts about Oneself, *44*
Sharing General Information, *45*
Sharing Snapshots, *42*
Stimulating Creativity in Expression, *36*
Thinking about Things, *38*
Treasure Chest, A, *42*
Using a Telephone, *98*
Was and Were, *27*
Went and Gone, *28*
What Can You Do? *34*
What Did I Like Best? *43*
What Goes with It? *37*
What Would You Do? *39*

Words That Describe, *35*
Words Which Arouse Emotions, *38*
Words Which Have Different Meanings, *30*
Words Which Have the Same Meanings, *30*

LANGUAGE (Speech Sounds)
Bell's Sound, The, *63*
Chick-Chick's Sound, *62*
Copycat Looking Glass, *63*
Elevator's Sound, The, *60*
Fluffy Cat's Sound, *60*
Frog Sounds, The, *61*
Gray Goose's Sound, *59*
Making Sound Baskets and Scrapbooks, *64*
Mrs. Fly's Sound, *61*
Mr. Crow's Sound, *61*
Mister Rooster's Sound, *59*
Pink Shell's Sound, *62*
Three Bears Talk, *63*
Timmy Teakettle's Sound, *59*

LANGUAGE AS A SOCIAL SKILL
Animal Picnic, The (Story), *50*
Cricket Who Didn't Listen, The (Story), *52*
Dish, The (Story), *58*
Duckling Who Wouldn't Say "Quack," The (Story), *51*
Gray Velvet Rabbit, The (Story), *53*
If Your Clothes Could Talk, *52*
Little Kittens, The (Story), *49*
Little Rooster, The (Story), *48*

LISTENING
Discrimination Game, *72*
Echo, *73*
Listen for the Last Number, *73*
Listening for Footsteps, *75*
Listening for Kitten Calls, *72*
Listening to Taps, *76*
Listening Treasure Hunt, *73*

Magic Whisper, The (Story), 75
Metronome, 76
Musical Bottles, 72
Noise Makers, 74
Raindrop Songs, 75
Sleeping Giant, 75
Sound Boxes, 73
Sounds We Hear, 73
Strange Noise, The (Story), 77
Where Is the Sound? 76

MOTHERS
Baby and Group Photographs, 207
Helping Mother, 197
Identifying Name, 207
Mothers Visit the Center, 204
Our ABC Book, 207
Scrapbooks, 206
What Mothers Can Do, 207

NEW YEAR'S
Happy New Year, 236
New Year's Bells, 236
On New Year's Day, 235

NUMBERS AND MEASURING
Alarm Clock, The (Story), 94
Bowling Game, A, 93
Calendars, 95
Clocks, 94
Concept of Pair, The, 93
How Far? 92
How Many? 92
If You're Glad It Is Monday, 97
Learning By Twos and Threes, 92
Little Cuckoo, The (Story), 95
Lonesome Little Penny, The (Story), 97
Making a Telephone Directory, 98
Making Comparisons, 91
Number and Measuring Concepts, 91
Poem for Measuring Myself, A, 100
Thermometer, The, 98
Using Linear Measure, 100

Weight and Measures, 100
Writing Numerals, 93

NURSERY RHYMES
Acting Out Nursery Rhymes, 134
Christmas in Mother Goose Land (Story), 232
Hey Diddle, Diddle, 146
Hickory, Dickory, Dock, 140
Hot Cross Buns, 147
Humpty Dumpty, 140
I'm a Little Teapot, 142
Jack and Jill, 146
Little Bo-Peep, 141
Little Boy Blue, 142
Little Jack Horner, 146
Little Miss Muffet, 145
Mary Is Absent, 245
Pease Porridge Hot, 147
Pussy Cat and Queen, 143
Pussy Willow, 144
Sharing a Nursery Rhyme, 44
Sing a Song of Sixpence, 141
To Market, To Market, 145
Two Little Blackbirds, 142
Wee Willie Winkie, 144

OBSERVATION
Animals' Eyes, 79
Close Your Eyes, 78
Eyes, 78
Find One Like Mine, 80
It Looked Like Spilt Milk (Story), 81
Magic Eyes, 78
Matching, 80
Poems about Eyes, 79
Seeing Shapes in Everyday Objects, 80
Talking about Pictures, 81
Things to Do, 79

PANTOMIME
Acting Out Familiar Traditional Tales, 135

307

Acting Out Nursery Rhymes, *134*
Around the House, *138*
Beating Rhythm, *137*
Elf in the Rain (Story), *137*
Five Big Elephants, *294*
Follow the Leader, *139*
Here Is a Tall Tree, *256*
I'm a Sunflower Tall, *179*
I'm a Tree, *177*
Little Brown Seeds, *262*
Little Duck (Story), *135*
Little Indian's Adventure, *226*
Making a Snowman, *261*
Pantomime All the Year Round, *138*
Picking Apples, *257*
Raggedy Ann, *179*
Tiger Walk, *292*
What Can I Do? *139*

PATRIOTISM
Abraham Lincoln, *239*
Abraham Lincoln Helps a Baby Pig (Story), *240*
George Washington, *241*
Lincoln Pennies, *239*
My Country's Flag, *237*
My Flag, I Salute You, *238*
Saluting the Flag, *238*

POETRY, RHYTHM, AND RHYMES
Bouncing Words, *21*
Christmas Rhymes, *25*
Classical Poetry Inspires Words, *22*
Drum Signals for Your Friends, *19*
Nonsense Rhymes, *21*
Pictures Make Poetry, *21*
Rhythm at Work, *20*
Riddles in Rhyme, *193*
Suggestions for Using Picture-Storybooks, *24*
Tell Us What the Seasons Say, *23*
Ten Fat Pumpkins, *224*
What Colors Tell Us, *23*
What Do Objects Say? *21*

What Do Rhythms Say? *19*
What Do the Pictures Say? *20*
What Poem Does the Music Make? *22*

RELAXATION
Alexander's Sleepy Time (Story), *180*
Baby Birdies, *178*
Fog Elf, The (Story), *182*
How Animals Sleep, *274*
Ideas for Relaxation, *177*
I'm a Sunflower Tall, *179*
I'm a Tree, *177*
Kitty Cat, *180*
Quiet Times, *176*
Raggedy Ann, *179*
Rest and Listen, *177*
Resting, *178*
Resting Time, *177*
Sleepy, Sleepy Place, The (Story), *181*
Sleepy Time, *178*
Wake-Up Story, *203*

ST. PATRICK'S DAY
St. Patrick's Elf, A, *246*

SEASONS (Nature)
Apple Buds, *254*
Autumn, *255*
Busy Squirrel, *255*
Cherries Ripe, *241*
Dear Little Tree, *260*
Dish Garden, The, *253*
Fuzzy Bumblebees, *266*
Here Is a Tall Tree, *256*
Here Is Mister Froggie, *277*
Ladybug, *275*
Little Brown Seeds, *262*
Little Brown Sparrow, *252*
Little Honeybees, *263*
Making a Snowman (Story), *261*
March, *265*
Miniature Forest, A, *254*

My Garden, *264*
One Little Bug, *276*
Pantomime All the Year Round, *138*
Picking Apples, *257*
Planting Seeds, *263*
Pussy Willow, *144*
Seasons, *254*
Sleepy Snowflakes (Story), *260*
Snowflakes, *259*
Special Days, *209*
Tell Us What the Seasons Say, *23*
Ten White Sea Gulls, *253*
This Little Cricket, *278*
Three Little Robins, *266*
Through the Year, *213*
Time for Growing, A, *262*
Time Sequence, *23*
Warm Clothes, *259*
What to Do with Leaves, *256*
What to Do with Seeds, *257*
Where Do They Go? *257*
Wind, The, *258*

SELF-IMAGE
Be a News Announcer, *45*
Big Hunt, The, *14*
Child's Picture, The, *11*
How Tall Am I? *13*
Identifying Me, *11*
Learning with a Globe, *14*
Monkey See and Do, *290*
Nobody Just Like Me, *9*
Parts of Your Body, *12*
Personal Possessions, *10*
Poem for Measuring Myself, A, *100*
Question and Answer, *14*
Roll Call, *32*
Sharing Facts about Oneself, *44*
Sharing Snapshots, *42*
Silhouettes, *11*
Soft Toys, *10*
Tall and Small, *13*
What Can I Do? *139*
What I Want to Be, *11*

SENSE PERCEPTION (See Colors, Smells and Tastes, Touch)
Applying Sensory Stimulation, *70*
Five Senses Poem, A, *69*
General Impressions, *68*
Gray Velvet Rabbit, The (Story), *53*
Impressions of the Woodland, *67*
Senses and the Seasons, *69*
Sensory Words, *37*
What Do the Pictures Say? *20*
Which Senses Are Used? *69*

SMELLS AND TASTES
Making Gingerbread and Popping Corn, *122*
Noses of Animals, *120*
Smelling Session, A, *120*
Smells and Tastes (Discussion), *119*
Taste, *121*
Tastes, *122*
When You Have a Cold, *120*
Your Tongue, *121*

SONGS
Happy New Year, *236*
Musical Flannelgraph, A, *144*
My Country's Flag, *237*
My Flag, I Salute You, *238*
Pussy Willow, *144*
Singing Time, *43*

SPANISH
Ardilla, *156*
Caballo, *156*
Conejo, *157*
Dos Patitos, *194*
Guajolote, *157*
Mariposa, *156*
Torteitas, *151*

STORYTELLING
Arranging Pictures for Storytelling, *172*
Picture File, A, *172*

309

Picture Window, The, *170*
Story Plates, *171*
Surprise Window, A, *163*
Using a Tape Recorder, *164*
What Do the Pictures Say? *20*
What Will the Picture Be? *172*

THANKSGIVING
Guajolote (Spanish), *157*
Indians, *224*
Indians and Trees, *223*
Little Indian's Adventure (Story), *226*
Making a Thankful Book, *223*
Prayer for Help, A, *221*
Pumpkin Faces, *40*
Six Little Pilgrims, *224*
Ten Fat Pumpkins, *224*
Ten Little Squirrels, *222*
Thanksgiving, *222*
Thanksgiving Dinner, *225*
Three Tepees, *225*

TOUCH
As Smooth As ———, *108*
Book of Feels, A, *107*
Clothespin Aprons, *109*
Experimenting, *109*
Feel and Say, *107*
Feeling Shapes, *107*
Feeling with Feet, *105*
Feet, *105*
Felt Mats, *109*
Fruits and Vegetables, *108*
Gray Velvet Rabbit, The (Story), *53*
Hand Prints, *106*
How Does It Feel? *104*
How Your Fingers Help You, *105*
How Your Hands Help You, *104*
Paint Printing, *111*
Play Dough, *106*
Recognition of Objects, *110*
Softest Thing, The (Story), *102*
Softie Toys, *107*

Sorting Objects, *111*
Talking about Your Skin, *103*
Tell What It Is, *109*
Touching, *13, 102*
Using the Hands, *106*
Winding Activities, *110*

TOYS AND EQUIPMENT
Bean Bags, *112*
Block Play, *129*
Bringing Toys to School, *128*
Equipment, *84*
Make a Toy Scrapbook, *128*
Make Your Own Thermometer, *99*
Making a Magnetic Flannelboard, *113*
New Things From Old, *130*
Odds-and-Ends Box, *129*
Table Playhouse, A, *128*

TRANSPORTATION
Airplanes, *190*
Big School Bus, *190*
Traffic Light, *189*
Train Ride, The (Story), *192*

VALENTINE'S DAY
Five Pretty Valentines, *237*
Valentine's Day and Devices to Use, *236*

WRITING PREPARATION
Artists, *116*
Drawing Around Hands, *117*
Preschool Drawing or Scribbling as a Preparation for Writing, *114*
Scribbles, *115*
Scribbling to Nursery Rhymes, *115*
Slates for Scribbling, *115*
Something to Draw, *118*
Things to Draw, *116*
What Is It? *117*

81-87

372.6 Scott, Louise Binder
SCO
　　Learning time with
　　　language
　　　experiences for
　　　young children

| DATE | | | |
|---|---|---|---|
| | | | |
| | | | |
| | | | |
| | | | |
| | | | |
| | | | |
| | | | |
| | | | |
| | | | |
| | | | |
| | | | |
| | | | |
| | | | |

ROSEDALE ELEMENTARY MEDIA CENTER
1200 OLD PHILADELPHIA ROAD
BALTIMORE, MARYLAND 21237

© THE BAKER & TAYLOR CO.